INTRANET
FIREWALLS

INTRANET FIREWALLS

Kevin Pagan
Scott Fuller

Contributing Author
Dennis Lone

VENTANA

Intranet Firewalls
Copyright © 1997 by Kevin Pagan & Scott Fuller

Library of Congress Cataloging-in-Publication Data
Fuller, Scott.
    Intranet firewalls : planning & implementing your network security
system / Scott Fuller, Kevin Pagan.
        p. cm.
    Includes index.
    ISBN 1-56604-506-1
    1. Computer networks—Security measures. 2. Intranets (Computer
networks)—Security measures. 3. Business enterprises—Computer
networks—Security measures. I. Pagan, Kevin. II. Title.
TK5105.59.F84 1996
005.8—dc20   96-31281
                                                            CIP

First Edition 9 8 7 6 5 4 3 2 1

Printed in the United States of America

Ventana Communications Group, Inc.
P.O. Box 13964
Research Triangle Park, NC 27709-3964
919.544.9404
FAX 919.544.9472
http://www.vmedia.com

Limits of Liability & Disclaimer of Warranty

Trademarks

About the Authors

Kevin D. Pagan

Kevin D. Pagan is an attorney specializing in civil trial law and representation of local governments. Currently serving as an Assistant City Attorney for the City of McAllen, Texas, Mr. Pagan has a bachelor's degree in accounting from Arkansas State University and a law degree from Southern Methodist University. He is a member of the Texas Bar Association and the American Bar Association. Throughout his more than 11 years as an attorney, Mr. Pagan has served as the network system administrator for two law firms and has helped those firms, and some of his other clients, develop network solutions for common business and legal challenges. He is the co-author of numerous computer books.

Scott Fuller

Scott Fuller is president of IDEAS and a former employee of EDS (Electronic Data Systems). IDEAS is a nationwide computer solutions firm that consults on a variety of MIS-related issues. Mr. Fuller has extensive experience in computer systems operation, networking, software engineering, and end-user education. With Kevin Pagan, he has co-authored six computer books. You can e-mail Mr. Fuller at ScottFuller@msn.com.

Dennis Lone

Dennis Lone's business card identifies him as "A writer, mostly." Writing is mostly what he has been doing since his college days (when he banged out newspaper copy on something called a "typewriter"). In his turn as an entrepreneur, he founded and ran a high-tech advertising agency in California's Silicon Valley for several years. Later, he moved to the Pacific Northwest, where he now lives and works as a freelance writer. Although most of the subjects he writes about are technical, he considers himself a non-technical person whose sympathies lie with the user who has to struggle with all the things that are supposed to make our lives easier.

Acknowledgments

As with any book on a cutting-edge topic, this book was created by a team that included many more people than just the authors. We want to express our appreciation to all of them, and mention a few by name:

To the folks at Ventana, especially Lynn, Judy, and Neweleen, who developed this project from a good idea into an actual book—not an easy task, especially during a hurricane! They stuck by us, even when the going got tough.

To the many software and hardware companies mentioned in the book that allowed us access to what is, by definition, sensitive information about security products.

And, finally, to our literary agents, Lisa Swayne and Bill Adler, who took a chance on us and didn't give up until we had a great project. A particular note of thanks to Lisa, who went above and beyond during the development of this book to make sure it stayed on track.

Dedications

From Kevin Pagan

Each time I write a book, I realize how much I owe to so many people. This book is dedicated to a few of those people.

To my terrific and loving family, Carmen, Alec, and Katie, who once again saw a lot less of me during weekends, evenings, and holidays than they deserved. My new law practice has meant much less free time, but they've still given it up willingly when asked. I love you.

To my parents, Herbert and Beverly Pagan—as time goes on I realize I can never say thanks to you as much as I should, but I try. Thank you.

To the great folks that are the "gang" at my "real job"—the Darling Law Firm: Bob, Sonia, Karen, Patti, Gracie, Marcy, Nelda, and Molly. They put up with me tinkering with their computers and actually seem to use the books I've written. And a special note to my boss, mentor, and friend, Jim Darling, who has taught me how to practice law and actually get things done. He has also given me a fresh perspective on computers, especially in realizing what they *can't* do. (Yes, your paper calendar is still faster than my electronic one.) I think that perspective appears in several places in this book.

And speaking of things computers can't do, creating free time for writing in a busy law practice is one of them. And that has put a lot more pressure on the last person I want to thank, my co-author and friend Scott Fuller. Once again, his technical expertise proved second to none in this book. This is our sixth book together, and by far the most ambitious. When you spend your holiday weekends eating pizza, surfing the Net looking for material, and arguing about what to put in and what to leave out, you learn a lot about a person, and Scott is one of the best. And, if you don't kill each other, you become pretty good friends. Thanks.

From Scott M. Fuller

In addition to the people who helped directly on the project, there are several more who helped me through their unselfish support and friendship. I wish to dedicate this book to a few of them.

Susan, my beautiful wife, whose love for me passes all understanding. I know deep in my heart that the next nine years of our marriage will be even more loving, more wonderful, and more special than the first nine. I look forward to every minute of it.

My wonderful children, Janessa, Michael, and Matthew, who entrusted "their computer" to me so I could use it to write. Thanks guys, now if I could only get you to put your shoes on before you go outside. Nevertheless, I love all of you!

Joe Herrera, my business partner and friend, who "took point" for me several times while I was working on this project. Everyone should be fortunate enough to have a partner like you. Thanks for everything.

Kevin Pagan, my co-author, friend, and "brother." This one has been one heck of a ride. They say "When the going gets tough, the tough get going." I see it differently: when the going gets tough you find out who your real friends are. You have been a true one. Thanks.

Contents

Introduction xix

Part 1: Firewall Concepts ////////////

1 The Basics 1

The Importance of Firewalls & Computer Security 2

The Evolution of Computer Crime 3

Why Intranets? 4

    The Growth of Intranets ■ The Appeal of Intranets

More About Computer Security 9

Why Firewalls? 11

2 Intranet Concepts 15

What Is an Intranet? 16

    There Are Internal Networks... ■ ...& There's the World
    Wide Web ■ When They Meet, You Get an Intranet

Intranets vs. Groupware 22

Intranet Hardware 23

Intranet Software 25

Intranet Services 27

Web (HTTP) Publishing ■ File Transfer Protocol (FTP)

TCP/IP Primer 37

Addresses ■ Addressing on the Internet ■ Addressing on an
Intranet ■ Subnets & Subnet Masks ■ Domain Names
■ Uniform Resource Locator (URL)

Planning Your Intranet 48

Implementing an Intranet 49

Step 1: Setting Up the Corporate Network ■ Step 2: Attaching a Web Server to the Network ■ Step 3: Connecting
Data to the Web Server ■ Step 4: Equipping the Users

3 Integrating Firewalls Into Overall Network Security

**Integrating Firewalls Into
Overall Network Security** 53

The FBI on the Internet............................... 53

The Importance of Network Security 55

Official Levels of Computer Security 57

Level D1 ■ Level C1 ■ Level C2 ■ Level B1 ■ Level B2
■ Level B3 ■ Level A

Types of Security Controls 61

Internal Controls ■ External Controls ■ Internal & External,
Hand in Hand

Approaches to Network Security 63

Allowing Access ■ Denying Access ■ Handling Exceptions

Designing a Network Security Policy............. 65

Step 1: Identify Security Issues ■ Step 2: Analyze Risk/Cost
■ Step 3: Implement Your Plan ■ Step 4: Review & Update
Your Plan

4 Firewall Concepts & Technology

Firewall Concepts & Technology 75

The Firewall Concept 76

Firewall Technology 78

Packet Filters ■ Proxy Servers ■ User Authentication

Component Certification 94

   NCSA Test Criteria

Firewall Configurations 98

   Screened Network (Packet Filtering Only) ■ Dual-homed
   Gateway ■ Screened Host ■ Screened Subnet ■ Other
   Firewall Configurations

5   Practical Firewall Implementation 109

Our Sample Corporation: Acme, Inc. 109

Security Issue: Defining the Internet Connection 112

   Solutions

Security Issue: Determining Who Needs Access 113

   Solutions

Security Issue: Identifying Weak Spots
in Information Flow 117

Security Issue: Managing Remote Access 118

   Solutions

Security Issue: Getting Information to Remote Sites.... 122

   Solutions

Security Issue: Managing Internal Access to
Sensitive Information 124

   Solutions

Security Issue: Virus Detection & Removal 127

Acme's Future 128

Part 2: Firewall Products ////////////////

6   About the Products 133

The Products 134

The Reviews 135

7   **Product Review: *BorderWare Firewall Server*** 137

Product Description 137

Transparent Proxies ■ Network Address Translation ■ Packet-level Screening ■ Secure Server Net ■ Virtual Private Network (VPN)

Platforms 140

Installing Firewall Server 141

Pre-installation Planning ■ Installation

Using & Configuring Firewall Server 144

Displaying System Activity ■ Viewing Logs ■ System Configuration ■ Proxy Configuration ■ Authenticated Access/Secure Logins ■ Alarms ■ Other Administration

8   **Product Review: *LT Auditor+*** 153

Product Description 154

License Metering ■ Hardware Inventory ■ Bindery Filter

Platforms 155

System Requirements 156

Installing LT Auditor+ 156

Starting LT Auditor+ & Selecting Server 158

Selecting a Server ■ Attaching to Other Servers

Configuring LT Auditor+ 159

Files/Directory Filters ■ Login Filter ■ Bindery Filter ■ Metering Filter ■ Auto-Delete/Purge Filter ■ Hardware Filter ■ Reports

9   **Product Review: *Modem Security Enforcer*** 165

Product Description 166

Benefits

The Operation of Modem Security Enforcer 168

Operational Overview ■ Customization Options

Platforms 172

Installing Modem Security Enforcer **172**

Configuring the Modem Security Enforcer **173**

Changing the User Password ■ Using the System
Administrator Menu ■ Stats: Displaying Access Statistics
■ List: Creating & Canceling Accounts ■ Parameters

Using Modem Security Enforcer **181**

Status Indicators ■ Indicator Lights

10   Product Review: *Internet Scanner* **183**

Product Description **183**

Platforms **184**

Installing Internet Scanner **185**

Downloading Internet Scanner ■ Disk-based Installation

Configuring Internet Scanner **186**

Some General Operational Settings ■ RPC Options
■ Network File System (NFS)-Related Options ■ Brute Force
Options ■ Firewall Options ■ NetBios Options

Using Internet Scanner **190**

Running a Manual Scan ■ Setting Up an Automatic Scan
■ Analyzing Scan Results

11   Product Review: *CyberSafe Challenger* **193**

Understanding Kerberos **194**

Kerberos Design Goals ■ Kerberos Security Levels

Using CyberSAFE Challenger **196**

Logging In ■ Administrating CyberSafe Challenger ■ Using
the CyberSafe Application Security Toolkit ■ Securing an
Application With the Security Toolkit

12   Other Firewall Products **203**

Directory Sites **204**

Firewall Fiesta ■ National Computer Security Association
(NCSA) ■ Serverwatch

Firewall Product Listing **205**

AbhiWeb AFS 2000 ■ AltaVista FireWall ■ ANS Interlock
■ Black Hole ■ BorderGuard 2000 ■ BorderWare Firewall
Server ■ Brimstone ■ Centri Firewall/Centri TNT ■ Challenger
■ CONNECT:Firewall ■ Controller ■ CryptoWall ■ CyberGuard
FireWall ■ Cypress Labyrinth Firewall ■ Digital Firewall for
UNIX ■ Eagle ■ ExFilter ■ FireDoor ■ FireWall-1 ■ FireWall
IRX Router ■ FireWall/Plus ■ Galea Network Security
■ Gauntlet Internet Firewall ■ Guardian Firewall System ■ GFX
Internet Firewall System ■ Horatio ■ IBM Internet Connection
Secured Network Gateway ■ I.C.E.Block ■ Interceptor
■ Internet Scanner SAFEsuite ■ INTOUCH NSA—Network
Security Agent ■ IWare Connect ■ KarlBridge/KarlRouter
■ LT Auditor+ ■ Mediator One ■ Modem Security Enforcer
■ NETBuilder Firewall ■ NetFortress ■ NetGate ■ NetLOCK
■ NetSeer ■ NetRoad FireWALL ■ NetWall ■ The Norman
Firewall ■ ON Guard ■ PERMIT Security Gateway ■ PORTUS
■ Private Internet Exchange (PIX) Firewall ■ PrivateNet Secure
Firewall Server ■ Secure Access Firewall ■ Secure RPC
Gateway ■ Sidewinder ■ Site Patrol ■ Solstice Firewall-1
■ SmartWall ■ SunScreen ■ TurnStyle Firewall System
■ WatchGuard Security System ■ WebSENSE

Part 3: Appendices ///////////////////////////

A   **E-Mail Privacy & Security** 227

B   **Other Firewall Notes of Interest** 267

C   **Other Informative Firewall Resources** 283

D   **Intranets Redefine Corporate
Information Systems** 289

Glossary 303

Index 311

Introduction

The proliferation of computers, networks, Web sites, servers, and every other type of silicon-based life on the increasingly crowded "information superhighway" has generated concern among many that the information on company computer systems may not be secure. There is good reason for this concern. What was once limited to harmless "hacking" has grown into full-fledged corporate espionage. The Internet, and more recently corporate intranets, have increased exponentially the number of users with access to various systems.

With more and increasingly valuable data residing on corporate systems, companies must now guard the three main doorways to their systems: internal access; external access (through, for example, the Internet); and the latest hybrid—intranets. In this book, we concentrate on intranets and the security known as *firewalls* used to protect those systems.

Who Needs This Book?

This book provides useful information for every member of your computer "team," including those who run and implement the network (such as systems administrators or system operators), the executives who make the decisions related to computer purchases, and even the everyday users of the system who may need to understand the basics of computer security and intranet operation.

This book contains information that will be helpful regardless of the size of your organization or the computer platform that you use.

Although we assume that you have some familiarity with basic computer concepts and operating systems, you need no knowledge of intranets, Internet protocols, or firewalls to use this book.

If you or your company has a computer network, and if your computers are accessible from beyond the confines of your home or office, you need to know about security. If your network uses Internet-style connections, or if you are thinking of using Internet technologies to improve the performance of your internal network, you need to know about firewalls. (The differences between conventional network security and intranet firewalls are explained in Chapter 1.)

A firewall is a collection of software and hardware components that implement an organization's security policy, usually to protect a network (or part of a network) from unauthorized access that originates from outside the protected network. For example, a computer network that is connected to the Internet should be protected from unauthorized access into the network from the Internet. Similarly, a corporate intranet (that is, an internal network that uses Internet-style technology) may have parts of the system that must be protected from other parts. A firewall system provides this protection.

Whether you design, administer, or simply use computers with outside access, the knowledge you will gain from this book may prevent you or your organization from making costly mistakes in your computer security.

What's Inside?

This book explains how you can use firewalls to protect secure areas of your organization's intranet. In doing so, this book also explains the basics of computer intranets and network security. After the basics, we explore more sophisticated firewall concepts and provide practical information for setting up and managing your own firewall system.

The book is divided into three main parts: Part 1, "Firewall Concepts," Part 2, "Firewall Products," and Part 3, "Appendices." We have selected five firewall products that we think help illustrate a variety of approaches. In Part 1 of the book, we refer to those products to help explain what goes into implementing an intranet firewall. In Part 2, we provide additional detailed information about those products, along with a listing of many other firewall products and vendors. Be sure to check out the appendices in Part 3, which offer valuable supplementary information on intranets and network security.

Here's a summary of the book's contents:

Part 1: Firewall Concepts

Chapter 1, "The Basics," provides all of the general information you need to see why your organization might benefit from intranet technology, why you need a firewall, why security is important, and other basic concepts related to intranet firewalls.

Chapter 2, "Intranet Concepts & Technology," covers the theory of intranet design and implementation.

Chapter 3, "Integrating Firewalls Into Network Security," discusses concepts and design strategies for implementing firewalls into your existing network security plan.

Chapter 4, "Firewall Concepts & Technology," provides information about firewall theory and construction.

Chapter 5, "Practical Firewall Implementation," uses a typical business as an example to provide practical information about how you can use intranet firewalls in your organization.

Part 2: Firewall Products

Chapters 6 through 11 contain more detailed background information about the products we have referred to in Part 1 of the book:

- BorderWare Firewall Server (Chapter 7)

- LT Auditor+ (Chapter 8)

- Modem Security Enforcer (Chapter 9)

- Internet Scanner (Chapter 10)

- CyberSafe Challenger (Chapter 11)

Chapter 12, "Other Firewall Products," lists numerous other
firewall products and their makers, with brief descriptions and
contact information. This listing also provides Web addresses
where you can get more information about firewall products.

Part 3: Appendices

Appendix A, "E-Mail Privacy & Security," is an excellent discus-
sion of e-mail security issues written by Sean Carton and Gareth
Branwyn and excerpted from their Internet Power Toolkit
(Ventana 1996).

Appendix B, "Other Firewall Notes of Interest," is a selection of
excerpts from the recently published National Computer Security
Association Firewall Buyer's Guide. We thank NCSA for letting us
reprint these excerpts, which give valuable tips on policing protocols and testing your firewall, and offer some thoughts on the
security implications of Internet Protocol version 6.

Appendix C, "Other Informative Firewall Resources," lists
security-related Usenet newsgroups, mailing lists, Frequently
Asked Questions (FAQs), and organizations.

Appendix D, "Intranets Redefine Corporate Information Systems," is a white paper written by Netscape Communications
Corporation and reprinted here with Netscape's permission.

The Glossary consists of a list of common terms found throughout this book and related technical journals and articles on
firewalls and intranets.

To start learning how to protect your computer system from
foes both internal and external, turn to Chapter 1.

Part 1:

Firewall Concepts

1 The Basics

This book, as the title indicates, is about *intranet firewalls*; that is, software and hardware systems designed to protect certain segments of your company's Internet-style network system from intrusion by people (or machines) that are not supposed to be there.

To help you fully understand this topic, this book employs a "building block" format. Thus, chapters later in this book that discuss, for example, the details of constructing an intranet firewall will build on knowledge that you have (we hope) gained from earlier chapters, such as the chapter on general firewall technology. In this way, you can develop a good foundation of knowledge about this rapidly expanding technology.

We also recognize, however, that some of you out there are not particularly concerned with the history of the TCP/IP protocol, nor do you care much about U.S. Department of Defense security-level classifications (both of which, by the way, are covered in this book). You are simply interested in the "big picture"—that is, gaining a basic knowledge of intranets, firewalls, why you might need a firewall, and where to go to get it. It is for you that we included this chapter. As you move closer to implementing your intranet firewall system, however, you will probably want to read the other chapters, too, as this material will help ensure that you end up with a system that meets your goals and needs.

In this chapter, we provide an overview of both intranets and firewalls, along with references to other sources of more detailed information (including chapters in this book).

////// TRAP

Please keep in mind the old adage that "a little knowledge can be a dangerous thing." This adage can apply especially to computer technology. We suggest the approach outlined in the preceding paragraph only if you are not the person directly responsible for installing and maintaining your organization's intranet. The "little knowledge" approach may be perfect, however, if you simply want to know what all those "tech" people are talking about when they ask you to sign the check for your own firewall.

The Importance of Firewalls & Computer Security

Security for your computer system is more important today than ever. The U.S. Department of Defense has estimated that their own computer systems were attacked 250,000 times in a recent year. If that many attacks are made on a single (albeit important) government system, how many more attacks are made against private companies' systems?

With that thought in mind, consider the following: Corporate espionage is at an all-time high and is still on the rise. Most companies are not prepared to deal with the corporate invaders, nor do they always even recognize that the intruders exist. Some companies still do not see how the threat affects them. The fact remains that the computer online society mimics the real society in which we live. Cyberspace contains many unscrupulous people, and they are continually hacking away at computer security systems.

The Evolution of Computer Crime

Over the last 10 to 15 years, companies have learned a lot about computer security, often the hard way. Let me (Scott) tell you a story from my own early computer experiences that illustrates the typical attitude (and state of the art) of computer security as recently as 10 years ago.

When I was on a field trip in high school, the local bank that we were visiting in my hometown of Germantown, Wisconsin, had the password to its computer system posted on the wall of the bookkeeping department in six-inch letters for the world to see. Then, as we walked past the modem rack, I noticed that each modem's phone number showed on an address label on the top of all the modems. Without even trying, the bank had armed me for mischief (or worse).

Of course, being the law-abiding soul that I am, I never did try to log in to the bank (had I wanted to, my 300-baud modem and Tandy TRS-80 may have posed some obstacles, anyway). Even at the time, though, it was shocking to me how easy it would have been to get into the bank's computer system, à la Matthew Broderick changing his high school science grade in *War Games*. At the very least, the "front line" security of the password and telephone numbers was compromised. This typified the state of computer security at that time, and represented the little attention paid to computer crime.

Fifteen years ago, large companies with extensive computer systems and hosts of modem connections were the principal victims of computer crime. The conventional wisdom was that computer "nerds" committed all the computer crimes and that such crimes were committed mainly against the large data processing companies where they worked, or had worked, as programmers. (Those were the days when most people also thought of computers as room-sized machines with thousands of blinking lights.)

The general public's knowledge of computers is obviously much more sophisticated today. This is largely due to the drop in the cost of the average personal computer, along with the exponential increase in its computing power. If you sit in a coffee shop today and listen to people, you will hear them talking about their computer at work not doing something the right way, or maybe the new Web site they found last night.

Just as the growth of computers and computer knowledge has happened at an incredible rate, so has computer crime. The super connectivity afforded by the Internet further extends the range of today's computer criminal.

Computer crime is an everyday issue for most companies, no matter what their size. Even the small, independently owned local department store must concern itself with this issue. We truly have moved to the next generation of computer crime.

As a result of all this online crime, the FBI's National Computer Crime Squad recommends the use of firewalls as a measure to guard against computer crime. Although the NCCS recognizes other security measures, it views firewalls as an excellent measure to protect your intranet against intrusion.

Why Intranets?

At this point, you may be wondering why your organization even needs an intranet. For that reason, we assume that you have not yet made the transition to an intranet system but are considering the various advantages and disadvantages of intranets.

With all the talk in the media about the Internet, do not be confused; an *intranet* is actually a network of computers, based upon Internet-style technology, that is completely *within* an organization. In fact, an intranet may be very similar to the LAN (Local Area Network) or WAN (Wide Area Network) that your organization has used for the last several years. These networks are generally based upon network "platforms" that use special network software (sometimes called *groupware*) that allows those computers to communicate with one another. Common examples are Novell, Lantastic, and Windows for Workgroups.

Intranets are also groups of computers used inside an organization; however, rather than traditional networking software, intranets use the same *protocols* (or communication techniques) that have been popularized by the Internet and its most-used service, the World Wide Web. Generally speaking, these protocols use systems such as TCP/IP (the standard Internet protocol) and other common Internet technology. (For a more detailed discussion of these protocols and systems, see Chapter 2.)

The Growth of Intranets

In the past few years, the Internet and the number of users on it have grown exponentially, making it truly the information superhighway. A side benefit of this explosive growth has been software developers' ability to test communication and data-transfer technologies on a huge scale.

Now, the astounding growth of the Internet is being repeated, but this time within the confines of the *firewall*; that is, inside the corporation. Many organizations are building intranets and using Internet and Web technologies to solve internal organizational problems. These problems were previously addressed by proprietary databases, groupware, and workgroup solutions, as noted previously. The use of Internet technologies within the corporate firewall is a much simpler solution that can also be a large cost saving.

Internet technologies such as TCP/IP, HTTP, Java, and so on have all been proven on the Internet and now are ready to be put to work within the MIS (management information system) world. Much of this is due to the fundamental simplicity, openness, and adaptability of these technologies. Their openness of design has been the product of global research and development effort to improve TCP/IP technologies to meet new demands and challenges. The resulting flood of software, most of it both free and high quality, makes the implementation cost for extending TCP/IP into the organizational network lower than any other network technology currently available.

The two most important functions of the Internet (especially the World Wide Web) are the mass publishing of information and the widespread sharing of data. These functions mirror the two biggest responsibilities of the MIS department of almost any corporation. Thus, a new niche for Internet technologies has opened in the protected waters behind the corporate firewall, and the intranet market has exploded.

The Appeal of Intranets

Why do users and MIS managers find intranets so appealing? The simplest answer is that intranets offer several advantages over traditional groupware or network software solutions. Intranets are fast, they work, and they scale to different users very well. These are basically the same advantages that led to the growth of TCP/IP on the Internet.

When you stop to think about it, the World Wide Web is a great deal more complex than any single organization, and yet it seems to satisfy an enormous user base fairly quickly and efficiently. The combination of low implementation cost and the simplicity of the interface (through the use of the various Web browsers) attracted the attention of many businesses. They saw Internet technologies as an easy way to solve their problems.

One very popular application that uses this technology is Federal Express's tracking software. FedEx has been very successful in its implementation of a Web-based package-tracking interface, which enables anyone anywhere on the globe with a browser and an Internet connection to track a package from pickup to delivery anywhere on the planet. Applications like this demonstrate the grand possibilities that could result from using the same technologies internally to solve corporate problems. If corporate users could travel anywhere on the planet and use their Web browser to log in to the corporate intranet, retaining the same access to data that they have at their desk, the corporate remote connectivity world would be a tranquil place.

In addition, the simplicity of TCP/IP, helped along by many other standards and open technologies, makes it possible and desirable to marry Web browsers to virtually any information source, from Structured Query Language (SQL) databases to highly proprietary information systems. Because the browser has evolved far beyond its original uses, it may well become the universal interface to all information resources in the future.

Of course, this is an evolving technology. The Web will become more complex as it develops into a system that can readily be used as a full client–server application platform, capable of easily integrating with other client–server protocols. The integration of Internet protocols with legacy systems will continue to grow in importance as new intranet technologies take hold. The result will be the increased integration of corporate data-access systems with inter-corporate communication systems and corporate-customer communications.

If an intranet produces essentially the same result as a "traditional" network, you might be curious as to why an organization would select the intranet protocols over a standard network package, especially if making that decision involves replacing the network software. Several reasons exist for an organization to go the intranet route, depending on a variety of circumstances.

Cost

As with most computer system decisions, a major factor is cost. Internet-type technology is, generally speaking, less costly for the same number of users than traditional groupware, especially as the number of users grows. In fact, many intranet software systems are available free or for very little cost. Groupware, on the other hand, can be quite costly—as much as $10,000 or more for a company with even less than 100 users.

Security systems will also reflect cost savings. For example, some of the less sophisticated firewall products described later in this book are available for a few hundred dollars (though some cost several thousand dollars or more).

Ease of Use

Another reason to use intranet technology is the ease of use that the system provides the end user; that is, the employee at the workstation who needs to use the information on your system, not necessarily understand the intricacies of how it got there. Because intranet technology is based upon the user-friendly atmosphere of the World Wide Web (WWW), the system is ideal for this situation.

Web technology, for example, allows users to intuitively search for and retrieve information by using graphical user interfaces (GUI). Thus, a user can simply point to information on a graphical screen and click to that information without any knowledge of how the system is actually moving from one information area to another.

Connectivity

Another important consideration is connectivity. If you have multiple users at remote sites (that is, sites other than where your primary computer data is located), intranets offer well-tested, easy-to-use protocols for remote connections. Remember, several million people a day "test" the Internet-style connection protocols by logging on to the Internet and World Wide Web. Generally, this is accomplished by simply clicking on the icon for an Internet provider's communication software or logging on to a traditional online service (such as Prodigy, CompuServe, or America Online) and clicking on the Web browser within that system. These providers are highly motivated to provide you with quick and easy access to the Internet.

LAN software providers, on the other hand, have (or had) far less reason to develop easy remote access to their systems. In fact, early on, the idea of even being able to log in to a local network from outside the office was not encouraged because of the security risks. When remote access became an issue, the network system providers relied primarily on outside vendors (PC Anywhere, for example) to fill this need. Thus, if you attempted to access your Novell 2.15 LAN from your home, the process involved several steps, including loading and running a communication package, connecting to the file server, and then logging in to the network. To make matters worse, because of the nature of traditional LAN software, the LAN would often attempt to transfer huge chunks of nonessential information over the telephone connection to your remote computer, making access times very inconvenient and sometimes intolerable.

Compatibility

Finally, compatibility is often easier with intranets than with standard networks, due to the larger (and ever-expanding) base of Internet-friendly software and information. As more and more organizations place information on the Internet, more and more software and document vendors are creating Web-compatible programs. For example, if you have purchased a word processing program in the last year, the word processor can likely already take a document you create and convert it into a Web-compatible format of some type. Thus, you already have the ability to use that same technology to create documents in, say, your Phoenix office, place them on your company's intranet, and retrieve and manipulate the documents when you visit your Dallas office.

 **TIP**

For more information about how intranets work, as well as more information about why your organization might benefit from using an intranet, see Chapter 2.

More About Computer Security

The nature of multi-user, networked computing introduces a variety of potential security problems that did not exist in the traditional office environment. If you keep sensitive data on a computer and if that computer is connected to an external network, then it is not sufficient protection simply to lock your office door. Unfortunately, securing your computer data from unauthorized access over a network can be complicated. It is not necessarily difficult or expensive, but it requires a working knowledge of what threats are possible and of what can go wrong. A comprehensive survey of computer security is beyond the scope of this book, and many details are likely to depend on your particular operating system and configuration. However, there are certain components of a proper security model that may be applied universally and that are very effective. One of these is the intranet firewall.

Computer security is limited, of course, in the sense that computers operate according to rules, and people want to be able to allow and deny access depending on a variety of circumstances, which are not entirely consistent and often have exceptions. It is important to design your security policy in a way that protects sensitive data without creating too many restrictions that impede authorized access.

As we have already suggested, the most important element in computer security is ensuring that users follow the security policy. Most problems result from insecure passwords or other simple mistakes. Faced with an elaborate system of locked doors, anyone who gains access to the keys will have little trouble entering. Even a form of data encryption that is practically unbreakable may be rendered useless if the keys become known or if a user carelessly disposes of a printout of the decrypted data. Stated baldly, the idea is this:

> *Any system that allows authorized access will always be susceptible to unauthorized access.*

Also, networked computer security is not a perfect analogue to building security, in the sense that it is easier to break into a computer undetected than to walk into a building undetected. People are less likely to notice and worry about securing a computer on their desk from invisible intruders. So the primary security concern should be to develop a good user management policy. This brings us to another important principle:

> *The effectiveness of any technology we apply to the security problem depends on the creation of a security policy that people will follow.*

Additionally, there is the problem of how to change the level of authorization for an employee who moves to a different department or leaves the company. A security policy that cannot adapt to such a change is flawed. In particular, knowledge of a department's internal operations and security policy should not be enough information to gain access; otherwise, former users would have the potential to cause a security breach, even accidentally. This is a very delicate problem, of course, because it is not desirable or even feasible to treat employees as potential intruders, but the risk is real and should be considered. This has to be addressed in both the security model (as we will see) and the user policy.

Implementing a sound security policy involves many issues, and we'll have more to say about it in later chapters.

Why Firewalls?

Now that you understand what an intranet is and have a general understanding of computer security, what exactly is a firewall? In short, a firewall protects your intranet (or various portions of your intranet) from unwanted users. A simple definition for firewall (discussed in more detail in Chapter 3) is as follows:

A firewall is a system (software, hardware, or both) that enforces an access-control policy between two networks.

Organizations that are connected to the Internet have used firewalls for several years as barriers between the organization and the Internet. As the popularity of intranets evolves, firewalls on intranet systems are becoming essential to secure corporate computing.

The most important thing to recognize about a firewall is that it implements an access-control policy set up by your organization. This security policy should be designed to best fit your organizational needs.

Figure 1-1 illustrates the basic design of any firewall technology or model.

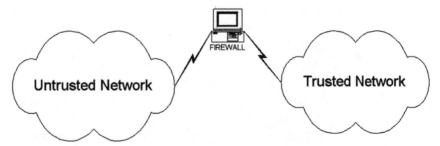

Figure 1-1: A firewall is placed between the protected (sometimes called trusted*) network and the external (sometimes referred to as* outside *or* untrusted*) network.*

A firewall performs primarily two functions: one is to block traffic, and the other is to permit traffic. (Obviously, the firewall must be able to distinguish between various *types* of traffic to determine which traffic should be permitted and which should be blocked.)

Typically, a firewall installation will place a greater emphasis on blocking traffic, not so much on permitting traffic. However, there are certain installations where the opposite emphasis would be the better choice.

If your organization is already using an intranet, chances are that the folks in your MIS department have already considered security issues, including firewalls. (If not, take this book to them!)

Even if security has been addressed, however, the use of firewalls may not have been a specific consideration when your organization implemented its intranet. Likewise, if you are just now considering intranets generally, you should consider whether (and where) you may need firewalls.

As discussed later in this book, a growing number of software vendors are now developing and selling firewall technology, either specifically for intranets or as "additional uses" of their Internet firewall packages. It may be that one of these "off-the-shelf" packages will fit nicely into your existing firewall plans. (For the relative advantages and disadvantages of the various packages, see Part 2 of this book.) In this book, we have selected five firewall products that are good examples of the variety of approaches you can take to secure a network. In Part 2, you'll find detailed information about the features and use of these five products. Chapter 12 lists vendors for many other firewall products, briefly describes the products, and tells where you can get more information.

In addition to the commercially available solutions, more ambitious MIS departments may want to create custom solutions either by modifying existing packages or by creating their own system using available Internet technology.

Whether you select an off-the-shelf solution (which is the fastest and easiest way to implement an intranet firewall) or take the more ambitious route of designing your own firewall system, the concepts discussed in this book should help you create an overall security system that integrates traditional security measures with firewall technology to help protect various areas of your intranet.

Just as the firewall in your car (located between the engine and the passenger compartment) keeps the heat and other "bad stuff" away from you, an intranet firewall can be thought of as a device to keep bad stuff out of your computer system. "Bad stuff" might be unwanted users, unwanted data, viruses, and so on, but in general, it is anything "out there" that you do not want "in here."

As suggested previously, the well-reasoned and sophisticated use of firewalls can provide many additional benefits to your organization. Just as a firewall between your company and the hackers on the Internet protects your data, a well-placed firewall between your accounting department and your personnel department might keep an overzealous employee from rearranging your balance sheet the day after you decide the employee's services are no longer needed.

Another simple way to think of firewalls is by comparison to secure filing cabinets and locked doors. Since the inception of the concept of "confidential information," those who have it have devised ways to keep it from those who should not have it. With the widespread use of computers, that confidential information need not necessarily be kept completely off your computer system to remain confidential. By implementing proper overall security systems (see Chapter 4) and the efficient use of firewalls on your intranet, the data can be safely placed on the system with a high degree of confidence that it will remain secure—perhaps even more secure than if it were locked in a filing cabinet.

Moving On

In this chapter, we have covered the basics of both intranets and firewalls, and discussed how each can be useful for your organization.

In the chapters that follow, we take a closer look at these same issues, to help you decide how to best use this new technology in your company.

2 Intranet Concepts

To help you fully understand the security needs in an intranet system, we first explore the concepts and foundations upon which intranets themselves are based. This chapter covers the basics of intranets, including the hardware and software they use, the services they can provide, and the protocols and data transmission methods they use. We also give you an overview of what's involved in planning and implementing an intranet.

Later chapters in this book make use of your working knowledge of these concepts; therefore, be sure that you understand the terms and concepts presented here. (On the other hand, if you are already familiar with the concepts behind intranets, you may wish to just skim this chapter or even skip it altogether.)

 **TIP**

You can find a glossary at the end of this book that will help you understand the terminology used in relation to intranet firewalls.

What Is an Intranet?

With the explosion of intranets within the corporate MIS world, many people are asking the question: What exactly is an intranet? You could read many articles on intranets and intranet technologies without ever coming across a definition of an intranet. Here is a simple definition:

> *An intranet is a private system that uses hardware and software developed for the Internet to provide communication, information management, and information publishing services within an organization.*

To understand intranets, it's helpful to go back in time to trace some of the significant developments in the world of computers.

There Are Internal Networks...

In the beginning, there were great, big computers called *mainframes*. The mainframe computer lived in its own specially constructed, temperature-controlled room where it was tended by specially trained computer priests and acolytes. When mortals wanted the computer to do something for them, they went to the computer room and asked very politely. Sometime—perhaps days—later, a stack of paper would be delivered to them with the computer's answer to their question. If the information they got wasn't what they really wanted, it could only be because they hadn't asked *exactly* the right question in *exactly* the right way. When that happened, they had to start all over again. This way of getting the computer to do things was called "batch processing."

By and by, a new kind of computing came to be: *interactive* processing. Computer terminals, comprising a display screen and keyboard, were placed throughout the organization and connected by cables to the mainframe computer, as shown in Figure 2-1. With interactive processing, people could work with the computer directly, asking the questions and getting the results on their terminals. That speeded things up quite a bit, but there were still a couple of drawbacks: First, the more people who wanted to use the mainframe computer at one time, the slower it went. Second, if the mainframe quit working for some reason, everyone was out of luck.

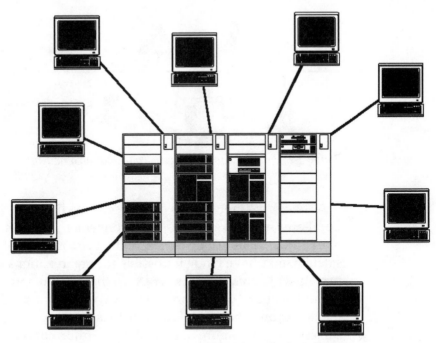

Figure 2-1: Terminals were connected directly to the mainframe.

Then came the personal computer. The advent of small, relatively inexpensive computers meant that users could have their own private computers right on their desks. No longer were they at the mercy of the mainframe.

There were a couple of new problems with personal computers, however. For one thing, having individual computers made it difficult for users to share information. Another problem was that each computer had to have its own printer and enough disk space to store all the work it was doing. Printers and disk drives were very expensive. Organizations soon found they were spending more for *peripheral* equipment than they were for the computers themselves.

To solve that problem, organizations connected their computers, printers, big disk drives, and other expensive peripherals on networks, as shown in Figure 2-2. With the right software, users on a network could send messages to each other, share files, and do their printing on high-speed, centrally located printers.

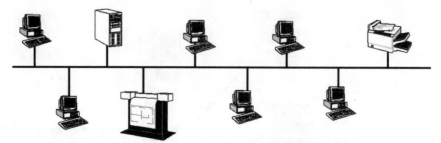

Figure 2-2: Personal computers were connected on a network.

Network technology has progressed steadily over the years. Local-area networks (LANs) offer convenient connectivity for workgroups. Fiber-optic cables, high-speed telephone lines, and satellite links have made it possible for organizations to build private wide-area networks (WANs) that span the world.

But in spite of the advances in networking, the model for managing and sharing information has stayed pretty much the same: If you can figure out whether the information exists on the network and where it is and what format it's in, and if you have the right kind of computer and the right kind of software and the right level of access permission, you can have the information.

...& There's the World Wide Web

Back when mainframes walked the earth, one of the main driving forces in computer technology was the U.S. Department of Defense (DoD). In 1969, the DoD's Advanced Research Projects Agency (ARPA) established the ARPANET network as an experiment in packet-switched networking. ARPANET-linked facilities were doing research for the military, enabling researchers to log in and run programs on remote computers. The network became an essential tool for sharing information through file transfer, electronic mail, and interest-group mailing lists.

In the late 1970s, the designers of ARPANET introduced TCP/IP (which stands for Transport Control Protocol/Internet Protocol), a pair of protocols that allows different kinds of computers to communicate over a network.

ARPANET was later split into two separate networks: MILNET, used exclusively by the military, and ARPANET, used by universities and other scientific bodies.

In 1986, the National Science Foundation (NSF) established NSFNET, a "backbone" network based on the ARPANET TCP/IP protocols that linked other networks at research and educational institutions.

This "network of networks" was the Internet (Figure 2-3). In the 10 years since its inception, thousands of networks and tens of millions of users throughout the world have joined the Internet. Along the way, commercial companies gradually took over running and providing access to the Internet, and the NSF eventually got out of the backbone business.

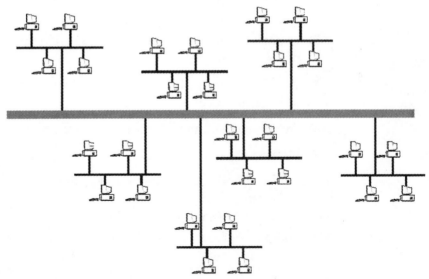

Figure 2-3: The Internet is a network of networks.

Although the Internet provided connectivity among networks, it didn't automatically make it easy (or even possible) for everyone to freely exchange information. On the contrary, the Internet was more like an international bazaar, with everyone talking at once in his or her own language. Those "languages" were protocols for exchanging information.

 **TIP**

You're going to hear the word "protocol" a lot in connection with the Internet and intranets. There are network protocols, communication protocols, and data exchange protocols. It will all become clear as we go along.

Here are some of the early data exchange protocols and their uses:

- Telnet, for logging into a remote computer and running it from your computer

- FTP (File Transfer Protocol), for copying files from large archives

- Gopher, for providing menu-driven access to documents, files, images, and software

- Usenet, for bulletin-board-style information exchange and news groups

- WAIS (Wide-Area Information Service), for creating indexes of information on the Internet

- Archie and Veronica, for searching for files

- Internet Relay Chat (IRC), for online, interactive chat

Not only were there lots of ways of doing things, but there was also information stored in lots of different kinds of documents and file formats, so even if you could find the information you wanted, there was no guarantee you would be able to copy it to your computer or use it when you got it there.

Once again, necessity gave rise to invention. In 1989, the European Laboratory for Particle Physics (CERN) began to develop the World Wide Web for its internal use. In January 1992, the foundation blocks of the WWW—the specifications for HyperText Markup Language (HTML), HyperText Transfer Protocol (HTTP), and the Uniform Resource Locator (URL)—were made public.

Here's how Tim Berners-Lee, who conceived the World Wide Web (W3) and developed the key specifications for it, describes his creation:

"The world-wide web is conceived as a seamless world in which ALL information, from any source, can be accessed in a consistent and simple way.

"The W3 principle of universal readership is that once information is available, it should be accessible from any type of computer, in any country, and an (authorized) person should only have to use one simple program to access it."

When They Meet, You Get an Intranet

As we said previously, intranets combine the concepts of the Internet with the organization's existing network infrastructure to produce a new way to manage and publish information. Intranets are attractive for several reasons:

- They are relatively inexpensive to build and maintain (after the underlying network is in place).

- They are easy to use. Both publishing information and retrieving information use fairly simple tools (although complexity is increasing).

- They can greatly improve information management and publishing in an organization.

As an example, a company with offices at several locations could put popular data, such as budgeting and marketing information, on intranet servers at various locations. Using common Internet-style software, users at other locations could then access the data on the company's intranet server. What's more, with just a bit of work, hypertext links could be added to the information so that users could easily request related information.

Indexing and searching software can help users find the files they want, and they don't have to worry about whether they have the right kind of machine or software to retrieve it.

With today's more advanced browsers, users can see full-motion video clips and play sounds. They can fill out forms, engage in discussion groups, store and retrieve information from databases, and even make appointments and reserve facilities online.

**TIP**

Technically, an intranet can support any of the services, such as those listed previously, that you can find on the Internet. As a practical matter, however, the dominant service on most intranets, as on the Internet itself, is World Wide Web publishing. Through the rest of this book, unless we specifically say otherwise, we use "intranet" and "World Wide Web," as they relate to protocols for networks, synonymously.

Most people who use an organization's intranet do so while connected directly to the organization's private network. However, the benefits of the intranet are also available to people who log on remotely over telephone lines. When they log on to their organization's intranet, they can access everything that their security level would allow on their conventional remote access, but with the ease of using a Web browser.

For example, consider how an insurance company might use remote access to its intranet. Insurance agents could log on to the intranet to get the most recent marketing literature together with the latest rates. With a laptop computer and access to a telephone line, they could make an online presentation tailored to the specific needs of the client, and then fill out and submit a form to get an immediate quote.

Claim adjusters in the field could log on to the "private Web" to research damage rates and other data that would help them work claims. And, of course, everyone could participate in the e-mail system.

Intranets vs. Groupware

Groupware is a broad category of software that has appeared in the last two or three years. It often includes facilities for functions such as sending and receiving e-mail, maintaining personal and group calendars, planning projects, and sharing documents. Groupware packages also provide ways to customize their capabilities or create group applications. The insurance company in our example could use groupware to provide its employees with the capabilities we described.

But World Wide Web software has one big advantage over most groupware software: It's a whole lot less expensive.

For example, a Lotus Notes application can cost $250,000 or more to install in a network of significant size. A corporate intranet, on the other hand, can be implemented for less than $10,000 and serve the same number of users.

Lower costs are making intranets more accessible to organizations that cannot afford the groupware price tag. For example, a small distribution company with 150 users spread throughout the country could justify an intranet implementation long before it could afford the equivalent groupware implementation.

Groupware will still have its market. Groupware has greater facilities for collaborative computing—applications that allow two or more people to work on a document simultaneously over the network—than intranets can currently offer.

Intranet developers are closing the gap between the two systems, however. Intranet browsers and servers are becoming more intelligent and capable, especially with the addition of programming facilities such as Microsoft's ActiveX and Netscape's Java technologies.

On the groupware side, the Lotus Notes server software can now act as a Web server, making it a type of hybrid groupware/intranet system. It seems clear that the two technologies—groupware and intranets—will merge over time, each incorporating the best features of the other.

Intranet Hardware

An intranet is a client/server system, as shown in Figure 2-4. The server is a computer that has two main functions:

- It runs the intranet server software.

- It usually stores some or all of the content that is available to users.

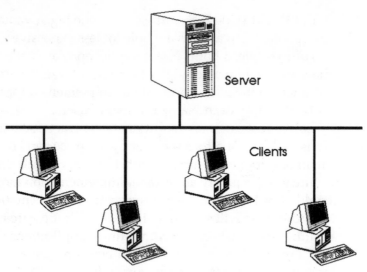

Figure 2-4: An intranet is a client/server system

For an intranet, the requirements for the server computer depend mainly on how many connections per hour it will be expected to handle.

 **TIP**

One connection equals one user requesting one page of information. If a user requests 10 pages of information in the course of a session on the intranet, that requires 10 connections.

A typically equipped modern personal computer—single Pentium 120 MHz processor, 32MB of random-access memory, 2GB hard disk—would be sufficient to handle a small intranet load. The load could be up to, say, a few hundred connections per hour.

When the connection load on the server gets too high, users will find themselves waiting a long time (several seconds) to get a page. Eventually, their requests will time out (the browser will get tired of waiting and give up) because the server can't get to their request fast enough.

When the server becomes overloaded, there are a number of things you can do to improve its performance:

- Add more memory to the server

- Add more processors to the server

- Add more servers and split the content among them

Almost any computer can be a client. All the client needs to do is run the World Wide Web browser software, which does not require a lot of processor power or memory. Clients can also be based on any technology, such as Macintosh, Intel, or Sun, as long as the platform is capable of running TCP/IP.

 **TIP**

Although it is true that browser software is relatively "light" in terms of its demands on the client computer, that situation is changing. Newer browsers, such as Microsoft's Internet Explorer 3.0, run to several megabytes in size, and they are happiest with a plentiful supply of RAM.

Intranet Software

The software that runs on the server computer and provides services such as World Wide Web (also known as HTTP) publishing, FTP file retrieval, and indexing and searching facilities is known as *server software*. Server software is available free on the Internet, and commercial packages such as Microsoft's Internet Information Server and Netscape Navigator are also available. Server software is available for a variety of operating systems, such as UNIX and Windows NT Server.

The software that runs on the client is called a *browser.* You use the browser to access and view Web pages. Because your intranet will use the same protocols as the Web, you can use any of the well-tested Web browsers already available—either free of charge or at a reasonably low cost on the commercial market. Perhaps the best-known Web browser is Netscape Navigator. Netscape provides the user with a variety of features, such as bookmarks (for keeping track of sites on the Web so that you can find them later), e-mail automation, and "hot" lists for storing the addresses of your favorite Web sites. Navigator is available commercially and, at most times, Netscape Communications Corporation allows downloading of a recent version (see Table 2-1 for the Web address).

Several other Web browsers are available. Table 2-1 provides a list of some of the Web browsers available free on the Internet.

 **TIP**

The Internet is a gold mine of free software. You can find everything you need to run a full-featured intranet. One word of caution: If you use software from the Internet, you may be on your own when it comes to getting it set up right and solving the inevitable problems that come up. Unless you're the adventuresome sort and feel comfortable poking around in the innards of computer applications, you might be better off spending a few dollars for well-designed, tested, and supported software.

Name	Web Address
Midas WWW	http://www-midas.slac.stanford.edu/midasv22/introduction.html
Mosaic	ftp://ftp.ncsa.uiuc.edu/Mosaic/
Netscape	http://home.netscape.com
Emacs	ftp://moose.cs.indiana.edu/pub/elisp/w3/
Lynx	ftp://ftp2.cc.ukans.edu/pub/lynx/
Internet Explorer	http://www.microsoft.com

Table 2-1: Some of the Web browsers available free on the Internet.

Intranet Services

When we described the fledgling Internet earlier in this chapter, we listed some of the services that were available then. All of those services are still available on the Internet. Chances are, however, you won't want or need all of them on your intranet.

Here's the suite of services and facilities you'll probably want:

- World Wide Web publishing

- FTP

- Some kind of indexing and searching service

- Some facility to run scripts

Web (HTTP) Publishing

The World Wide Web is by far the most popular service on the Internet. In fact, for many people, the Web *is* the Internet. (That's why, as we said before, we're using the words as synonyms in this book.)

The World Wide Web is based on HTTP. HTTP defines how browsers and servers communicate and move information back and forth.

 **TIP**

There's that word again: protocol. *Now we have three layers of protocols: the HTTP uses the Internet Protocol over a network that has some kind of network communication protocol. One would think the Internet was invented by the State Department.*

HTTP uses a "request and response" process. The browser on the client computer sends a request to the server for a particular page of information. The server receives the request, finds the requested page (file), and sends it to the browser. HTTP then forgets about the whole transaction. The browser and the server maintain a connection only long enough to process the request.

////// TRAP

Let's clear up some potential confusion here. As stated, the server and the client maintain a logical connection only long enough to process a request. However, they remain physically connected over the network. If you connect to your intranet remotely over a telephone line, the telephone connection remains open until you quit the session, even though the server and browser aren't talking to each other.

HTTP is usually used to send HTML files to the browser, but it can send any kind of file. If the browser cannot display the file, it will start another application (called a *helper* application) to display it, if possible. If it can't find a helper application, it will give the user the option of saving the file to disk.

HyperText Markup Language

The primary language used to create Web pages is HTML. HTML uses commands called *tags* embedded in a text file to tell the browser how to display the file.

Figure 2-5 shows an example of a Web page and the HTML tags that control its display.

HTML started out as a fairly simple markup language but, like everything else in the computer world, it's getting more complex all the time. An official HTML standard is published by the World Wide Web Consortium, but companies that produce browser software like to add unique extensions to the set of tags their browsers understand, to give them a competitive edge.

For example, Microsoft's Internet Explorer lets you use a special tag in an HTML document to create a marquee in which a line of text crawls across the page from one side to the other. A browser that does not support this tag will not display the marquee effect. (It should, however, display the line of text in a fixed position on the page.)

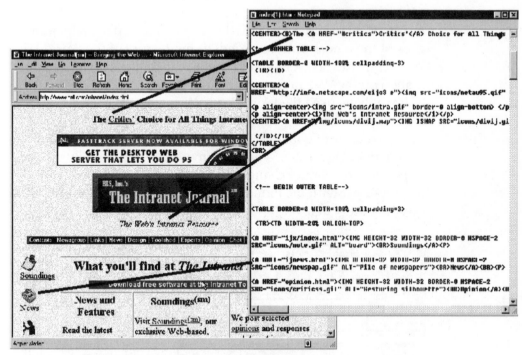

Figure 2-5: HTML tags control how a Web page is displayed.

This example illustrates one of the irritating "gotchas" in the Web: All browsers do not support all the same extended HTML tags, so you can't count on them all to display the same page in the same way. (All should, however, display the *standard* set of tags.) For your intranet, it would be a good idea to standardize on one browser to be used by everyone, so you will always know what tags it can understand.

In the early days of the Web, creating a document in HTML format meant typing the content in a text editor and then adding HTML tags by hand. Nowadays, there are authoring tools, such as Navigator Gold, FrontPage, and others, that are very much like word processors. They let you create documents and add formatting and effects without ever having to touch an HTML tag. Instead, the tools add the tags behind the scenes as you create the document.

Hypertext

Hypertext—links that can take the user to a new page with a single click of the mouse button—is a defining feature of the World Wide Web. Hypertext is what gives you the capability to manage information on the Web in new, highly effective ways.

If you have used the World Wide Web, you have used hypertext. It shows up usually as colored text—a label, a section title, a word or two in a sentence, or even a portion of an image—as shown in Figure 2-6. When you move the mouse pointer over hypertext, the pointer changes to a pointing hand. When you click the hypertext with the mouse, something happens. Usually, you go to another page.

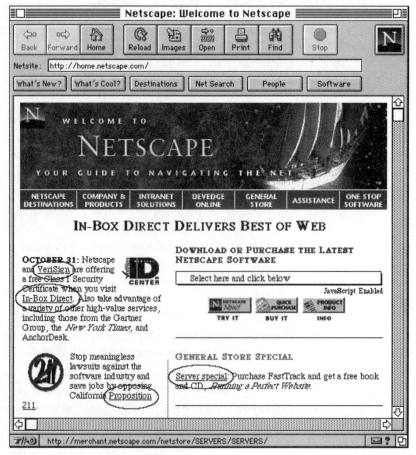

Figure 2-6: Hypertext links take you to other pages.

To illustrate the power and benefits of hypertext, compare publishing a several-page technical document on the Web with publishing the same document in traditional printed form, such as a book.

A book presents information in a certain order determined by the author or publisher, and the information is meant to be read from the beginning to the end. The table of contents in the beginning of the book and the index in the back are there to break down the larger body of information into smaller chunks to help you find the specific information you want without having to read the entire book. Nonetheless, books are essentially linear in their presentation of information.

In contrast, the Web is essentially nonlinear. In effect, the author puts the content on the Web in pieces (called *pages*), which you can view in any order, thanks to hypertext.

Each hypertext link contains information that identifies a different page (or a different part of the same page), as shown in Figure 2-7. (That information is called a Uniform Resource Locator, or URL. More on that shortly.) When you click on a hypertext link, the browser uses the identifying information to request the other page from the server or to jump to the other location on the page you're already viewing. Either way, the new information is displayed for you immediately.

Figure 2-7: A hypertext link contains a Uniform Resource Locator.

 **TIP**

The term hypertext link *is often collapsed into* hyperlink.

Hypertext links can be used in many ways. The table of contents for the Web-based document can be made with hypertext links so that you can go directly to any part of the document. Words and phrases in the text can be linked to definitions or more detailed information. They can even be linked to information outside of the document, such as other documents on the same subject.

Hypertext links can also be used with images such as maps and drawings. Using special Web-page authoring software, areas of the image can be made "hot"—turned into hypertext links. When users click that part of the image, they are taken to another page.

For example, a Web-based weather reporting service could show a map of the United States with each state outlined. When you want to find out about the weather in your state, you click within the state's outline, and the page of weather information for that state appears.

Using hypertext links, Web authors can produce "rich" documents that can be the launching pad for almost endless exploration of a subject.

Common Gateway Interface (CGI)

The Common Gateway Interface (CGI) adds power and versatility to the Web by enabling the user to run small programs called *scripts* on the server.

For example, suppose that you work in a real estate office and you want to set up an intranet. Your intranet Web site could contain photographs and descriptions of properties for sale. Potential buyers could browse through available properties on a computer in your office rather than have to drive all over town to look at them.

You would also like to help potential buyers figure out what their loan payments and financing costs would be for any house that interested them.

To do that, you would create a special Web page—a form—that contained blanks where the buyer would type the total price of the home, the down payment amount or percentage, the length of the loan, and the assumed interest rate. After the buyer had entered the information, he or she would click a button on the page to have the system perform the calculation.

The browser would send the information to the server. It would also send the name of a script for the server to run.

When the server received the information and saw that it contained the name of a script, it would automatically forward the information to the Common Gateway Interface. The CGI would start the script and feed it the loan information.

The script would calculate the monthly payment and financing costs and return them to the server, which would send them in a new page back to the browser. The browser would display the new page to the user.

All of that could happen on an intranet in a fraction of a second (given that the network is fast enough and the server isn't busy with other requests).

CGI scripts can be written in any computer language. PERL is the traditional language for scripts, and Visual Basic is also popular. If you don't want to write your own CGI scripts, hundreds are available on the Internet to perform a wide variety of tasks.

 **TIP**

Newer, more efficient technologies are beginning to replace CGI for running scripts on the server. One is ISAPI, which is built into Microsoft's Internet Information Server. ISAPI makes better use of the computer's resources when running scripts.

In addition, Microsoft's ActiveX technology makes running programs possible both on the server and on the client.

Indexing & Searching

Go back for a moment to the book example we used to illustrate hypertext links. Imagine that you could tell a book exactly what you wanted to read about, and the book would rearrange its pages and present just those that contained the information you wanted. That's the concept behind indexing and searching on the Web.

A number of software tools are available for indexing and searching content on the Web (both HTML-format pages as well as other types of files, such as Word documents). The indexing tool goes through all of the content and builds a list that shows all unique words and the names of the files in which they appear.

 **TIP**

In truth, a well-done index in a book can be more effective in helping you find what you want because it can show relationships among topics that aren't apparent to the indexing engine in a computer. It takes a thoughtful, experienced human who understands the content of the document to produce a truly useful index.

When users want to find particular information, they use the search tool. They submit a request, called a *query*, to find certain key words. The search tool looks through the index and returns a list of all files that contain the words.

For example, if users wanted to find information about the commercial fishing industry in the Pacific Northwest, they might search for the words "Northwest" and "fishing." That search would find the information they wanted, but it would also find a lot they didn't want, such as information about sport fishing. (See Figure 2-8.) By adding words to their query, they could narrow the results.

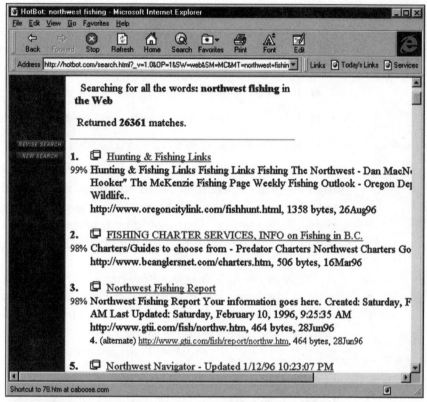

Figure 2-8: Results of a query.

 **TIP**

Indexing and searching tools don't all operate the same way. Take a look at several different services that use search engines on the World Wide Web, such as Yahoo!, HotBot, and Magellan, and you'll find that searching for the same words on different services will return different results.

If you want to index and search your own data in this way, you'll need to get search engine software. Many commercial and free search engines are available, such as Isearch, which you can download from http://www.cnidr.org/.

File Transfer Protocol (FTP)

File Transfer Protocol, one of the original Internet protocols, is used to copy files from a server to a client. FTP lacks the glamour of the World Wide Web, but it's still useful. It has three advantages:

- ■ It can copy any file, no matter what format it's in.

- ■ It can copy to and from different kinds of machines.

- ■ It's the fastest way to copy large files.

For example, suppose that you wanted to publish a software manual. You could break the manual down into small chunks and make each a chunk a Web page, complete with hyperlinks to other parts of the manual. That would be fine for viewing the manual online in a Web browser, but some people still prefer to read printed copies of large documents.

The user could print each Web page, but that would take a long time. A better approach would be for you to make the document available in its original form on an FTP site. Using his or her browser, the user would go to the FTP site and select the document from a list of available files. (See Figure 2-9.)

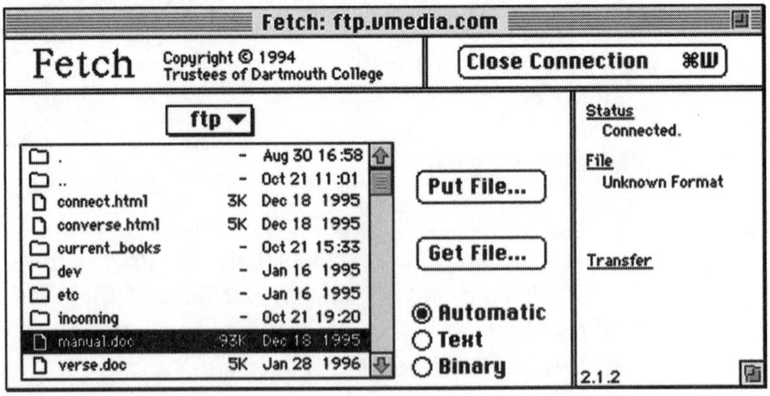

Figure 2-9: An FTP site shows a list of files that can be downloaded.

The document would be copied to the user's computer. FTP would open the document if the user has the appropriate application, or it would let the user save the document on his or her disk.

TCP/IP Primer

TCP/IP are the standard network protocols used on the Internet. Because the building blocks of the Internet are also used to build intranets, you will find that the TCP/IP protocol is used as the network communications protocol on most intranet sites, also.

////// TRAP

We're going to clear up some more "protocol" confusion before we lose points for bad grammar. TCP and IP are two separate protocols. They are used together on the Internet and intranets, however, so they are often run together and referred to as a single entity.

The TCP/IP technology was developed by the United States Department of Defense in the late 1960s and early 1970s, for use on ARPANET. The government needed a protocol that could be used on a variety of computers and network types. Today, TCP/IP is the basis for the Internet and intranets.

To illustrate how networks and TCP/IP work, we use a railroad as an analogy, as shown in Figure 2-10. (We hope we don't get derailed.)

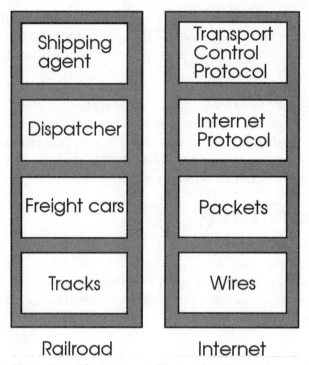

Figure 2-10: The Internet is like a railroad, sort of.

 **TIP**

The "official" network model is the seven-layer OSI Reference Model, defined by the International Organization for Standardization. We're not attempting to describe the OSI model here.

The first thing we need is a way to physically move things from here to there. For a railroad system, that's the rails and the structure that supports them, the locomotives that pull the trains, the crews that run the trains, and the rules of the road that the crews follow.

 **TIP**

You may suspect that the word rules *really stands for the "p" word—*protocol. *You're right. The most common protocol for the physical network is Ethernet.*

For a network, things are moved by way of wire, fiber-optic cable, satellite link, or other physical medium for moving electrical signals from one place to another; the connections to computers; devices that route signals from place to place; and the rules that govern how these things work together.

When you ship freight on a railroad, it's carried in a freight car. On a network, data is carried in a *packet.*

If you're going to ship freight on your railroad, you'll need someone to figure out what route each freight car should take to get it to its destination. That person could be called the *dispatcher.* Note that the dispatcher doesn't care what's *in* the freight cars. He or she just knows where they need to go and figures out how to get them there.

On the network, the dispatcher's role is handled by the Internet Protocol. It receives "freight"—data—from TCP in the form of *datagrams.* IP's job is to find the best route for the datagram. IP doesn't give a hoot what's in the datagram.

IP passes the datagram on to the network, where it's placed inside a packet and sent on its way.

Finally, our railroad has agents who take care of shipping and receiving freight. At the shipping end, the agent loads the freight, puts a shipping label on the container, makes careful records of what needs to go to whom, and then checks to make sure that it gets there undamaged. On the receiving end, another agent checks the freight cars as they arrive, unloads the freight, and notifies the shipper that the shipment arrived.

TCP does similar work on the network. It breaks the sender's message down into datagrams, numbers them, sticks an address label on them, and gives them to IP for shipment. On the receiving end, TCP checks the datagrams as they arrive to make sure that they haven't been corrupted, notifies the sender if a damaged datagram needs to be re-sent, and assembles the datagrams in the right order to re-create the original message.

 **TIP**

A more detailed description of TCP, IP, and Ethernet can be found at http://www.rutgers.edu/Computing/Network/Internet/Tech/ tcp-ip/3/.index.html.

In the network world, the terms *datagram* and *packet* are often used synonymously, but they are different. A *datagram* is the unit of data TCP works with. A *packet* is a physical chunk of user data and other information that is transmitted over the network. The size of a packet varies with the network technology, such as Ethernet or X.25. Usually, one packet carries one datagram, but that is not always the case.

Addresses

Addressing is one of the most important topics to understand about the Internet and intranets. Later in this book, you'll see how addressing plays a major role in making your firewall secure.

Just as the address for your house must be unique from every other house so that mail can (usually) find its way to your door, every computer on an organization's intranet must have a unique address to allow computer information to flow to and from those computers. In both cases, addresses are composed of different elements that, when combined, provide a unique address.

Consider a hypothetical home address: 123 Main Street, Burgville, AZ 98765 USA. Probably thousands of homes across the country have the same street address. But when the street address is combined with a city, state, ZIP code, and country, the complete address distinguishes one house from all the others.

An IP address is a 32-bit string containing four elements called *octets*, each of which is a number from 0 to 255. (That is the range of numbers that can be expressed by one 8-bit byte.) For example, a typical 32-bit IP address would look like this in notation:

```
10111011 10010001 11001000 01101011
```

Each group of 8 bits is an octet. This address would be more commonly written:

187.145.200.107

The latter format is called the *dotted decimal* form because the octets are expressed in base 10 ("decimal") and they are separated by dots. Each octet corresponds to a group of 8 bits (1 byte) in the 32-bit IP address. For example, 187 is written in binary as 10111011, the first octet in the bit string.

The Internet and intranets use IP addressing to identify computers. An IP address is normally divided into two parts: the network part and the host part. The network part identifies the network to which the computer is connected. The host portion of the address identifies the particular computer within that network. It is possible to have more than one IP address that refers to the same computer. So, it is more accurate to say that an IP address identifies a computer's interface to the network, and that a single computer may have multiple interfaces. This may seem a fine distinction, but it will become important later in our discussion.

As you'll see in a moment, this two-part address scheme enables network operators to come up with a unique address for everything from the smallest intranet to the Internet itself.

Addressing on the Internet

Internet addresses are assigned by the Internet Network Information Center (InterNIC). InterNIC was started by the National Science Foundation, but is now operated by AT&T and Network Solutions, Inc. For a fee, InterNIC assigns blocks of Internet addresses to large organizations and Internet service providers (ISPs).

 **TIP**

For more information about InterNIC, visit its World Wide Web site at http://whois.internic.net.

There are three classes of Internet IP addresses, as shown in the following table:

Class	Address Range*	Example	Maximum Computers per Network
A	1.x.x.x through 126.xxx.xxx.xxx	47.18.102.74 = network 47 host (computer) 18.102.74	16,777,214
B	128.1.x.x through 191.255.xxx.xxx	132.14.104.3 = network 132.14 host (computer) 104.3	65,534
C	192.1.1.x through 223.255.255.xxx	200.106.8.209 = network 200.106.8 host (computer) 209	254
*Some addresses are used for special purposes, hence the missing numbers in the address ranges.			

Table 2-2: IP address classes.

 **TIP**

There are more than 4 billion possible IP addresses, but because addresses are assigned in blocks, many possible addresses wind up not being used. As a result, InterNIC is running out of address blocks.

Address classes are important to you if you are an ISP who plans to provide Internet connections to the public or if your company wants its users to be connected directly to the Internet. In those cases, you will need a class of network addresses that gives you enough host addresses to meet your needs.

If you just want to have a connection between your organization's network and the Internet, however, all you need is an account with an ISP and a proxy server (more about proxy servers in later chapters). The ISP will assign a single IP address (instead of a block of addresses) to your account. (You can sign up for additional accounts if you need more capacity for Internet traffic.)

Addressing on an Intranet

Addressing is a lot simpler on an intranet. As long as you follow the four-part, dotted-octet format, *you get to make up your own addresses.*

It's not good practice to just assign addresses out of the blue, however. It's better to have a plan that will allow your intranet to grow and change.

For example, if you have a large corporation, you might set up an intranet addressing scheme like this:

Octet	Meaning	Example
1	geographic region	10 = U.S. 20 = South America 30 = Europe
2	major business division	10 = product A 20 = product B 30 = product C
3	department	10 = manufacturing 20 = engineering 30 = marketing 40 = sales 50 = accounting
4	individual computer	1 - 255

 **TIP**

On an intranet, the IP addresses do not need to correspond to the physical arrangement of the organization's network. The preceding example would work whether the company had one large network or individual networks for each of the levels shown.

In this scheme, the address 10.20.50.102 would identify a computer in the U.S. product B accounting department. The address 30.30.10.2 would identify a computer in the European product C manufacturing department.

As you can see, there is plenty of room in this scheme to add more organizational units. This scheme will handle up to 255 computers in the lowest organizational level (the department, in this case). If you foresaw a need for more computers, you could use the first and second octets to represent the organizational unit, and the third and fourth to identify individual computers.

Subnets & Subnet Masks

A *subnet* is a division of a larger network. Thus, the network 199.47.x.x is a subnet of the network 199.x.x.x.

A *subnet mask* (also called a *netmask*) is a 32-bit number, usually expressed in dotted-decimal form, that enables IP to distinguish the network part from the host part of any IP address. It can also be used to distinguish one group of computers from another group on the same network. It does that by *masking*, or hiding, part of the address.

Subnet masks are very important to the proper functioning of an intranet and to successful implementation of a firewall.

Look at the simple case first. To distinguish the network part of an IP address from the host part, the decimal numbers in the octets that represent the network are set to 255. For example, a class A address has a subnet mask of 255.0.0.0, because only the first octet is used to identify the network. A class B address has a subnet mask of 255.255.0.0, and so on.

Things get a bit complicated when you want to split one of the first three octets. (Okay, they get *very* complicated, but we can do it.)

Suppose that you used the scheme we outlined previously to set up your intranet addressing. The network address for the U.S. product A engineering department is 10.10.20.0. (The 0 in the fourth octet stands for any number from 1 to 255.) Just when you've got everything working smoothly, the engineering department hires 200 more people. It can't handle that many people with the 254 host address assigned to it. What can you do?

 **TIP**

*If there were a sensible way to divide the group into two parts—
for example, if they were on two different floors or in two different
buildings—you could simply add network 10.10.25.0 and put part
of the group on that network.*

You decide to split the third octet in the existing address and
use part of its address range for hosts. To do that, you need to
create a custom subnet mask.

Look at our network address in both decimal and binary
representations:

Decimal	10	10	20	0
Binary	00001010	00001010	00010100	00000000

A subnet mask tells IP how many of the binary digits in each
octet are used to specify the network. In the existing address, all of
the bits in the first three octets are used to specify the network, so
the existing subnet mask looks like this:

Decimal	255	255	255	0
Binary	11111111	11111111	11111111	00000000

To split the third octet, you'll use some of the 8 bits to specify
the network and the others to identify computers. To give the
engineering department plenty of room to grow, you could use the
left-most six bits for the network address and the right-most two
for hosts. That would also leave room for you to split the third
octet again in the future if necessary.

Your custom subnet mask would look like this:

Decimal	255	255	252	0
Binary	11111111	11111111	11111100	00000000

With this new subnet mask, the Engineering Department could have the following IP addresses for its computers:

```
10.10.20.0
10.10.21.0
10.10.22.0
10.10.23.0
```

Remember that the 0 in the fourth octet stands for any number from 1 to 254. Thus, with this simple change to the subnet mask, you quadrupled the number of computers you can have in the engineering department.

Now take a closer look at what's happening with that third octet.

In the original address, it took the fourth, fifth, and sixth bits (counting from the left) to represent the decimal value 20. The two right-most bits weren't needed to represent the network, so, by masking them off from the network bits, they could be used to represent hosts:

Decimal	Binary	Mask
20	00010100	11111100

Two binary digits can represent decimal numbers from 0 through 3. Thus, the 8 bits can now represent four decimal numbers:

Binary	Decimal
00010100	20
00010101	21
00010110	22
00010111	23

If you had needed more host addresses for the engineering department, you could have changed the subnet mask to use more of the right-most bits to represent hosts.

Domain Names

A string of numbers, such as an IP address, isn't very easy to remember, and making a mistake when you type it is easy. Names are much easier to use.

On the Internet, the Domain Name System (DNS) takes care of translating names you can understand into IP addresses that the Internet routers can understand. The DNS is a system of computers, called *name servers*, distributed throughout the world that maintain lists of domain names and the IP addresses that correspond to them.

InterNIC is in charge of registering domain names in the five most commonly used top-level domains, which account for most of the domain names in the United States. Those domains are as follows:

- COM   Commercial entities

- EDU   Educational institutions, now limited to four-year colleges and universities

- GOV   Government agencies other than the military

- ORG   Miscellaneous organizations that don't fit anywhere else

- NET   Computers that are part of the Internet infrastructure (such as network providers' computers, administrative computers, and network node computers)

For example, if MegaByte Software Company wanted to be on the Internet, it could register the domain name MegaByte.com. If MegaByte wanted to add other domain names for divisions of the company, such as sales or product support, it would contact the administrator of the name server that maintained its DNS information and register the names sales.megabyte.com and product_support.megabyte.com.

Intranets use the same name-to-number translation system, but it's easier to manage because you don't have to deal with organizations outside of your own. Your intranet can have its own name server with which you register domain names and their corresponding IP addresses.

Uniform Resource Locator (URL)

Every file on every computer on the Internet has a unique label called a Uniform Resource Locator (URL). The same is true for the files on an intranet. URLs enable the user to request the files.

URLs follow a standard format that includes the protocol to be used to retrieve the file, the domain name and server name, the path to the file, and the filename. Here is an example:

```
http://www.ideas.com/services/consulting.html
```

- http signifies that the protocol is hypertext transfer

- www.ideas.com is the domain name of the server computer where the resource is located

- services is the path to the file (the directory in which it is stored)

- consulting.html is the name of the file

Planning Your Intranet

Although developing an intranet is still easier than implementing a groupware solution, some design issues are important to the success of the implementation.

 **TIP**

Before starting the actual implementation of your intranet, you will certainly want to consult additional sources, such as Build a Microsoft Intranet *(Ventana, 1996) and* Build an Intranet on a Shoestring *(Ventana, 1996).*

Before you implement your corporate intranet, consider the following issues:

- External Security. Because of its ease of use and the easy availability of intranet-style software on the Internet, security on an intranet is very important. Everything from access control down to file management is an important issue. We highly recommend using firewalls at critical locations.

■ Internal Security. Web servers are already becoming a common desktop tool, and eventually, these servers may well be able to share not only text and graphics but also audio and video, just like Internet Web servers. Therefore, many of the users in your company may quickly become proficient at creating Web sites. The policies to control their use need to be a consideration.

■ Development Tools. Getting the right tools to the application development team so that the applications can be quickly developed, and creating standards to be applied across intranet applications, are important issues.

■ User Training. You should make sure that the users can make the most of the intranet applications.

■ Administration and Management. You need to consider how the intranet will be managed and by whom.

■ Legacy Support. Consider the connection of the new intranet technology to the old corporate data system. You can either link the intranet to the older data system, or you can convert the data to run on the new system. Naturally, the particulars of this issue will depend on your situation.

■ Basic Network Infrastructure. This is an important consideration. You must have a good Internet Protocol (IP) network in place for your intranet to work. If not, you will have to decide on a course of action for either assimilating or eliminating legacy network technologies that will not or cannot be converted.

Implementing an Intranet

In this section, we discuss the general steps involved in building an intranet. Companies that already use the UNIX operating system can build an intranet on that platform. Still, learning UNIX or even using UNIX is not essential to constructing an intranet: Many software developers have brought the necessary tools to both the Macintosh and PC platforms. Picking the right tool for the job can make all the difference.

Step 1: Setting Up the Corporate Network

This is the first and sometimes most difficult step in setting up an intranet. Before you can build the rest of the intranet, you must first lay the TCP/IP network protocol groundwork. Intranets are centered around this protocol, and almost all intranet applications require it. Many groups have IP *subnet* addresses, therefore allowing them to link an intranet to the Internet. Any part of the corporate network that you wish to have accessible via the intranet must have TCP/IP protocol running beneath it. Many times, this protocol can simply be added to your current protocols.

Step 2: Attaching a Web Server to the Network

Plenty of shareware and free HTTP servers exist that can get a basic intranet off the ground. As the need develops for more advanced options, such as maintaining and monitoring your Web site, you can migrate to a mid-range commercial Web server. The top-of-the-line Web servers have features such as data encryption, security, and links to corporate databases. Some firewall servers act as Web servers. The Web server can run a different operating system than the rest of your network. The TCP/IP protocol will enable the connectivity between the two systems.

Step 3: Connecting Data to the Web Server

Start with a survey of your organization to find out what kind of information you want to put on the intranet, where it is, and what format it's in. That information will drive the way you set up your Web site.

If you are planning to provide access to a lot of corporate documents, you should consider linking your Web servers to a document database, enabling users to search, view, and manage documents, as well as translate documents to HTML, all on the fly.

Content must be coded in HTML, the World Wide Web's universal language format. This can be done by adding HTML codes to text documents by hand, or by using automated tools that translate documents into HTML format.

Step 4: Equipping the Users

You must educate the users before you can successfully launch your intranet. This is a good point in the process to get that done.

You should select a Web browser that best fits your situation. As for Web browsers, Netscape Navigator is the most popular and offers the best built-in Java application support and other cutting-edge features. If you do not need these sophisticated tools, you might consider any of the several free Web browsers available.

Users will also need to know how to produce pages for the Web. You can equip them with a Web-page authoring tool such as Microsoft's Front Page, or you can teach them HTML.

 **TIP**

For more information on building an intranet, or for information on the steps involved, please refer to the following publications: HTML Publishing on the Internet *(Ventana, 1996);* Official HTML Publishing for Netscape *(Netscape Press, 1996);* Official Netscape Navigator Gold 3.0 Book *(Netscape Press, 1996)*

Moving On

In this chapter, we described how intranets are essentially internal organizational networks based upon Internet protocols and technologies. We examined the main Internet protocol (TCP/IP) and how computers on networks are addressed and exchange data.

In the next chapter, we discuss the security creature called the *firewall* and how they can help your corporate intranet remain secure and safe from unwanted data transfers.

3 Integrating Firewalls Into Overall Network Security

Intranet firewalls can play a major role in the security plan of your organization. Firewalls will likely be only one part of your organization's overall security plan, however. Therefore, in order to properly use firewalls in your intranet, you should have a good understanding of network security in general.

In this chapter, we examine several issues related to overall network security and look at how intranet firewalls fit into the total network security picture.

The FBI on the Internet

As noted in Chapter 1, criminal activity related to computers and computer networks is on the increase—both in terms of amount and sophistication. Therefore, your overall computer security plan should take into account the latest risks and increasing likelihood that any particular system (including your intranet) will be the target of a computer "attack."

The FBI now has a special department, the National Computer Crime Squad (NCCS), to deal with this relatively new area of crime. Its job is to try to protect the country's computer systems from "hackers." The squad is trying to curtail the tidal wave of computer crime mainly by studying computer crime, computer criminals, and the techniques of the computer criminal in order to produce recommendations for MIS and other computer professionals.

You can find the FBI and the special unit on the Internet at the address shown in Figure 3-1.

Figure 3-1: The address for the FBI Web page on the Internet is www.fbi.gov.

If you log on to this Web site, you will find information that the National Computer Crime Squad has compiled through its numerous investigations of computer crime. This site has many suggestions to help you protect your organization's computer systems and network against computer crime.

The Importance of Network Security

Earlier this year (1996), the U.S. Department of Defense announced that its computer systems were attacked 250,000 times in the preceding year. Even more disturbing, most of these attacks went undetected. The extent to which these attacks affect national security is still undetermined. The majority of the detected attacks, however, were against computer systems housing sensitive and classified information. Two-thirds of these attacks were considered successful, with the intruders (hackers) stealing, modifying, or destroying data on the system.

With that sobering thought in mind, consider the following: Corporate espionage is at an all-time high and is still rising. Most companies are not prepared to deal with the corporate invaders, nor do they always even recognize that the intruders exist. Some companies still do not see how the threat affects them. The fact remains that the computer online society mimics the real society in which we live. Cyberspace contains many unscrupulous people who are continually hacking away at security systems on various computer systems. Some people who may not be so unscrupulous outside cyberspace transform into first-rate hackers when they are on the prowl in cyberspace, for reasons that we will leave for psychologists to decipher.

Consider, for example, the recent episode at a nationally known financial institution. One of the organization's employees was assigned to handle the accrual of interest and verification of amounts to the institution's interest-bearing accounts. This employee noticed that, because of errors in rounding small amounts, very small discrepancies existed in the amounts credited to the customer accounts, and certain small amounts were "dropped off" as a result.

With this information in hand, and because the institution had insufficient internal protection from this employee's department to the new account department, the employee logged into that department and created a variety of new accounts with fictitious names. Next, the employee created a simple program for the system that performed the accruals to note any account that had the "dropped off" amount (usually a few cents or less). The program was also instructed to route a credit for that same amount to the new accounts. Even though it was a few cents at a time, with this calculation performed thousands of times daily, the accounts quickly accumulated substantial sums of money. Several years elapsed before the institution realized what was happening.

As a result of all the online crime, the FBI's National Computer Crime Squad recommends the use of firewalls as a measure to guard against computer crime. Although the NCCS recognizes other security measures, it views the use of a firewall as an excellent measure to protect your intranet against intrusion.

The other measures recommended by the crime unit are the following:

- *Login banner warning against unauthorized access*. This notice, which appears on the screen at login, warns unauthorized users that they are entering a protected system.

- *Keystroke-level monitoring*. This security measure involves actually trapping and recording (in a file) all of the keystrokes performed at certain workstations. These files are reviewed by the administrator to ascertain whether unusual patterns, such as numerous failed login attempts, are generated from particular stations.

- *Trap and tracing service from telephone company*. This service allows your company to intercept incoming telephone calls and trace them to their origin; it can help catch and eliminate unauthorized remote access.

- *Caller ID*. This service (now popular even among household consumers) identifies the number and name of the person calling into a system and can be a first step toward identifying and eliminating unauthorized remote access.

- *Call blocker*. This service (related to Caller ID) allows certain telephone numbers to be blocked from your telephone system. For example, if your modem (remote-access system) has received large numbers of calls from a local university dormitory, you can block calls from that number. (You might also want to make a phone call yourself, to the university authorities.)

- *Data encryption*. You can "scramble" your data by using encryption and decryption software, which makes logging into your system less attractive to most hackers.

- *Firewalls*. Among all these security measures, firewalls can be the most protective because they can be customized and installed at the most critical points in your system, as described throughout this book. When a firewall is used in conjunction with some of these other security measures, you will have an excellent security plan for your company's data and your intranet.

Official Levels of Computer Security

To help computer users identify and solve computer network security issues, the government decided to try to classify computer systems by their security risk and protection. Thus, a few years ago, the U.S. Department of Defense put forth criteria for differing levels of computer security. The resulting "Orange Book" (officially, *Trusted Computer Standards Evaluation Criteria*) contains these classifications of levels of computer security.

These classifications are rarely seen in commercial software packages. However, by reviewing these classifications (that move from the lowest level of security to the highest), you should get some idea of the various security risks inherent in some systems and perhaps gain some insight into how to reduce or eliminate those risks.

Level D1

This is the lowest possible level of computer security. The entire computer system is untrusted. The hardware and operating system are easily infiltrated. Additionally, the standard for a D1-level computer system states that there is no authentication for users; that is, any person can use it without challenge by the computer system. The system requires no user sign-on (requiring the user to provide a user name) or password protection (requiring the user to provide a unique code word to gain access). Anyone can walk up to the computer and start using it.

Examples of D1-level computer systems are the following:

- MS-DOS

- MS-Windows 3.x and Windows 95 (not in workgroup mode for which user must sign in)

- Apple's System 7.x

It is easy to compromise all these operating systems because they do not require user authentication.

 **TIP**

Each level of security defined in this system is progressively more secure than the preceding level. Thus, all C levels afford more security than all D levels, and C2 affords more protection than C1.

Level C1

The Discretionary Security Protection system, or level C1, dictates that the hardware is afforded some level of security (for example, a hardware-locking mechanism requiring a key to gain access to the computer) and that the users must log in to the system before use. Additionally, Discretionary Access Control, which is part of C1 protection, allows the systems administrator to set access permissions to certain programs or data.

Examples of popular level C1-compatible computer systems are the following:

- UNIX systems

- XENIX

- Novell 3.x or higher

- Windows NT

Where level C1 protection fails is the point at which users gain access to the root level of the operating system. Because this level does not control the various levels to which users have access after they enter the system, users are free to move anywhere in the system. Thus, at this level, they can manipulate the configuration of the system and gain further access than the systems administrator may desire, allowing them, for example, to change and control user names.

Level C2

Level C2 dictates several features to address the shortcomings of level C1. Level C2 introduces the enhanced feature of controlled-access environment (user authorization levels). Because it is based on more than user permissions, this feature further restricts users from executing certain system commands.

Authorization levels enable the systems administrator to create groups of users who are granted access to certain programs or levels of directory access.

User permissions, on the other hand, grant the user, on an individual basis, permission to access the directory where the program is located. If other programs or data happen to be located in the same directory, the user's permission will automatically grant the user access to that information as well.

Level C2 systems may also use system *auditing*. The auditing feature tracks all "security events" such as logins (successful and failed) and systems administrator tasks such as changing user access and passwords.

 **TIP**

By differentiating between security events and administrator tasks, the auditing features provide an additional level of protection. For example, if a hacker successfully logs in to the system, the audit "trail" for that event might be unremarkable. If the hacker then proceeds to manipulate passwords or user access, however, the audit trail will also record this event. This allows the true administrator to recognize an attack that might have gone unnoticed if it were recorded only as a security event. (Some systems even permit the audit log to be written to a hidden file, thus making it even more difficult for the hacker to cover his tracks.)

Again, popular operating systems that are capable of obtaining level C2 certification are as follows:

- UNIX systems
- XENIX
- Novell 3.x or higher
- Windows NT

Level B1

Label Security Protection, or level B1, supports multilevel security. The term *label* here means that every object in the network is identifiable and protected in the security protection plan. *Multilevel* refers to the fact that security is installed at a variety of levels (network, application, workstation, and so on), affording greater overall security to sensitive information.

Security levels such as secret and top secret exist. These are the computers belonging to real "cloak and dagger" stuff, such as Department of Defense and National Security Agency systems. At this level, objects (such as disk volumes and file server directories) must be under access control and cannot have their permissions changed by the owner.

Examples of computer systems that meet any level-B security protection vary by operating system. Government agencies and defense contractor installations house the majority of level-B computer systems.

Level B2

This level is also known as Structured Protection. Level-B2 security dictates that all objects on the computer system are labeled and that devices (such as workstations, terminals, and disk drives) have security levels assigned to them. For example, a user might have access to a workstation but might not have access to a disk subsystem that contains payroll data.

Level B3

Security Domain, or level B3, states that the user's workstation or terminal is connected through a trusted path to the network system. Additionally, this level provides the introduction of hardware to protect the memory area of the security system.

Level A

This is the highest level of security found in the Orange Book. This level also is sometimes referred to as Verified Design. This level, like all previous ones, incorporates the features of the levels below it. Level A brings the additional requirement that the design of the security system undergo scrutiny. Qualified security individuals must analyze and approve the design. Also at level A, all the components that comprise the system must come from secured sources; that is, sources that are protected by security of a level sufficient to ensure their integrity. The security measures also must guarantee that no tampering with the components can take place in distribution. For example, a tape drive is carefully tracked from the factory floor through the distribution process to the computer room at the level-A facility.

Types of Security Controls

Two basic types of security controls exist for you to use to protect a computer network system: internal and external controls. The vast majority of this book discusses internal controls, but for completeness, we briefly discuss the other type as well.

Internal Controls

Internal controls are simply the controls that are internal to the computer system itself. Passwords, firewalls, and data encryption are examples of internal controls. Internal controls are effective only if they are accompanied by some level of external controls as well.

External Controls

External controls cover the part of the system that the system cannot address itself. The three general categories of external controls are as follows:

- Physical
- Personnel
- Procedural

Physical controls are the physical security measures that protect the computer system. Locked doors, air-conditioned rooms (that ensure that the system operates within acceptable parameters), and keyboard locks are examples of physical controls. As intra-networking becomes more common, the role of physical controls continues to diminish. In a large intranet, guaranteeing that any system other than your own is physically protected is impossible.

Personnel controls are the techniques and policies that an employer uses in deciding who to trust with the organization's computer system. As an employee gains a higher level of access to the computer system, the scrutiny of the employee should be increased. This can range from interviews with previous supervisors to a background investigation or even a polygraph test. All this depends on the particulars of your installation.

Procedural controls are the measures taken to ensure that the information on the computer system is handled only by those who need to handle it. These controls also address how new software is installed and how the system is maintained.

Internal & External, Hand in Hand

Internal and external controls should function together to create a complete security system. Although trading off one for the other is possible, internal and external controls complement one another most of the time. For example, having a crucial database server be password protected wouldn't do much good if it were left in the hallway for anyone to steal or damage.

The general rule of thumb is that if an exposure can be eliminated by either an internal or external control, the internal control should be used. External controls are usually more expensive and harder to implement. In addition, procedure controls are notoriously error-prone because they rely on people.

Approaches to Network Security

Basically, two approaches exist for handling every network security issue. You either allow someone access to something, or you deny access to something. The criteria for the access or denial of access is unique to every installation.

Allowing Access

Allowing a user access to a resource is an act of inclusion. In this approach to security, you specify what characteristics a user must possess in order to be given access. These criteria should somewhat match the nature of the resource being shared.

For example, the payroll system should be accessed only by the users working in the payroll department. To accomplish this, the systems administrator would create a group of users called "payroll" and grant that group access to that resource. If a new employee ("Michael") is hired for the position of payroll clerk in the Payroll Department, he is added to the payroll group, and Michael automatically has the same level of access as anyone else in that group. This is the act of inclusion.

One example of a potential pitfall with the inclusion concept occurs if Michael is transferred out of the Payroll Department to the General Ledger Department. In the new department, Michael is granted access to the general ledger system by his inclusion in another group called "general ledger." The potential problem becomes a real problem if someone forgets about Michael's inclusion in the payroll group, and his access there is not removed. Now you have inadvertently granted access to the payroll system to someone outside the payroll group.

To prevent this problem, procedures should be defined for granting users access to a group. For example, procedures should be implemented that require a user's whole security profile (that is, the areas in the system to which the user should have access) to be analyzed and updated each time the user is transferred. Also, if possible and supported by your operating system, safeguards should be programmed into the software that require you (or at least remind you) to remove users from other groups when they are added to new groups.

Denying Access

To deny a user access to a network resource is an act of rejection. In this approach to security, you specify characteristics that will cause a user to be denied access. You are rejecting the user's access based on a set of criteria. These criteria somewhat match the restrictions placed on the shared resource.

In the example of our payroll clerk, Michael, you might deny access to the payroll system if someone were trying to access the system at 2:00 in the morning. In this case, the systems administrator might set after-hours as one of the criteria for denial of access.

Handling Exceptions

The two approaches in network security described previously often work together. Taking the example of the payroll system, you would both allow access and deny access to the same resource as part of your protection to that resource. This is an excellent way to handle *exceptions*. Exceptions can be a significant issue when looking at network security. Often, you have the security of a network resource all planned out, and someone throws an exception at you that foils your plan. Then, you must back up and look at the resource in the light of these two approaches, whereupon you can work the exception into your plan.

For example, if someone legitimately requires access to the payroll system at 2:00 in the morning, then an exception (perhaps at the user level) must be implemented to allow that access. You can only hope that this exception (and others) can be allowed without compromising overall network security.

Designing a Network Security Policy

Every organization that has an intranet with outside or interdepartmental connectivity needs to have a *network security policy*. A network security policy is a statement of your network security plan. A network security policy is also the blueprint from which you design and build your network's defenses against intruders, both internal and external. A good network security policy is an essential part of building effective intranet firewalls.

Identifying significant network security issues before implementing firewalls is important. Of course, identifying these significant network security issues is easier said than done. Doing so involves discussing network services with all appropriate users, and determining which resources you will allow users to access and which ones you will restrict because of security risks.

An effective network security policy should cover the concerns of network administrators and yet be acceptable to the network users. It needs to cover all the potential security risks without impairing the use of the network.

The following sections discuss suggested steps in creating an effective network security policy.

Step 1: Identify Security Issues

To implement an effective network security policy, you must identify all the important network security issues at your installation. Your consideration of the issues must go beyond your current situation to encompass your future plans for your intranet or network.

While you review the different network security issues, be sure to include all network resources. Leaving anything out of the consideration can weaken the overall security plan and cause an inaccurate risk analysis. The following is a basic list of the areas (or resources) that should be considered:

- Hardware
- Software
- Data

- People
- Documentation
- Supplies
- Overprotection

To start a network security policy, ask yourself several questions:

- What resources need to be protected?
- How important is each of these resources?
- Who are the potential "intruders"?
- How likely is the threat?
- What is needed to guard against this possible intrusion?
- Does the cost of defense balance with the likelihood of the threat and the importance level of the resource?

Because they have the knowledge of the day-to-day interworkings of the computer system or their department and can therefore offer valuable insight, you should involve the whole MIS staff and the department heads in considering security issues. The implementation of the network security policy will also benefit from having as many people involved in the process as is practical. If department heads are involved in the process from the beginning, they will feel that the new network security policy is partly their idea. This will help a great deal with their acceptance of the security policy and its successful implementation.

The use of an outside consultant also can be very useful in this step. An outside consultant can offer insight and suggestions that he or she has seen at various other installations. Additionally, a qualified consultant will be aware of the latest approaches and technologies in computer security.

At this step, you also should review all the different network resources (described shortly) and view them in light of the two approaches to network security (access and denial) to decide which approach the network security policy will take with respect to the different network security issues.

Hardware

Your security policy should encompass everything that is part of the computer system at your installation, including: workstations, servers, routers, terminal servers, data drives, communication lines, modems, printers, keyboards, and spare equipment.

Software

Make sure that you include all the software that exists at your installation. Include operating systems, applications, source code, utility programs, and original and duplicate diskettes. If someone places a "Trojan horse" type of computer virus on an original application disk, and that disk is loaded onto the system by a systems administrator, the overall network security is compromised.

Data

Consider all the data on the system. Remember to include the data that isn't online, such as data tapes, backup tapes, removable drives, and archived data. After you have identified all the data, consider who in the organization should have access to that data.

Also, you should consider why the data is important. That is, is the data critical because it will be difficult to re-create, or is it critical because it is confidential? If re-creation of data is the prime concern with some particular data, then a good system of redundancy (such as tape backups) may be more important than access security. On the other hand, if the data is important because, for example, you don't want anyone outside the organization to *have* the data, access is the key issue.

People

This is the easiest area to overlook in this step. Consider all the users and the support people needed to keep your system afloat. They are an important factor in the risk analysis. If you are looking at a network resource that isn't necessarily all that important in terms of confidentiality, you might not attach much importance to it. If this resource represents several hundred man-hours to create or duplicate, however, you would be wise to give it a higher overall importance.

Documentation

This is another area that can be easily overlooked. Documentation on certain types of hardware and software products discusses the management of the security features of that product. Would you want someone to know the procedure for bypassing the administrator's password on the firewall computer? Of course not. Yet, if you don't factor the location of the documentation into your security policy, you could compromise it.

Supplies

Even computer system-related supplies should be factored into the mix. This will ensure a more accurate risk analysis. For example, because of the ongoing problem of computer viruses, many companies now have a strict policy prohibiting disks brought from home to be used in a company computer until the disk has been checked by the systems administrator.

Overprotection

It is possible to focus so intently on protection of data that you engage in the computer equivalent of padlocking the door and forgetting where you put the key. While careful consideration must be given to who in the organization will have the ability to control overall access, thought must also be given to what will happen if the one and only person with "supervisor" password access to your Novell network leaves to join a fishing expedition in Alaska (this has actually happened). Be sure that there is redundancy in the organization's ability to *access* information, as well as in the ability to *deny access.*

Step 2: Analyze Risk/Cost

You can perform a risk analysis of the network system in several ways. The method that we discuss in this section uses a simple cost/risk matrix (see Figure 3-2).

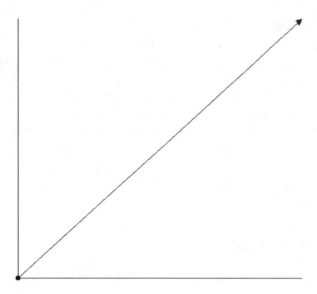

Figure 3-2: Cost/risk evaluation matrix.

This method does not produce a detailed list of probable or expected losses. It does, however, show management the high-risk exposures that can be addressed cost effectively.

Start by listing all the exposures (that is, security risks) that have been identified by your MIS team or consultant. The exposures on the list should be ranked on a scale of 1 to 100. The higher the likelihood of a particular exposure, the higher the score. The risk of a user cracking the systems administrator's password and "reconfiguring" a gateway would receive a low score. The risk of tampering with an unprotected, stand-alone computer system that monitors all long-distance calls would, however, receive a very high score.

 **TIP**

You should create this list in a spreadsheet program, such as Microsoft Excel or Lotus 1-2-3, that can produce three-dimensional graphs.

Next, rank the exposures again, this time according to the cost of the loss on a scale of 1 to 100. Using the previous examples, the cost of correcting the gateway settings would most likely be low. The loss of long-distance phone tracking, however, could be high. At this point, you need to consider all the factors carefully to ensure that you have an accurate cost estimate.

Finally, rank the items on the list a third time, this time according to the cost of implementing corrective procedures for each exposure on a scale of 1 to 100. (When several corrective procedures are available to the job, you should pick the least-expensive option.)

 **TIP**

Sometimes, a corrective measure is just a policy change or a new company policy.

Now, you should plot each of these exposures on a three-dimensional graph to show the matrix (see Figure 3-3).

Figure 3-3: A simple graphical representation of the cost-versus-risk analysis described in this section.

If you produce the list on a spreadsheet program, plotting the exposures should be quick and easy.

 **TIP**

You may want to print the graph on a color printer. This will help in the presentation of your cost-risk analysis.

At this point, you should see all the exposures and how they rate on the three different axes. Of particular interest are the exposures demonstrating the highest risk at the lowest corrective-measure cost. These are found on the matrix near the lower-left corner, where the cost axis and the risk axis meet. These should be addressed first.

Step 3: Implement Your Plan

After you complete the cost-risk analysis, deciding which measures should be implemented first should be easy. Depending on the scope of what needs to be done and the budget with which to do it, you should start with the corrective measures that apply to the exposures that, again, display the highest risk at the lowest corrective-measure cost. These are generally policy changes.

Generally, firewalls can be found in the "high-risk, low-cost" area of the graph. Firewalls can protect many large areas of concern and potential exposures at a comparatively low cost. They are excellent starting points for your initial security changes. The first safeguards that you implement should have a big effect for relatively low cost for several reasons:

- Other departments will see faster progress and be more cooperative as the implementation progresses.

- Management will see things happening and feel that the money is being wisely spent.

- If you have not received all the money allotted by the budget for everything that needs to be done, having fast initial progress will help you obtain the remaining funds.

■ If the budget is cut later, you will have already protected the most important exposures.

As the initial implementation of security devices and policies occurs, you can roll out the next or the rest of the corrective measures that seem practical or necessary. Keeping these corrective measures from greatly disrupting the workflow of the users is important. If you create a user-unfriendly system as a result of accomplishing a complete "lock-down" of system security, you will have failed. The users won't use the system, so you won't have anything to protect, anyway. Your goal in this process is to make the security checkpoints and barriers as transparent as possible to the end user.

Step 4: Review & Update Your Plan

An important step to include in your network security policy is a fixed (and recurring) time frame for reviewing the whole policy. As new hardware and software are added to your network or intranet, the security requirements will change. If no predefined time or procedure for reviewing the security design exists, the review probably will never happen. The review period will obviously be different for every organization. It should be done at least once a year, however, no matter what the size of the organization.

 **TIP**

In addition to the periodic review of your security, you should also plan to review security after any significant changes are made on the system, such as major application upgrades or operating system changes.

In this final step, you should also designate a group of people in your organization to serve as a security review team. This team of employees can make the process of reviewing the network security policy easier and more effective. Depending on the complexity of your original network security policy, you might consider using an outside consultant in this process. The review team should review the network security plan for the following concerns:

- New exposures

- Old exposures that no longer exist

- Security violations since the last review

New Exposures

The first areas to consider during the review process are the new exposures that might now exist due to new additions to the network or new software installations. Some attention may have been paid to them at the time they were implemented, but an examination of how their security measures fit into the overall network plan should be considered as part of the periodic review process.

Old Exposures That No Longer Exist

The next areas to investigate are the old exposures that are gone. If certain parts of the network have been eliminated or have been diminished in capacity, their protective measures may need to be diminished according to new situations. You don't need to spend significant resources protecting something that may no longer present much of a threat of exposure. The resources may be better used on a different area that was perhaps discovered in the first part of this review process.

Security Violations Since the Last Review

Learning from past mistakes can be the most valuable tool in preventing new ones. A careful review of the past security violations can show you the areas of exposure that may not have been properly secured. Additionally, you may discover some trends in the violations that will enable you to take corrective measures.

For example, if you notice during the review that every violation of the payroll system has occurred after hours and over the phone lines, you could limit the use of the payroll system to the regular business hours period, and update your firewall computer so that that branch of the network will not accept any requests for access to the payroll system after hours.

Moving On

In this chapter, we have looked at problems related to overall computer network and intranet security. We also have provided a framework for establishing network security to address those problems, including the places in the system where firewalls might provide a viable solution.

In the next chapter, we'll describe general categories of firewall technology and how they can be used to implement your security policy. Then, in the following chapters, we look at some typical firewall packages provided by software vendors that you might use in your company intranet.

4 Firewall Concepts & Technology

Now that you've analyzed your security risks and developed a comprehensive security policy, you're ready to put it into effect by building your firewall.

Not very long ago, building a firewall meant writing your own software and configuring your own hardware. If you have the resources, there might be good reasons for taking that approach. For one thing, you would get a system precisely designed to meet your needs. Also, attackers wouldn't be able to study your system's documentation to learn its weak points, as they can with commercial products.

But doing it yourself takes a lot of time and resources, so most organizations buy the products they need for their firewall. In order to understand the competing products and decide which is best for your needs, you have to start with a good understanding of what firewalls are all about.

We wrote this chapter to give you that foundation. We will describe the key technologies used in firewalls, and we'll show you how those technologies can be put to work in basic firewall configurations. This information will help you decide which firewall solution is best for your organization.

There are a lot of firewall products on the market, and they don't all fit nicely into the categories we'll describe in this chapter. Many products combine features from more than one category, blurring the distinctions between them. As this young (only five or so years old) industry matures, it is evolving toward new definitions of firewall products.

The terminology used to describe these products is also a little blurry. The glossary at the end of this book provides the most commonly accepted definitions of firewall terminology as of this writing.

So, your best protection in the maelstrom is a good understanding of the basics.

 **TIP**

When you start looking for products for your firewall, use caution. The field is changing rapidly, with new products being introduced every month. Some of those products combine some features of different kinds of components, such as proxy servers and screening routers. That may seem like a more convenient and efficient way to go, but be certain that the product doesn't leave out the features you really need.

There is no precise firewall vocabulary, and terms tend to be used in slightly different ways by different people and different manufacturers. Don't be afraid to ask the salesperson to explain the terms they're using, even if they are common ones. Don't assume that you're both using the same term to mean exactly the same thing.

The Firewall Concept

"Firewall" is a blanket term that can be defined as follows:

> *A firewall is a system (either software or hardware or both) that enforces an access control policy between two networks.*

Thus, your firewall is the manifestation of your security policy.

A firewall is not a single computer program or piece of equipment. In fact, a firewall could be empty space. If your security policy is to provide absolute protection against penetration from the outside, the surest way to achieve that policy is to eliminate all paths by which someone could connect with the network. The firewall in this case would be the complete *lack* of connection with the outside world.

Figure 4-1: No computer is an island.

However, in a world that is becoming increasingly interconnected, such a drastic security policy would probably not be appropriate for most organizations. As a practical matter, firewalls comprise hardware and software that, in theory, block all unwanted communication between networks while allowing acceptable communication to pass back and forth. "Communication," as used here, means any kind of transaction between networks.

"Unwanted communication" can be anything from a completely innocent errant message, such as a misaddressed e-mail message, to a willful attack by someone who is intent on stealing or damaging your information. In practice, complete protection from unwanted communication and complete freedom for acceptable communication are antithetical, so firewall design requires judgment, compromise, and the acceptance of some level of risk.

Implementing an effective firewall is more complicated than buying an anti-virus program for your personal computer. Simply plugging a firewall product into your intranet probably won't give you the protection you need. (In fact, that approach may *increase* your risk if it leads you to a false sense of security that causes you to overlook vulnerabilities.) Setting up a firewall that effectively implements your security policy requires you to evaluate firewall technologies, select the ones that best suit your needs, and then set them up correctly.

In the rest of this section, for convenience, we'll talk about firewalls as lying between your intranet or internal network and the Internet. However, we don't mean to overlook the possibility that it may be equally important for you to defend one part of your intranet from users on another part.

Firewall Technology

Firewall technology generally falls into one of two categories: *network-level* or *application-level*. Even though, as we said before, most firewall products now contain features of both categories, it's still useful conceptually to discuss these categories separately.

Network-level technology guards the entire network from unauthorized intrusion. An example of a network-level technology is packet filtering, which simply reviews all information coming into a network and rejects the data that does not meet a predefined set of criteria. Another technique employed in network-level firewalls is the use of an authorization server that checks the authenticity of the user's login.

Application-level technology controls access on an application-by-application basis. For example, proxy servers can be set up to permit access to some applications, such at HTTP, while blocking access to others, such as FTP.

Packet Filters

In Chapter 2, we described a packet as a unit of information that moves across a network. A document, for example, is broken up into a series of packets for transmission from one computer to another. When the packets arrive at their destination, the data in them is assembled to recreate the document.

Each packet has two parts: the data that is part of the document and a *header*. If the packet is an envelope, then the data is the letter inside of the envelope and the header is the address information on the outside. (See Figure 4-2.) (Of course, since we're talking about computers, it's really more complicated than that, but you get the idea.)

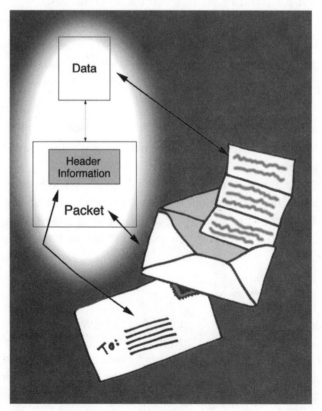

Figure 4-2: A packet is like a letter.

Just as the post office sorts mail by the address information, a packet filter (also called a screening router) can sort (filter) packets by the information in the header.

 **TIP**

The terms packet filter *and* screen router *are more-or-less interchangeable. In this book, we use* packet filter *to refer to the technology or the process that is taking place and* screening router *to refer to the thing that's doing it.*

To be technically rigorous, the packet contains three sets of header information—one each for three layers:

1. The transport layer, which includes Transport Control Protocol (TCP), User Datagram Protocol (UDP), or Internet Control Message Protocol (ICMP).

2. The Internet layer, which includes Internet Protocol (IP).

3. The network access layer, which includes Ethernet, Fiber Distributed Data Interface (FDDI), and so on.

Packet filtering uses information from the transport layer and IP headers.

Screening routers operate by comparing the header information with a table of rules set by the network administrator to determine whether or not to send the packet on to its destination. If there is a rule that does not allow the packet to be sent on, the router simply discards it.

 **TIP**

Screening routers are placed between the network they are intended to protect and the external world (usually the Internet, but possibly another part of the organization's internal network). They can be set to filter network traffic in either or both directions. Packets moving from the protected network to the external world are called outgoing *packets; those moving the other direction are called* incoming *packets.*

For each packet, the router applies the rules sequentially, starting with the first one, until it finds one the packet fits or until it runs out of rules.

For example, suppose a router had three rules in its table (greatly simplified for this example):

1. Don't accept any packets from Fred.

2. Accept all packets from Sylvia.

3. Don't accept packets addressed to Roy.

Now suppose a packet arrives from Sylvia. The router checks the first rule, but that doesn't fit the packet, so it goes on to the second rule. The second rule does fit, so the router passes the packet on to its destination; there's no need to check the remaining rule.

 **TIP**

Different routers do different things when they run out of rules. Some always deny the packet while others may or may not deny it. To be safe, you should enter a final rule in your table to deny any packet that didn't match any other rule.

Because rules are applied sequentially, their order in the table is very important. You will need to take a great deal of care to avoid having an overly permissive rule that allows a packet through when it would have been rejected by a later rule.

Let's take another look at the example we just used. Suppose the packet that arrived from Sylvia was addressed to Roy. It was passed by rule two, while it would have been rejected by rule three.

The process is like sifting gravel through increasingly finer screens. Each screen excludes some rocks and lets others through. If you get the screens out of order, you'll screen out rocks that you really wanted to let through, and vice versa.

Following is a very simple example of a table of rules. In real life, the rules table could have scores or even hundreds of rules, and the rules would probably be based on more elements of the header information. Also, these rules apply only to incoming packets.

- Rule 1: Don't allow packets from a particular host, called TROUBLEHOST.

- Rule 2: Let in connections into our mail gateway (using SMPT), located at Port 25 on our host.

The rules table could look like this:

Rule No	Action	Local Host	External Host	Local Port	External Port	Description
1	Block	!	TROUBLE-HOST	!	!	Block packets from TROUBLE-HOST
2	Pass	SMPT-Mail	!	25	!	Allow packets to our mail gateway
3	Block	!	!	!	!	Block everything else

! = Any value allowed

 **TIP**

For clarity in the example, the local and external hosts are identified by name in the table above. In an actual table of rules, they would be identified by their IP addresses.

When a packet arrives at the screening router, the process works like this:

1. The packet filter extracts the information it needs from the packet header. In this example, it uses the local and external host identification and the local and external port numbers.

2. The packet filter compares that information with the rules in the table.

Cisco Routers

One of the most common routers in use today is the Cisco router, produced by the manufacturer of the same name. This router performs traditional routing functions (that is, routing IP packets from one location to another), as well as screening functions.

The Cisco Router uses a concept called *Access lists*. These lists are essentially collections of the rules described earlier in this chapter. The lists are used to determine whether particular IP packets are permitted to pass the router or are denied that access. This router can screen both incoming and outgoing packets.

Although the syntax for specific Cisco access lists is beyond the scope of this book, a few typical lines from the system illustrate the function of this screening router. (In the material that follows, the code is in the first line and the explanation follows in parentheses.)

```
.no ip source-route
```

(Deny all "source-routed" packets. Source routing is a typical method of hacking and involves address spoofing. That is, attempting to use a legitimate internal source packet, usually obtained by intercepting outgoing messages, to get back into the protected system.)

```
.access-list 101 permit tcp any any established
```

(All incoming packets that are part of already established TCP connections are allowed to pass.)

```
.access-list 101 deny tcp any any range 6000 6003
```

(Blocks all services that list connections in with the designated port numbers.)

3. If the packet is from TROUBLEHOST, no matter what its destination, discard it.

4. If the packet makes it past the first rule (it's not from TROUBLEHOST), check to see if it's intended for port 25 on our SMTP-Mail host. If it is, send it on; otherwise, discard it.

5. If neither of the first two rules apply, the packet is rejected by rule three.

To appreciate the importance of the order of the rules, try reversing rules 1 and 2 in the example, and see what happens if a packet arrives from TROUBLEHOST addressed to the port 25 on our SMTP-Mail host.

Rule No	Action	Local Host	External Host	Local Port	External Port	Description
1	Pass	SMPT-Mail	!	25	!	Allow packets to our mail gateway
2	Block	!	TROUBLE-HOST	!	!	Block packets from TROUBLE-HOST
3	Block	!	!	!	!	Block everything else

! = Any value allowed

The packet will satisfy the criteria of rule one and be passed on, thus violating our policy of denying all packets from TROUBLEHOST.

Also notice that in order to be sent on, a packet must not only *not be blocked*, but must be affirmatively *allowed to proceed*. In other words, if a packet is not expressly entitled to proceed, it is blocked. Returning to our original example, a packet from GOODHOST directed toward port 144 (News server) would not be blocked by Rule 1, but it also would not be passed by Rule 2. It would wind up at rule 3, where it would be blocked.

If you wanted to accept packets from GOODHOST, you would need to add a rule to do so, such as:

Rule No	Action	Local Host	External Host	Local Port	External Port	Description
	Pass	!	GOOD HOST	!	!	Allow packets from GOOD HOST

This rule would go after rule 1 and before rule 3.

Packet filtering rules are usually based on some or all of the following header information:

■ IP Protocol Type.

■ IP source address.

■ IP destination address.

■ Contents of the IP Options field. This field is sometimes used to contain specific instructions for how the packet is to be routed through the network. That's called *host routing*. The only legitimate use for host routing is in testing, but attackers will use it to try to get around screening routers. Therefore, if there is anything in this header field, the packet is highly suspect.

■ TCP source port number.

■ TCP destination port number.

■ TCP ACK flag. The ACK flag is used to indicate whether a packet is the first packet in a connection or is a response to another packet.

We can't remember enough from our college statistics class to tell you how many combinations of these elements are possible, but it's a big number.

 **TIP**

For a listing of the port numbers assigned to various protocols, with notes about associated security vulnerabilities, see "Policing Protocols" in Appendix B. This information was provided by the National Computer Security Association.

The Drawbridge Packet Filter

Another typical packet filtering system, the Drawbridge Packet Filter, was developed by Texas A&M University. You can locate this software by accessing the FTP server, *net.tamu.edu*, and using a path of */pub/security/ drawbridge* with a file name of *drawbridge-2.0a.tar.gz*. (This product was designed and programmed by David Hess, Douglas Lee Schales, and David R. Safford.)

Drawbridge is copyrighted but is freely distributed. It uses a PC with two ethernet cards or two FDDI cards to perform the filtering. It is composed of three different tools: Filter, Filter Compiler, and Filter Manager. It operates on both incoming and outgoing packets.

To use the software, first create a filter source file. Then the included Filter Compiler creates filter tables that are stored, manipulated, and accessed by the filter manager component.

Rather than the access lists of Cisco's router, Drawbridge uses tables for the host, class, reject, and allow rules that the compiler creates. After creating the tables, the software then examines packets as they pass through the PC onto which the software is installed.

Again, a comprehensive review of all the possible filtering matrices is beyond the scope of this book. Here, though, are some sample lines from the filter language:

```
<smtp in-out>
```

(Allows Simplified Mail Transfer Protocol connections in either direction.)

```
<1-65535 out>
```

(Allows all outgoing connections.)

➡

```
Define normal <smtp in>, <gopher in>;
```
(This allows incoming mail and gopher connections. It actually creates a group called "normal" that includes incoming gopher and mail connections.)

As you can see, Drawbridge allows for a variety of filtering rules; we have touched on only a very few. For example, specific addresses (say, *195.55.55.0*) for various computers can also be filtered using similar statements.

Inspection Module

If the header information listed above doesn't give you enough elements for setting up rules, you can use a packet filter that has an inspection module, such as the Solstice FireWall Module (see Chapter 12). An inspection module looks at more of the header information; some can even look at the application data itself. An inspection module gives you much finer control over packets. For example, by inspecting the application data, the module can deny packets that contain certain application commands, such as the FTP put command or the SNMP set command.

State Evaluation

State evaluation is a technique that was developed to overcome a problem posed by the User Datagram Protocol (UDP).

UDP is an alternative to TCP that is often used for services that are query/response oriented, such as Domain Name Service, where one computer sends a request to a name server and the name server replies with the requested information.

The header of a TCP packet contains an indicator called the ACK flag. When the ACK flag is set, it means that the incoming packet is a response to an earlier outgoing packet. If the flag is not set, the packet is not a response to an earlier outgoing packet, and therefore is suspect. It's common to set a screen rule to allow incoming packets that have the ACK flag set and reject those that don't.

For example, suppose you want to allow your users to have access to the World Wide Web, but you don't want people on the Internet to have access to your intranet Web servers. When a user requests a page from the World Wide Web, the packets that are returned by the Web server will have the ACK flag set, because they are in response to the user's request. Your router should let those packets through.

On the other hand, if a packet from the Internet shows up that doesn't have the ACK flag set, it means the packet is not in response to a user's request, but is the first packet in an attempted connection initiated by someone on the Internet. Those packets should be rejected.

UDP doesn't use an ACK flag or any other similar indicator, so there's no way for the screening router to know whether an incoming packet was sent in response to an earlier outgoing packet. The only safe thing to do in that situation is to reject the packet.

That's where *state evaluation* comes in. A screening router that has the state evaluation capability, such as the FireWall-1 router, "remembers" the original outgoing packet for a certain length of time (set by the system administrator). If an incoming packet that corresponds with the original arrives within the timeframe, the router allows it to go through. The incoming packet must be from the host and port to which the outgoing message was sent, and it must be addressed to the host and port from which the outgoing message came.

Here's an analogy that's illustrative, if not precisely accurate. Suppose you go to a theater to see a movie. Part of the way through, you decide you want to leave for a few minutes. On your way out, the doorman stamps your hand with a rubber stamp. When you return, the doorman admits you because you have the rubber stamp symbol on your hand. That's (sort of) the TCP method of theater-entrance control.

In a UDP theater, however, you don't get your hand stamped, so the only way you can get back in is if the doorman remembers you. If the doorman can do state evaluation, you're in luck.

 **TIP**

A packet filter that does state evaluation is sometimes called a stateful *filter.* Stateful *is a linguistic double-back-flip, a back-formation from* stateless, *which is itself a back-formation from* state—*all of which may lead you to conclude that computer jargon has reached a sad* statefulness.

Proxy Servers

The second broad category of firewall technology is *application-level* technology. Devices in this category are called *application gateways*, which are computers running *proxy server* software.

A proxy is something that acts on behalf of something else. A *proxy server* is software that acts on behalf of an application that is trying to communicate from one network to another. Proxy server software can run on a machine by itself or along with other software such as packet filters.

A proxy server is like a border checkpoint between the internal network and the external world. Applications on both sides can communicate with the proxy server, but they can't communicate beyond it. The proxy server receives communication from one side, checks to make sure the communication is authorized to proceed, and—if it is—initiates a connection to the communication's destination and sends it on its way.

(A typical proxy server is the Firewall Server from BorderWare, described in Chapter 7. This product also demonstrates the trend toward combining firewall technologies; in addition to typical proxy capabilities, it also includes packet screening.)

For example, suppose there is a proxy server between your organization's intranet and the Internet. While the boss isn't looking, you decide to get onto the World Wide Web and check out the latest Dilbert cartoon.

You type the URL for Dilbert's home page (http://www.unitedmedia.com/comics/dilbert/) in your browser. The browser appears to send the request to the WWW but, unbeknownst to you, your intranet name resolution is set up to send the request to the proxy server.

The proxy server checks rules the administrator sets up to make sure your machine is authorized to visit the World Wide Web and that the site you want to go to is not prohibited. Then the proxy server sends the URL on to the Internet.

When Dilbert's home page is returned from the Internet, it is addressed to the proxy server. The proxy server receives the page, has a quick chuckle over the comic strip, readdresses the page, and sends it on to your machine. If you're lucky, it all happens before your boss figures out what's going on.

If someone initiates a contact from the Internet to a site on your intranet, the same process takes place in reverse. The proxy server receives the contact, checks the rules, and makes a connection on the intranet side if the contact is authorized. For example, if someone on the Internet wanted to request a page from an HTTP server on your intranet, they would address their request to your proxy server. The proxy server would readdress the request and forward it on your intranet, then reverse the process to send the requested page.

Application gateways have additional capabilities. They can log information about what passes through them, such as what users connected with what sites at what times. That can be valuable information for uncovering attempted penetrations of the network.

Some application gateways also store pages from the Internet that are requested frequently. When a user requests a page that is in the server's cache, the server can supply the page itself, rather than having to go out to the server on the Internet. That makes for much faster service for the user.

In addition to the application gateway, there's another kind of proxy server called a *circuit-level gateway*. The difference between them has to do with application protocols. An application gateway understands the application protocol that wants to use it. In fact, application-level proxy servers are written for specific services. If the gateway doesn't have a proxy server for a particular service, that service can't get through the gateway—period.

That's a disadvantage because the proxy server is limited in the application protocols it can handle. It's an advantage because the proxy server can look into the application protocol information to find out where the connection is supposed to go. The proxy server can even go so far as to inspect the contents of the packet and accept or reject the connection based on what the user is trying to do. For example, a proxy server for FTP can be set to reject a connection if the packet contains the "put" command. (The put command is used to write a file to the FTP site. If someone wanted to infect your site with a virus, they might use the FTP put command to do it.)

A circuit-level gateway doesn't know anything about the application protocol. It just sets up a connection from one network to the other (if the connection meet is permissible under its rules) and gets out of the way. That's an advantage because the proxy server can handle any protocol that comes along. It's a disadvantage because the proxy server can't inspect the application protocol information to find out where the connection is supposed to go. The application that is using the circuit-level proxy server has to tell the server what to do with the connection.

BorderWare's Firewall Server and Cypress's Labyrinth Firewall are two examples of products that include circuit-level proxy technology.

//////// TRAP

Note that using proxy applications requires a high-performance system; otherwise, a serious bottleneck of traffic is created.

User Authentication
The firewall technologies we've described so far are based on granting or denying access based on the machine or service that's trying to gain access. Another kind of security, called *user authentication,* is based on the person who is attempting to gain access to the network.

User authentication has two parts:

1. Determining that the user is who he or she claims to be.
2. Determining what that person is allowed to do on the network.

Positively identifying the person is the tricky part. The most certain way to verify a person's identity is visual identification; that's why most driver's licenses and ID cards carry photos of the owner. Measuring some characteristic of the person—their fingerprints, the details of their retinas, or their voiceprint, for example—is another good identification method. Unfortunately, the present state of computer technology does not make it easy to use these methods across a network.

The next-best identification method is to check for something that only the correct person would know or have. Traditionally, the thing a person should know has been a password.

Relying on something the person possesses is more common outside of the computer field. One such thing that is familiar to everyone is a key. If you have the key, you are presumed to be authorized to go where the key will admit you. A familiar, higher-tech version of the metal key is the plastic access card that carries identifying information on a magnetic stripe. When the card is passed through a reader, the information is sent to a central computer, which decides whether the holder of the card is authorized to go where they are trying to go. The computer then either unlocks the door, or it doesn't.

Passwords have some well-known shortcomings. The longer a password goes without being changed, the more likely it is to be discovered by someone who shouldn't have it.

Passwords that are easy to remember, such as common words, are also easy to deduce. Passwords that are difficult to deduce, such as random strings of letters and numbers, are hard to remember. If a password is too hard to remember, people will write it down, making it easier for someone else to learn it. (The image of a password written on a yellow sticky note and stuck below the computer monitor screen is all too familiar.)

Authentication Server

Nowadays, there are software solutions called *authentication servers* that use a variety of techniques to produce short-lived, one-time passwords.

For example, the TIS Internet Firewalls Toolkit authentication server uses a *smart card*—similar to a slim pocket calculator—from Digital Pathways in a challenge/response system. When the user logs on to the network, the authentication server produces a random number and sends it to the user.

The user enters a personal identification number—basically, a password—into the smart card to turn it on. Then they enter the challenge number. The card encrypts the challenge number using a secret key stored in the card and displays the result. The user types the result into the computer and sends it to the authentication server.

The authentication server encrypts the challenge number using the same key as the smart card and compares its result with the result sent back by the user. If the two results match, the computer concludes that the user is who he or she says and allows the user to access the network.

Another approach to authentication is taken by CyberSafe Challenger, which is a commercial implementation of Kerberos, a system developed by Massachusetts Institute of Technology to provide security over networks.

When the user logs in to the network and enters a password, the Kerberos server sends a "ticket" to the user's computer. The ticket is a one-time password that identifies the user's computer to other devices and applications on the network. (The ticket expires after a period set by the systems administrator.)

To the network user, the Kerberos system is transparent after the initial authentication. After authentication, users have access to any application that incorporates Kerberos and to which the user is authorized.

In addition to authentication, Kerberos also provides secure transmission across the network through the use of encryption, and it detects alterations to communications.

For more information about CyberSafe Challenger and Kerberos, see Chapter 11.

Component Certification

A firewall is something like a parachute: You'd like to be sure it's going to work when it's needed, but you'd rather not try it out yourself. That's where the National Computer Security Association (NCSA) comes in. As far as we know, they don't jump out of airplanes, but they do test firewall components to make sure that they work.

According to its literature, NCSA is a trade association of 30,000 members that provides a number of services relating to computer security, including testing, training, research, "underground reconnaissance," consulting, and certification.

In its certification program, NCSA sets up the firewall product to be tested on a laboratory network, subjecting it to attacks from both inside and outside the network. Products that meet NCSA's test criteria (see sidebar) are certified by the organization.

NCSA Test Criteria

As this book is being written, NCSA is updating its test criteria. Here is a draft of the updated version, reprinted with permission from NCSA. This draft is still subject to revision.

NCSA FWPD Criteria

Version 1.5c

Draft for FWPD Discussion

"Strawman 1"

I. Functionality Requirements

The product under test will be installed and configured to support the service requirements listed below. In the event that multiple means are available for supporting a feature, the "most transparent" mode will be used for supporting internal users, and the "most restrictive" used in supporting external users.

Operating system facilities which do not directly support the service/security requirements of the firewall will be disabled insofar as is possible.

1. Services to Internal Clients
   a. Telnet through firewall to external networks.[*]
   b. FTP through firewall to external networks.[*]
   c. HTTP through firewall to external networks.[†]
   d. SSL and/or SHTTP through the firewall to external networks.
   e. SMTP mail through firewall to external networks.
   f. DNS—external FQDNs must be resolvable by internal clients.

   [*] SOCKS may be used in meeting these requirements.
   [†] HTTP may be provided via a proxy/cache or by filter.

2. Services Provided to External Users
   a. FTP access to a server located on the internal network or a service network.[*†]
   b. HTTP access to a server located on the internal network or a service network.
   c. SSL and/or SHTTP access to a server located on the internal network or on a service network.
   d. SMTP mail must be deliverable to clients on internal networks.[‡]
   e. DNS—some form of "presence" must be configurable.

   [*] FTP service need not be anonymous.
   [†] If an authentication key device is required to access a service, the vendor must supply the device to NCSA for testing.
   [‡] Products which proxy (as opposed to filtering) SMTP traffic will be required to resist known sendmail-type attacks.

[This requirement is included as a clarification of the existing testing policy.]

3. Firewall Management
   a. The console of the firewall system must be securable, requiring a password authentication for access.
   b. If a remote management capability is provided for use over external networks:
      - A one-time password mechanism must be utilized.
      - An encrypted link mechanism must be utilized.

c. If a remote management capability is provided for use over internal networks, an IP address must not be the sole mechanism for administrator authentication.

II. Security Requirements

Upon demonstration of the functional requirements in section I, the configuration under test will be subjected to the following tests. The tests will be tuned utilizing full knowledge of the test configuration and its components, reducing the impact of "security by obscurity." The same set of attacks will be mounted from the internal network, as if an attacker had gained access to a system on the internal network.

To receive certification, a product (as configured to meet the requirements of section I above) must resist all attacks listed in this section, in accordance with the following criteria:

- No measure of administrative control of the firewall or the underlying operating system may become available to the attacker as a result of the attacks applied.

- No protocol or data content other than that specified in section I must pass the firewall and be carried on the internal network.

- Denials of service: The product under test must not be repeatably rendered inoperable by any network-based attack, unless the product has a documented fail-safe mechanism for removing itself from service according to a policy.

Products which do not meet these criteria will not be certified. [The FWPD Certification Contract is the authoritative document governing procedures for certification, resolution of certification problems, and decertification.]

During testing, network monitors will be utilized both on the protected network and on the segment outside of the firewall.

1. ISS Security Scanner

The most current production version (and/or beta release) of the ISS Security Scanner product will be configured with full knowledge of the firewall and systems it is protecting. All possible modes/attacks will be configured and enabled regardless of applicability to the configuration under test.

The ISS Security Scanner represents an aggregate of common threats known and repeatable at the time of its release. NCSA will continually update to the latest production release and/or beta release of this product as part of its ongoing testing.

a. External Scan
   The scanner will be run against the configuration under test from a non-adjacent subnet.

b. Internal Scan
   The scanner will be run against the configuration from a "trusted" internal system.

2. Port Scanning

   A port scanning tool will be run against the configuration under test, for the purpose of determining conformance to the service requirements in section I. Scans will be run from both the "trusted" internal net and an untrusted non-adjacent subnet.

   Information from the scans will be compared with the service requirements (Section I).

3. NCSA Tools

   As part of its network security advocacy role, NCSA collects and builds tools for use in penetration testing and vulnerability assessment. Generally these tools incorporate emerging attack methodologies, and or demonstration code for publicized exploits.

   NCSA will apply tools from its inventory to the configuration under test based on OS-type, firewall type, and active ports/services (as revealed by II.2).

   In the event of a successful exploitation which compromises the firewall platform or the protected network, the vendor will be provided with information regarding the attack's "signature" and on-wire protocol traces. In only the rarest of cases (where such methods do not provide the vendor with sufficient information to remedy the problem) will NCSA consider releasing the tool which facilitated the breach of security. Any such release of code would require execution of an NCSA Malicious Code Agreement*.

One of the tools NCSA uses in their testing is Internet Scanner from Internet Security Systems. This product is available to anyone who wants to monitor the security of their network. Internet Scanner "patrols" your network, checking for holes and alerting you to potential security breaches.

Internet Security Systems programs Internet Scanner to simulate known ways in which attackers try to penetrate networks. The tool reports the security breaches it finds during the simulated attacks.

For more information about Internet Scanner, see Chapter 11.

Firewall Configurations

We've described the basic components of a firewall, but we haven't yet described a firewall. Using the same components but arranging them in different configurations, you can come up with different kinds of firewalls that have different strengths and weaknesses. That's what we'll cover in this section.

Screened Network (Packet Filtering Only)

The simplest kind of firewall uses only packet-filtering software running on a screening router to let the good guys in and keep the bad guys out. This configuration is shown in Figure 4-3.

All traffic into and out of the intranet must pass through the screening router, where rules determine what traffic will be allowed through.

Benefits of the Screened Network

Packet filtering is easy to employ for small, uncomplicated sites. If there is already a single router between your network and the outside world, you may be able to simply add packet filtering software to it. In one step, you have added protection for your entire network.

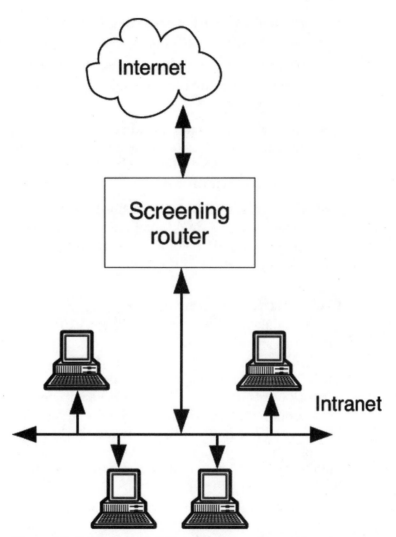

Figure 4-3: A simple firewall that uses a screening router.

Packet filtering doesn't require any changes to applications your users are running, and it doesn't require users to learn any new tricks. Users won't even know the screening server is there unless they try to do something that's against the rules.

Disadvantages of the Screened Network

Screening routers have a number of shortcomings:

- They have little or no logging capability, so the network administrator cannot easily determine if the system is or has been under attack.

- The table of rules can quickly become very large and complex, and the rules are difficult to test. As the table grows in size and complexity, the likelihood of having holes in the rule structure increases.

- The biggest disadvantage of this type of firewall is that you are relying on a single component for protection. If that component fails, it could leave the door to your network wide open, and you might not even know it.

Dual-homed Gateway

Using a single proxy server by itself, you can set up a *dual-homed gateway*, as shown in Figure 4-4.

A dual-homed host is a computer with two network interface cards (NICs), each with its own IP address. If a computer on one network wants to communicate with a computer on the other, it must connect with the IP address that it can "see" on the dual-homed host. The proxy server software checks its rules to see if the connection is permissible. If it is, the proxy server software initiates the connection to the other network through the second NIC.

An example of a dual-homed host is the SmartWall gateway.

─*//////* **TRAP**

If you are setting up a dual-homed host, make sure the routing capability of the operating system is turned off. *If routing is left on, traffic is routed from one NIC to the other without going through the proxy server software.*

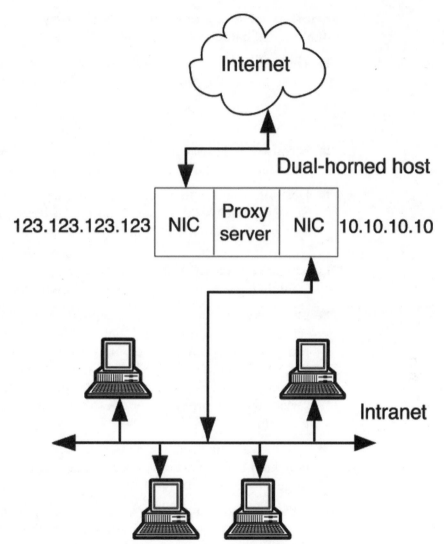

Figure 4-4: A dual-homed host has two IP addresses.

Benefits of a Dual-homed Gateway

A dual-homed gateway has some attractive features:

- The main advantage is that the gateway provides a complete separation of the protected network from the outside world.

- Proxy servers provide logging that can help in detecting attacks.

- Because it is a host computer, it can be used for services such as authentication servers as well as proxy servers.

- DNS information does not pass from the protected network to the outside world, so names and IP addresses of site systems are hidden from Internet systems.

Disadvantages of a Dual-homed Gateway

As you might expect, there are also some drawbacks:

- The proxy server needs to be designed specifically for each service that needs to use it. (That used to mean a separate proxy server for each service. Newer proxy servers, such as the AltaVista FireWall, can handle several services, but not just any service that comes along.) If you want to add a service that the proxy server doesn't handle, you have a problem.

- If IP forwarding becomes enabled in some way (as could happen if the operating system is reinstalled and someone forgets to turn off routing), all security is lost.

- If the dual-homed gateway is the only component of the firewall, you have a single point of failure that could jeopardize your security.

To the Ramparts!

A term that is heard frequently in discussions of firewalls is *bastion host*.

A bastion host is a computer running proxy software that is exposed to the world outside the network it is intended to protect. The term does not denote a particular kind of firewall configuration; bastion hosts are used in all of the arrangements described in this chapter except the screened network, because that arrangement doesn't use a proxy server.

In addition to the configurations described here, there is another kind of bastion host called a *victim machine* (also called a *sacrificial lamb*). A victim machine is exposed to the outside world, so communications (and attacks) are directed to it. Behind the victim machine, you build a strong defense to keep intruders out of your internal network. You might even go so far as to remove all network links to the victim machine, so there is no physical way for intruders to get past it and into your network.

The victim machine contains only information that you are willing to share freely with anyone, and only minimal services. As a policy matter, you are willing to sacrifice the machine rather than make it possible for someone to penetrate your network. When the attacks come (and they will), you simply rebuild the contents of the machine, if necessary, and carry on.

Screened Host

A screened-host firewall uses both a screening router and an application gateway to achieve a higher level of security than you could get with either one by itself. This configuration is shown in Figure 4-5.

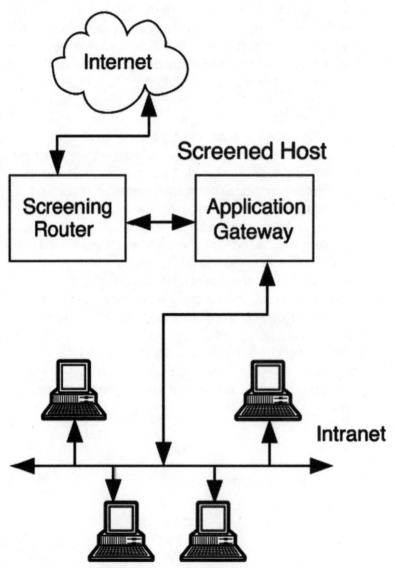

Figure 4-5: The screened-host Configuration.

In a screened-host firewall, all traffic from the Internet is directed to the screening router, which filters traffic according to the rules it has been given. All traffic that satisfies the rules is forwarded to the application gateway. In most cases, all traffic that is addressed to any machine other than the application gateway is rejected.

In this case, the application gateway has only one network interface card (that is, it is not a dual-homed gateway). The proxy server software on the gateway applies its own rules and passes permissible traffic on to the protected network.

Benefits of a Screened-host Firewall
The benefits of the screened-host firewall include:

- The configuration is more flexible than a dual-homed gateway firewall. It can be set up so that the screening router passes some traffic directly to sites on the intranet instead of to the application gateway. You might want to do that if, for example, you have an HTTP server set up as a sacrificial lamb that doesn't require protection.

- The rules for the packet filter can be less complex than for a screened-network configuration because most or all of the traffic will be directed to the application gateway.

- If either component fails in an "open" condition, so that it no longer blocks anything, the other component still affords some measure of protection.

Disadvantages of a Screened-host Firewall
The disadvantages of this configuration include:

- The two components of the firewall need to be configured carefully to work together correctly. For example, the router has to be set up to route all traffic to the proxy server. Even though the rules for the packet filter may be less complex, the overall job of configuring the firewall may be more complex.

- The flexibility of the system can lead to the temptation to take shortcuts that can subvert security. For example, users might try to set up connections directly to the router to avoid the proxy server. Administrators need to be more diligent in adhering to security policy.

Screened Subnet

The screened-subnet firewall adds another screening router to the screened-host configuration to create a subnet that is sometimes called the *demilitarized zone*. (In case you haven't noticed, the field of firewalls is rife with martial images.) A screened-subnet firewall is shown in Figure 4-6.

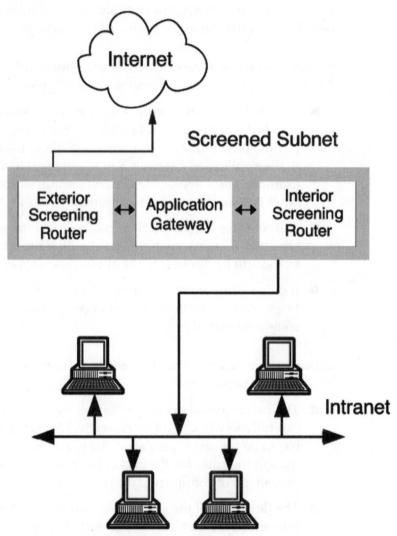

Figure 4-6: A screened-subnet firewall.

The demilitarized zone is the gray-shaded area in the illustration. In addition to the application gateway shown, this subnet could also be used for information servers, modem pools, and other systems that require carefully controlled access.

The exterior screening router and the application gateway function as they do in a screened-host firewall. The interior screening router provides additional protection between the application gateway and the protected network. Think of the interior router as a fall-back defense in case an attacker gets through the exterior router and application gateway.

Benefits of the Screened-subnet Firewall
The chief benefit of the screened-subnet firewall is another layer of protection. To gain access to the protected network, an attacker would have to go through two routers and the application gateway—not impossible, but more difficult than with a screened-host firewall.

Disadvantages of the Screened-subnet Firewall
The screened-subnet firewall has a few drawbacks:

- It's the most expensive configuration (of those described here) because it requires the greatest number of machines and software modules.

- With three machines, including two routers with their rule tables, configuration of the overall system can become quite complicated.

Other Firewall Configurations
You can come up with variations on the configurations described here to suit your security policy. You might want to use more bastion hosts to separate traffic for different services. You could add more layers of screened subnets to deal with traffic to and from networks with varying degrees of trustworthiness.

The point is that there are no hard-and-fast rules for how a firewall should be set up. Just remember a couple of guidelines:

- First and foremost, keep your security policy in mind and make sure your firewall faithfully implements it.

- Avoid the temptation to take shortcuts around more burdensome aspects of the security policy. Effective security sometimes means inconvenience.

- Keep it as simple as possible. More is not necessarily better, especially if adding more elements to your firewall makes it impossibly complex to set up and administer, or so difficult to use that users resort to unauthorized shortcuts.

Moving On

This chapter explained general firewall technologies and basic firewall configurations. It gave you a starting point for deciding on what type of firewall would work best for your organization. In the next chapter, you'll see how a hypothetical company determines its security needs and subsequently chooses firewall components and designs to meet them.

5 Practical Firewall Implementation

Now that we've reviewed the concepts and theories behind intranets and firewalls, we discuss how they can be put into practice in the real world.

In this chapter, we create a hypothetical corporation with the original name *Acme, Inc.* Using Acme as our example, we show you how and where firewalls can be used in a company's intranet to enhance overall security.

The purpose of this chapter is not to explain in technical detail how each item discussed would be accomplished, but to show approaches that this hypothetical company might use to solve common problems. The chapter is organized by business task, as opposed to computer design, to illustrate where and how security, including firewalls, might be an issue.

Our Sample Corporation: Acme, Inc.

Acme, Inc. is a small manufacturing company that produces a single product—the ever-popular widget. These products are sold wholesale only to a fairly large base of retailers throughout the country.

For our example, we keep Acme's organization simple and straightforward. Here is what the organizational chart might look like.

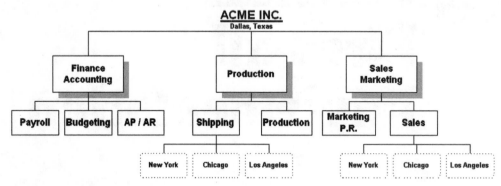

Figure 5-1: Acme's organizational chart shows a simple management structure with functions consolidated in three main departments: Production, Sales/Marketing, and Finance.

Acme has recently undergone a major change in management philosophy with the stated goal of technologically upgrading operations and easing the flow of information around the company.

To carry out its newfound commitment to technology, Acme first determines to use intranet technology for connectivity between areas of the corporation and, further, to connect the offices within each corporate area via intranet technology as well. Users in the same department and located in the same physical office will network using peer-to-peer technology, such as Windows 95 or Windows NT.

At the outset, Acme decides that it will use a design team for the intranet that includes not only the MIS employees, but also representatives from each major department, including manager-level employees as well as "front-line" employees, such as a sales representative and a production line supervisor, to ensure that the system actually works for the people who need to use it.

Acme management also has instructed all salespersons to exchange their paper sales books for notebook computers and has further decreed that all employees from first-level managers on up install computer workstations at their desks. The company has also recently exchanged its aging mainframe computer (used mainly for accounting) and its hodgepodge of LANs in various offices for a unified system using Windows NT as the main platform and using intranet technology for connectivity between offices, where appropriate.

Acme, like many other companies, has also determined that it will have a presence on, and allow its employees access to, the Internet.

Acme's corporate headquarters are in Dallas, Texas. The main management functions take place there.

The main production facility is located in New Orleans, with distribution points in New York, Chicago, and Los Angeles. Located with the shipping centers are the regional sales offices. These sales offices manage the salesmen in their respective regions, but report to Dallas for overall management functions.

For simplicity, we assume that all significant financial functions occur in Dallas and that the data for those functions also is stored primarily in Dallas. We also assume that all of the functions in a particular city (for example, Chicago) are physically located in the same building.

Acme's daily operations involve salespersons soliciting and taking orders from customers and passing those orders to their regional offices, and the regional offices passing the orders to both the shipping facilities and the home office (for accounting purposes).

The shipping facilities fill and ship orders, notifying the production facility in New Orleans on a daily basis as to activity so that production can be adjusted to meet anticipated demand.

In the sections that follow, we concentrate primarily on areas of computer security, including those areas in which firewalls will help the company meet its security needs.

This chapter is organized by setting out security issues and then providing sample solutions to those issues.

Security Issue: Defining the Internet Connection

As a first step toward expanding customer accessibility and upgrading the company's image, Acme management decides that a presence on the World Wide Web (WWW) is essential. To accomplish this goal, the company considers two general approaches, with security a primary concern.

First, the company could purchase, install, and run its own Web server system, perhaps from the company's headquarters in Dallas. Acme is a widget manufacturer, however, with no great desire to create a new department that deals primarily with the constantly changing atmosphere on the Web. Also, there is some legitimate concern that an internal Web server might inadvertently create unnecessary security risks. After considering all factors, including long-range cost, start-up time, and so on, the company opts for another approach: hiring an outside company to create and manage the corporate Web page.

 **TIP**

If a company's MIS department is sufficiently experienced in WWW page creation and management (as Acme's may become), or if the information on the Web site is particularly critical (for example, must be updated on a regular basis), the company would likely opt to create and manage its own page.

Solutions

Thus, like many companies, Acme retains the services of a professional Web server provider. This company consults with Acme, determines its goals, target markets, and potential for expanding business via the Web, and then designs an attractive Web home page for Acme, Inc. The page is up and running in a matter of a few days.

Initially, only information about Acme products is available, but shortly thereafter, Web users will have the ability to send e-mail messages to any of Acme's regional sales offices, generating a call back from the appropriate salesperson.

By keeping the Web server completely off-site, Acme has created a presence on the Web while also minimizing any security risks. This site, which is designed to attract outsiders, will be managed with a minimum of direct connection to any computer at Acme. In fact, the system could be created so that *no* information flows *out* of Acme via this channel—for example, incoming mail would be passed through the office of the professional Web server onto Acme's central SMTP (Simplified Mail Transfer Protocol) system, and outgoing mail would be filtered by a firewall. This system could be protected with a firewall product (such as a packet filter) that allows only the one-way passage of SMTP (or other e-mail protocol) data.

Other data that the Web provider might need for the home page, such as announcements of new products, updates on product availability, special promotions, and so on, could likewise be transferred via some secure method—via floppy disks, or a one-way e-mail service on the company's intranet, and so on—such that no files need be transferred via the Internet for this service.

Security Issue: Determining Who Needs Access

To protect computer data, and as we discussed in Chapter 4, the first step is determining who needs data and who does not. Further, in any computer network, including Acme's, a conscious effort must be made to decide which users in the organization need to communicate with other users and who those other users are. Often, without much input from operational managers, computer networks are created that simply "hook everybody up" to some central network or hub, thereby allowing everyone (at least initially) access to everything on the network.

Acme, as the forward-thinking company that it has recently become, realizes that a field sales representative does not normally need direct access to the same computer resources (or data) that, for example, an engineer in the production plant needs. Thus, Acme starts by analyzing the data currently in place on its computer system, factors in the new data that will be available under revised procedures, and then determines who needs access to the various types of data.

Solutions

Accordingly, Acme determines to organize the intranet by establishing internal servers for each major department. Each server will serve as the host for the data *generated* by the department. For example, the Production Department server will host product design data, production figures, and shipping records. The Sales/Marketing Department will host sales orders, invoices, and product sales information. The Finance Department server will host financial data such as customer account information, budgets, payroll, and so on.

Acme next determines that, where possible, data will be available only to individual users on an "as-needed" basis; in particular, users will not normally have access to data outside their own department. Thus, a field sales representative will not have direct access to engineering data, and shipping clerks will not have access to budgeting information, and so on. Employees at higher levels in the organization will have expanded access, however, as appropriate for their function. For example, the Vice President for Finance will have access to almost all data anywhere on the intranet, except for highly sensitive engineering data, which he or she will not likely need very often. (The president, who authorizes the funds for the system, will, of course, have access to anything the president wants.)

Table 5-1 provides a partial list of the data that Acme identifies, along with the people who need access and the intranet server where the data will reside.

Information	Department where created	People who need access	Server where data is located
Sales Orders	Sales/ Marketing	All sales, production managers, billing	Sales/ Marketing
Shipping Records	Production	Shipping clerks, sales managers, customer service (Finance Dept.)	Production
Invoices	Production	Sales managers, sales reps, all accounting	Production
Customer Accounts	Finance	All sales, all accounting, production managers	Finance
Production Data	Production	All production, sales managers	Production
Product Information	Sales/ Marketing	All departments	Sales/ Marketing
Product Availability	Production	All sales, all production, finance managers	Production
Design Information	Production	Production managers only (design team)	Production
Corporate Budgets	Finance	Department heads only	Finance
Payroll and other financial information	Finance	Production and sales department heads, all accounting	Finance

Table 5-1: This table shows where various information inside Acme is created and how it is shared.

From the table, you can see that various departments create and share a variety of bits of information. Using this table as a guide, the people responsible for building the intranet can ascertain where to place and how to share data.

Another benefit of advance planning of data sharing is that it enables changes to be made fairly easily. For example, after Acme's intranet is up and running, the employees and sales staff find that most inquiries from customers come not to the Finance (accounting) Department, but to the sales office for the area where the customer is located—that is, the regional office for the salespersons who took the order. Therefore, even though Finance creates the customer account information, Acme finds that response time is greatly enhanced by moving the customer account information onto the Sales Department server. For this reason, the MIS team sets up the system so that customer data (such as the account histories, transaction ledgers, and so on) are placed on the server for the appropriate sales office, as well as the Finance server at headquarters.

Acme's managers can also quickly request additional access to information, if it becomes apparent that such access is warranted. For example, the Finance managers may discover that they need access on a regular basis to the Production figures, in order to help them plan cash flow, next year's budget, and so on. In Table 5-1, under the "People who need access" column, "Finance managers" are added to the row for "Production data," and the MIS department is notified of the change. From there, appropriate changes are made in security to allow Finance managers in the area of the Production server with Production figures.

Keep in mind that Table 5-1 is a guide only. In other words, access to data need not be inflexible; using the matrix in the table as a guide, you can make changes with a minimum amount of confusion and redesign of systems. The point is to get the users of the information actually communicating with the "gatekeepers" (MIS team) about what they need.

In Figure 5-2, we can see how Acme begins the process of setting up its intranet.

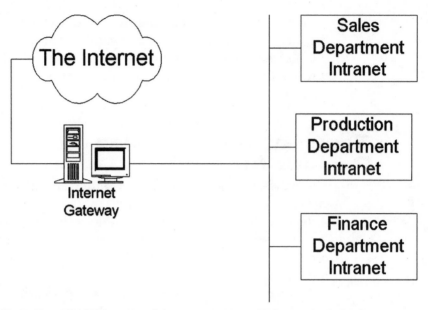

Figure 5-2: The beginnings of the Acme intranet with a server for each department.

Security Issue: Identifying Weak Spots in Information Flow

Before actual implementation, Acme's MIS employees carefully consider all security issues, as outlined in Chapter 4. Among those issues most important to Acme are the following:

- Limiting access to servers with remote (that is, dial-up) access capabilities

- Securing sensitive design data

- Preventing employees who should not have access to certain information from getting that information

In order to carefully consider security issues, we walk through the steps that show how various types of information are generated and used. Along the way, we examine how and where firewalls can help Acme ensure the integrity of its intranet.

To be sure that the planning steps outlined previously will actually work in the day-to-day operations at Acme, the company intranet design team outlines the path that information follows through the company. Throughout the process, security is a prime concern.

Security Issue: Managing Remote Access

The heart of Acme's operations is getting and filling orders from customers. Thus, it is vitally important that sales representatives' orders are processed quickly and efficiently on the new intranet. It is equally important, however, that the process by which those orders will now be transmitted (that is, through the company's intranet) be secure.

In the past, each order was taken on a paper order form while the sales representative sat at his or her desk or shared a cup of coffee with the customer. These paper forms were then photocopied and faxed to the central sales office, where the orders were telephoned to the nearest shipping point. The written order forms were forwarded by mail a few days later, with copies going to the shipping point and the main office for billing.

The shipping center shipped the products and forwarded a copy of the shipping documents to the main office for billing.

Acme decides to automate this process from the point of sale forward, using the new technology, including the intranets and remote accessibility.

First, sales reps take the orders from the customers and input the information into computer order forms on their notebook computers, which they never leave home without. At the end of the day, they compile the orders into single data files for transfer to the regional sales offices.

Next, whether at home or on the road, sales representatives begin the process of uploading the sales orders onto the company's FTP (File Transfer Protocol) order sites, located at each of the regional sales offices. This is accomplished by using communications software on the notebook computer to dial into the regional office's "modem center" via a cellular phone built into the notebook computer.

Solutions

As noted previously, anywhere an organization uses a standard telephone line for remote access, a danger exists that the number, and thus the line, may be attacked by a hacker. Anywhere that a hacker finds a modem answering the phone, a variety of attacks may begin on the system. For example, computerized hacking programs that repetitively dial modem numbers and attempt to intercept password data, or programs that dial the modem and attempt to download a virus file, are common. Acme recognizes this danger and takes steps to protect this doorway into its system.

Because this remote accessibility is a potential security risk point, Acme decides to use a two-stage firewall at this point in its system. This decision is made for two reasons. First, Acme wants an extra "layer" of protection for the modem system due to the potential security risk inherent with dial-up type systems. Second, whatever system protects the modems will not sufficiently prevent unauthorized access from within the corporation. That is, there may be employees inside the organization with legitimate need and access through the remote access system who do not have access to all data inside that firewall. For example, Bob Smith, the new salesperson, will need to have remote access to the sales server, but, once inside, he does not need the same access as the regional sales manager, who may have access to sensitive information, such as the evaluation of Bob's request for a raise.

In addition, the Sales server must be protected from those users who do not access the server through the remote access system at all, but rather have access through internal channels. Again, Bob may have a desktop PC with access to this server, but he does not need access to sensitive, managerial-type data.

To carry out this two-stage firewall protection, Acme decides to use the Modem Security Enforcer, described in Chapter 9, that requires users to call in, and pass a two-step password test, then hangs up the system and calls the user back at a preestablished telephone number (thus the necessity of the built-in cellular telephone in the notebook computer).

 **TIP**

Note that the use of Modem Security Enforcer in this example, or the other products mentioned in the examples that follow, is not an endorsement of that product over some other product—it is just a method of showing how real-world products can be used in a real-world situation. Some other approach or product might work just as well.

After the salesperson successfully passes through the modem security, the salesperson encounters the second firewall located on the Sales/Marketing Web server. For this firewall, Acme chooses a product that works by using more traditional firewall protection, such as a proxy server. In this case, Acme uses Borderware Firewall Server (described in Chapter 7), which accepts the data from the salesperson's notebook-generated order file and passes it through to the FTP site on the intranet.

Any data that comes back to the notebook during this process is protected by means of a Network Address Translation (also provided by Borderware's Firewall Server), which changes the actual internal addressing on information sent out to the remote computer. Therefore, even if a hacker should manage to intercept some of the outgoing data, the addressing has been changed by the firewall server, and "spoofing" (see Chapter 4) of this address will not allow the hacker back into the system.

The order is then combined with the other sales representatives' orders collected at the internal FTP site and downloaded by the regional sales offices for forwarding via internal (that is, inside the firewall) systems to the regional sales manager for that manager's records.

Figure 5-3 shows what the Sales/Marketing portion of the Acme intranet looks like.

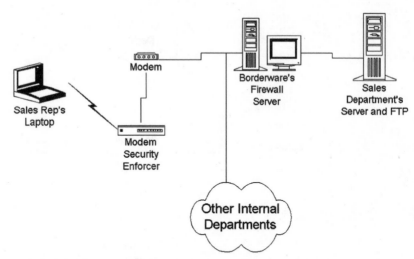

Figure 5-3: Here is the Sales/Marketing part of the Acme intranet with the firewalls added.

A process similar to that described here is used for transferring the data from the three sales offices to the main office. That is, the sales orders are combined into a single, larger format order and transferred to the various offices and the appropriate shipping points. Here, however, no public telephone lines are used. Rather, dedicated "T1" telephone lines are used to move the data from the sales offices to the shipping point and main office internal FTP sites, respectively.

Figure 5-4 shows a simple diagram depicting the flow of the information.

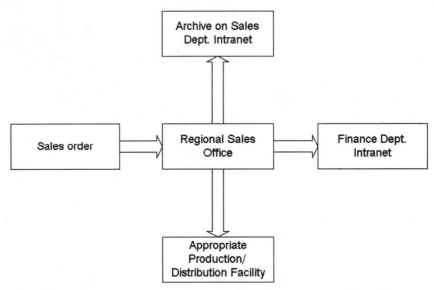

Figure 5-4: This diagram shows a typical sales order as it travels from the point of sale to the production and shipping facilities.

Security Issue: Getting Information to Remote Sites

In addition to receiving sales orders, the regional (and central) sales offices must make available to the sales force the latest information concerning changes to product lines, pricing information, shipping delays, and so on. As with previous tasks, Acme is not only concerned that this information be made available but also that the process of making it available be as secure as possible.

Also, as noted previously in Table 5-1, all offices (sales, marketing, and finance) must be able to access production figures and shipping times from the main production facility.

Solutions

These tasks can be accomplished using a secure e-mail system. Thus, the Acme intranet design team decides that, due to the need to pass queries and other short messages among various employees, the primary intranet system will be supplemented with a dedicated mail server system to handle only internal e-mail.

Figure 5-5 shows how the revised Acme intranet block diagram looks.

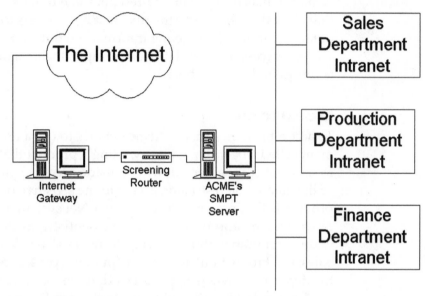

Figure 5-5: This is the revised Acme intranet, this time with the e-mail server added.

The design team decides to protect the e-mail server with a firewall product that includes a dual-homed gateway system with a mail forwarder, which protects the information by carefully screening incoming and outgoing data from the mail system to ensure that the only information that passes is mail protocol information (SMTP) and that the information is protected via the firewall's proxy server system. (See Chapter 3 for more details on these systems.)

Second, both the marketing and production facilities can use Web server-type systems to create internal "home pages" for access by intranet users. These home pages can contain information concerning the latest marketing strategies, production notices, shipping delays, and so on. These intranet home pages should be protected using the same firewall technologies described earlier in the section, such as dual-homed gateways, screening routers, and so on.

Security Issue: Managing Internal Access to Sensitive Information

Acme's Finance Department presents some unique challenges in that all of the other departments must have access to some of the data (for example, budgeting information) but should not be allowed access to other data (for example, the president's expense account) in that department.

Solutions

To accomplish these tasks, Acme decides to use a unique arrangement called a *tri-homed* gateway, using a product that allows Acme to segregate the server, allowing outside access to only a portion of the data while restricting access to the sensitive data. One such product is Borderware's Secure Server Net system. By using this three-pronged approach, Acme can essentially create an intranet within an intranet, thus allowing "outsiders" (such as the folks in Sales and Production) access to a "public" (yet secure) server in the department where appropriate data can be stored.

Meanwhile, both the public portion of the Finance Department's network and the rest of the Acme intranet are separated by the firewall from the sensitive portions of the financial data.

Figure 5-6 shows how the Finance Department can effectively be segregated into two "subnets" using the Secure Server Net concept.

A similar approach could be used in any department that has both information that should be available company-wide *and* data that should be used within that department only.

For example, Acme closely guards its production process, which it believes gives it a competitive advantage over its chief rival, Beta Company. Therefore, Acme restricts access to that information to those in the company who really need to know the information, such as engineers and the production managers. For that reason, another Secure Server Net (that is, a tri-homed gateway) might be used to allow intranet-wide access to shipping and production output data, while restricting access to sensitive production engineering data to those within the department.

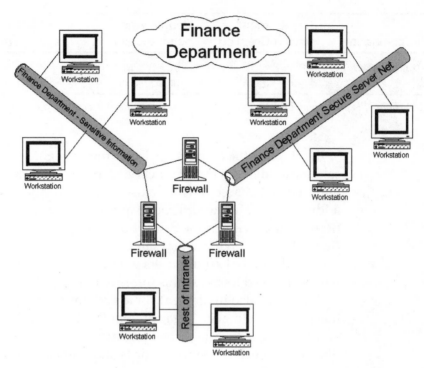

Figure 5-6: Acme's Secure Server Net approach to controlling data in the Finance Department.

In addition to the firewall placement matters mentioned here, Acme will also employ other, more traditional, computer security measures. For example, all users will have unique user names and passwords, providing an additional level of security inside the firewalls. These passwords will have relatively short expiration dates and will be changed approximately every 60 days to help limit damage from compromised passwords.

By using these passwords, Acme can control the information available to specific individuals within departments. Again referring to a portion of Table 5-1, note in the following Table 5-2, for example, the people who need access to "sales orders" information.

Information	Department where Created	People who need access	Server where data is located
Sales Orders	Sales/ Marketing	All sales, production managers, billing	Sales/ Marketing

Table 5-2: This portion of Table 5-1 shows the people who need access to sales information.

In this case, the entire Sales Department is given access to the sales order data. In the Production Department, however, only the managers need access. Thus, a user with a Production Department address will be allowed through any security (including a firewall) that protects the Sales/Marketing server. Once inside that firewall, however, the actual sales order data will be password-protected, and only those users with the appropriate password will be allowed to access this information.

Acme will also implement some systems administrator-level measures to help guard against unauthorized access. For example, audit trails will be established on particularly sensitive data or directories (such as payroll records and files containing sensitive design data) so that the administrator can routinely examine which users are accessing the data. Unusually high numbers of unsuccessful login attempts, both internally and externally (via remote-access gateways), will generate messages to the administrator. These login attempts will be traced to the stations attempting to log in to ascertain whether an employee has a problem typing his or her password, or whether the employee is trying to go somewhere he or she shouldn't go.

These audit trails will be implemented as part of the firewall protection for the particular server in question. In our example, the Finance Department will already be using BorderWare Firewall Server (due to the need to create the Secure Server Net, described previously), and, therefore, that product's auditing/ reporting features will be set up to perform the audit trail functions described.

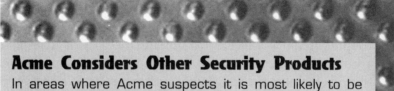

Acme Considers Other Security Products

In areas where Acme suspects it is most likely to be attacked, it might also use a product such as Intranet Scanner (the NT version of Internet Scanner), described in Chapter 10.

With Intranet Scanner, Acme can "patrol" its intranet system for attacks of various types. Intranet Scanner works by simulating network attacks and reporting security breaches it finds during the simulated attacks.

The Intranet Scanner scans your system, automatically testing for more than 135 security vulnerabilities, such as weak passwords (that is, passwords that are easy to re-create) or holes in UNIX system architecture. Internet Scanner examines hosts, services, ports, daemons, and domains. With this product, Acme can scan the system at any time and can also configure the software to scan automatically at regular intervals. Based upon the results of those scans, Acme can take the appropriate corrective measures.

Security Issue: Virus Detection & Removal

Virus detection and removal software will be used on all Acme computers (desktop and notebooks), and employees will be instructed that no floppy disks should enter the company facilities without being checked for viruses by the designated computer person in that office.

Acme's Future

With the firewalls and other security measures described in this chapter, Acme will begin to automate the flow of essential data around the company. At the same time, the company will ensure with each new phase of automation that sensitive and proprietary information is protected and, as important, that the company's intranet is guarded from outside attacks by unscrupulous hackers.

In the meantime, Figure 5-7 shows what our completed Acme intranet system looks like.

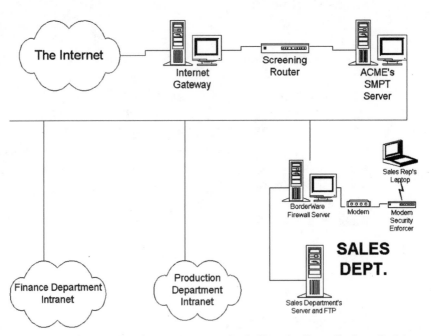

Figure 5-7: The completed Acme intranet, including the firewalls described in the chapter.

Moving On

Now that you have examined both the theory behind intranet firewalls and how that might be used in practical applications, we go on to examine some of the products available to help you build and manage those firewalls.

The following product review chapters are designed to provide a more technically detailed explanation of how the products work, along with their potential uses. These chapters will be especially useful for those in your organization who will actually decide which firewalls to install and how to use them.

Part 2:

Firewall Products

6 About the Products

In Part 1 of the book, we explored firewall strategy and implementation, using several commercially available firewall products as examples along the way. These varied products range in sophistication from simple system monitors to complete firewall and intranet servers that can provide numerous levels of high-end protection for your system.

In Part 2 of the book, we provide more detailed information about those particular products (Chapters 7 through 11), along with a listing of additional products and vendors (Chapter 12). As you examine the product descriptions in Chapters 7 through 11, remember that most of the products in this category are designed to serve as firewalls between internal networks (such as LANs) and the Internet. As described in Part 2, however, many of the same concepts used in those applications will work just as well in your intranet. Simply consider your intranet as a mini-version of the Internet/LAN configuration. Thus, the area or areas that you want to protect are equivalent to the LAN, and the rest of the system is equivalent to the Internet.

 **TIP**

Your system may actually have several areas that need protection from other areas; you may therefore need several firewall locations. This is especially true in larger organizations.

In the following chapters, products that have uniquely Internet applications are noted.

The Products

We have selected a variety of the more common firewall-related products to cover in the following chapters. As mentioned previously, most of these products have been in use for a while, having been used to protect systems from attack through the Internet. Some of these have specifically been modified for use with intranets, while others can be used in intranets "as is" or with very little modification. In all cases, documentation from, or conversations with, the manufacturers have verified that the products are useful in intranet applications.

Among the products reviewed, you will find some that work on specific platforms (such as Novell Netware or Unix) while others work on all platforms.

The products that are included do not represent all of the available products. The inclusion of a product here does not mean that we endorse its use over some other product; likewise, the exclusion of a product does not mean that we do not consider it useful. For purposes of demonstration, we looked for products that represented a variety of approaches. We selected those for which we were able to obtain software and the necessary information from manufacturers. (Most of the companies that produce these products are, understandably, extremely busy trying to develop and adapt their products for the quickly expanding intranet market.)

Keep in mind also that a firewall is, in simplest terms, supposed to deny or allow access to a computer system based upon security criteria supplied by the computer system owner. Thus, any product that performed that function had the potential to be included in this section. Some of these products are primarily hardware, whereas others are software products. A few are hybrids of both.

The Reviews

The product reviews that follow are meant to accomplish two goals: first, to provide you with an overview of the particular product reviewed, and second, to help you decide whether that product (or a similar product) would be useful in your system.

To that end, we have included in the reviews a variety of information about the products, including a brief overview of how and where we think the product would be useful.

In addition, we have included, in some cases, detailed information about how to configure and use the product. These sections are not intended to be substitutes for the users' guides for these products. We thought that by including this information, however, we might provide some insight into the capabilities of the product that would help you decide whether that product would work in your system.

Moving On

In the next chapters, we take an in-depth look at several intranet firewall products, including:

- BorderWare Firewall Server (Chapter 7).

- LT Auditor+ (Chapter 8).

- Modem Security Enforcer (Chapter 9).

- Internet Scanner (Chapter 10).

- CyberSafe Challenger (Chapter 11).

7 Product Review: BorderWare Firewall Server

In this chapter, we will review a software firewall system by Secure Computing Corporation, called Firewall Server, version 4.0. This firewall product is essentially a software application, although it requires a dedicated computer (the firewall server computer) to operate.

Firewall Server, originally designed to protect secure networks from the Internet, provides a variety of security features that you can use to protect various segments of your intranet from unwanted intrusion. For example, Firewall Server allows only *Telnet* and *FTP* through the firewall, and these only with *CrytpoCard* or *SecurID* cards for security.

Product Description

This product is produced by Secure Computing Corporation. You can contact them at 1-800-334-8195, or www.border.com on the Web.

Firewall Server was originally designed, as were most firewall products, to protect internal networks from unwanted access via the Internet; however, in discussions with the authors, Secure Computing technicians have indicated that the product works well in intranet applications. Because, as noted throughout this book, an intranet firewall serves a similar function to an Internet firewall, Border's claims of adaptability are easy to believe.

 **TIP**

Because Firewall Server was originally designed for use with the Internet, the software also serves as an Internet "gateway," allowing the secure network users access to the Internet. In this chapter, we will concentrate on the access control features of the software, rather than the Internet connectivity features.

The central security features of Firewall Server (described more fully below) include the following:

■ Transparent Proxies

■ Network Address Translation

■ Packet-level Screening

Transparent Proxies

Firewall Server uses a proxy system to control access through the firewall, thus creating an application-level gateway. By employing a *transparent* proxy system, Firewall Server eliminates the need for drastic application modifications and further eliminates the need for allowing users to log directly into the firewall.

Using transparent proxies allows the use of "off-the-shelf" network applications and allows those applications to work directly through the firewall.

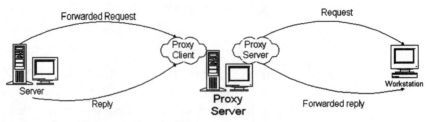

Figure 7-1: Transparent Proxy concept.

Proxies are essentially connections made through the firewall. Connections made from the internal side of the firewall (i.e., outbound proxies) are accepted by the firewall and rewritten on the external side of the firewall so as to appear to have come from the external address of the firewall. This keeps the address of the internal computer secure from any outside machine.

Inbound proxies, that is connections made from the external world to the internal network, are made to the external address of the firewall. The firewall then "proxies" the connection through to the internal network to the correct destination. Again, the address of the internal machine is never seen in the packet information on the external network.

Network Address Translation

As discussed in the preceding chapters, all IP packets contain unique addressing information that identifies the user from whom the packet originated. Even modestly sophisticated hackers can intercept these packets and obtain the user address, allowing access back into the network.

Firewall Server translates all outgoing IP addresses from the secure system into a single "BorderWare" address. This process effectively hides the internal addresses from any unauthorized users, providing another level of security.

Packet-level Screening

Firewall Server also provides packet-level screening, also known as "routing," as described in Chapter 4. Packet-level screening provides a filter through which all data packets must pass as they cross the firewall from the secure network to the outside world. By using criteria established by the systems administrator, the filter examines information in the packets (such as source address, destination address, and so on) against certain rules to screen unwanted packets. Using this packet-level screening, Firewall Server authenticates each data packet at the "kernel" level (sub-parts of the packet), thus providing yet another security level.

Secure Server Net

In addition to providing standard "two-sided" firewall protection between the secure portion of your intranet and the external network, Firewall Server makes it possible for you to provide a "triangular" configuration for separating certain segments of your intranet from each other. In this way, you can provide limited access into sections of an otherwise secure intranet. BorderWare calls this segment of Firewall Server the Secure Server Net, and it was designed to address the Internet/internal net need for a secure server that is inside the firewall, yet accessible from outside the firewall. This same feature can be useful for intranets as well.

For example, assume that your accounting department, located on your company's intranet, must be secured by a firewall from the rest of the system. However, one particular computer in the accounting department (containing budget request forms and prior-year budget information) must be accessible to the entire intranet. By using the Secure Server Net feature, you can configure your budgeting computer as a type of secure server, thus allowing limited access to the services on these computers, while protecting the rest of the accounting department from the outside. When configured in this manner, Firewall Server is actually acting as two separate firewalls, protecting each internal system.

Virtual Private Network (VPN)

Firewall Server 4.0 also contains a module called Virtual Private Network, or VPN. VPN is a method of securely connecting two Firewall Servers in remote locations (such as the home office and a satellite office) via the Internet.

Using VPN, the software creates an encrypted data "tunnel" through the Internet, allowing data to pass in a secured fashion through this much less expensive medium.

Platforms

Firewall Server contains its own, proprietary operating system. Therefore, the software must be installed on a stand-alone computer system.

You cannot load or run any other applications on the same computer with the firewall software. That is, the computer used for Firewall Server will be a "dedicated" firewall server machine.

System Requirements

BorderWare recommends the following hardware components for the Firewall Server software:

- Intel 486 or Pentium

- 16MB RAM minimum; 32MB recommended

- CD-ROM required (software supplied on CD)

- SCSI hard disk with 500MB minimum, 1 GB recommended

- Ethernet card for secure network and ethernet card for intranet-connected network

- Color VGA card or PCI video cards are supported.

 **TIP**

BorderWare provides support only for certain SCSI controllers and certain ethernet cards—be sure to contact the manufacturer prior to obtaining the hardware if you plan to use this system.

Interface

Firewall Server uses a graphical user interface (similar to a Microsoft Windows 3.11 interface), which allows for easy configuration and administration of the firewall software.

Installing Firewall Server

As noted earlier in this chapter, Firewall Server software is installed onto a dedicated computer using its own operating system. Thus, the first step in installing the product is obtaining and properly configuring your computer hardware. Once that is accomplished, you should consider your specific intranet configuration and security needs before proceeding.

Pre-installation Planning

Installing certain options in Firewall Server (such as the mail server) and setting up disk partitions can only take place at installation time and can only later be changed by re-installing the software; therefore, be sure to carefully consider how you want to configure your firewall before launching the installation.

Security Issues

Obviously, the first consideration for any firewall installation should be your intranet security needs. You should ascertain which segments of the intranet need access to which other areas and which may need "secure server" access (secure servers are described in the preceding sections).

By reviewing your overall network security plan (see Chapter 3), you should ascertain which services and computers need to be protected and, thus, where those systems should be in relation to the firewall server.

Selecting Firewall Server Components

As mentioned above, this software package comes with a variety of components, or modules, some of which you may not need in your intranet environment. For example, because Firewall Server is designed as both a firewall and Internet gateway, the package contains a Mail Server, a News Server, and the Secure Server Net (described above). If your intranet does not need these modules, make that decision at the outset, as installing (or not installing) these components can only be done at installation time, and these choices can only be changed by re-installing the software. (You may need the Secure Server Net if you allow Internet access into some portion of your intranet, and you may also need it if certain segments of the intranet will have only limited access to other areas of the intranet. The practical implications of this type of system are discussed in some detail in Chapter 5.)

Installation

The actual installation of Firewall Server is accomplished by using a floppy disk (the Installation Diskette) and a CD, which contains the main portion of the software.

 **TIP**

Throughout the installation process, keep in mind that Firewall Server was designed to function in an Internet/internal network environment; therefore, some of the terms and steps described are geared toward that environment. However, if you simply think of the secure network portion of your intranet as the internal network, and the "outside" portions of your intranet as the Internet, the process is almost identical.

The installation is straightforward and is accomplished by means of onscreen menus and options that guide you through the process. During the first part of the installation, you will be asked to decide several issues and provide basic information, such as:

- Disk partition parameters

- Software serial numbers

- Time zone information

After this basic information is in place, you will select an option called "Initialize Installation." The software will begin configuring your system and will ask for the following specifications, which you will probably want to know in advance.

- Organization's domain mame (may be slightly different in an intranet vs. an Internet environment)

- Firewall Server Host name

- Internal (or secure network) IP address

- Internal transceiver type

- Secure Server Net (if installed) IP address

- Secure Server Net subnet mask

- Secure Server Net transceiver type

- External IP address

- External subnet mask

- Service provider IP address

- External transceiver type
- External router IP address

After this information is provided, Firewall Server will ask you to configure your internal, or secure, network. Simply follow the instructions provided, and the installation and initial configuration will be completed.

 **TIP**

As you will see later in the next section, Firewall Server is "administered" both from the dedicated computer, called the "Firewall Server Console," and by selected users of the system from other computers on the intranet. These other users perform administration using "Remote Administration Console" features accessed through a Web browser, such as Netscape. Therefore, as you configure the system during installation, you need to decide which users will have Remote Admisnistration access and configure those users accordingly.

Using & Configuring Firewall Server

After installing Firewall Server, day-to-day use and administration of the software is the next concern. However, because the software uses the dedicated server concept, administration is fairly simple.

Some administration of Firewall Server 4.0 takes place at the dedicated computer on which the software runs, which BorderWare calls the Firewall Server Console (FSC). Other administration, however, is done by authorized users from "remote" locations, that is, locations other than the dedicated server. These users administer the system through a set of menus (accessed with Netscape) called Remote Administration Console (RAC). Some administration features are available from either location; however, other features are available exclusively from one or the other. In the sections that follow, we will note if a feature is available at the FSC or through RAC only.

Firewall Server uses a series of administration menus. Selecting the appropriate menu takes you directly to the area to be administered through a series of submenus.

To access the functions of the FSC, press the Esc key until the Configuration Password screen appears, then enter the password. The main FSC menu appears and contains the following menus:

- Admin
- Backup/Restore
- Diagnostics
- NameServer
- Support

From these menus, you can access a number of submenus, some of which we will look at in the sections that follow.

Displaying System Activity

To display and monitor the activity on your system, select the Diagnostics menu, then select System Activity. This option retrieves and displays information about the status of the Firewall Server software and your server.

This feature allows you to view a variety of information about your system, including CPU usage, Network resource usage, and the type of network services in use at the time.

Viewing Logs

As with any continuously monitoring security device, event logs are an integral part of Firewall Server's functions. Depending on the specific configuration options you select, you can obtain detailed logs regarding a variety of security activities on the server. Each log contains information about events that have occurred on the server during the log time period.

For example, the log for Connection Requests lists all of the connections made with the firewall during the logged period.

Each message contains the date and time of the connection request, the address and port of the user who requested to be connected, the destination address and port, and the status (successful or failed) of the connection request.

Firewall Server produces a variety of reports, and the detailed format of each report is included in the software documentation. The main reports that are available include:

Report Type	Description
General Messages	This reports lists all the kernel packet filter (kpf) rule information for service types that have "log rejected packets" enabled and services that have "log packets" turned on.
Kernel Messages	This report file lists all the core system messages.
Cron Messages	This report lists all log entries for clock time run procedures.
Mail Received	This report contains all the mail received by the firewall's SMPT server and includes the source and destination information for each piece of mail.
Mail Routing	This report lists all of the mail that used the firewall's mail router and includes the source and destination information for each piece of mail.
Mail Sent	This file lists all of the mail sent by the firewall's SMTP server. The source and destination information for each piece of mail sent is also logged.
News Received	This file lists all of the news items sent to the firewall.
News Sent	This report lists all of the news items sent by the firewall.
News Errors	This report lists all of the errors logged by the firewall due to handling of news items.

Report Type	Description
Connections Request	This report lists all of the connections made with the firewall and includes the date and time of the request, the source address and port of the user who attempted the connection, the destination address and port that the user attempted to reach, and the status of request.
Authenticated Access	This report contains a list of all the log entries for users who attempted to access the system from an external source. These entries include messages for the challenge and response authentication.
Alarm Conditions	This report lists all of the log entries for triggered alarms.
Admin	This report contains all the log entries for general administration.
Outbound Proxies	This report file lists all of the log entries (except FTP) for outbound packets that pass through the firewall.
FTP Proxies	This report lists all of the log entries for FTP packets that pass through the firewall.
Inbound Proxies	This report file lists all of the log entries (except FTP) for inbound packets that pass through the firewall.

Keep in mind that each log is maintained on a cumulative basis, and new files for each log are created each time a log reaches 100KB or 500KB in size (depending on the type of log). Thus, your server hard disk will, depending on usage and events, quickly begin to fill with stored activity logs.

////// TRAP

Once a series of logs fills up and creates five log files, the oldest log is automatically deleted. Therefore, your systems administrator should review the logs periodically to ensure that no useful data is inadvertently lost.

You can retrieve the log files from your internal network using FTP services.

System Configuration

Using the Admin menu and the various submenus, you can customize certain aspects of your server and the software. From here, you can also administer passwords and perform other administrative functions.

The main functions performed from the Admin menu are:

- Changing configuration password (this is the password required to change any configuration options)

- Applying software updates

- Updating license information

- Display software patches

Other routine configuration activities are also available in this area.

Proxy Configuration

Firewall Server uses a transparent proxy system as one of the centerpieces of the security side of the software. In order to accomplish this, the system must be configured to properly handle proxy applications. (The software's proxy system was described at the beginning of this chapter.)

To configure inbound and outbound proxy information, first log in to the RAC system using Netscape and your computer as follows.

1. Start Netscape.

2. In the Go field, type: http://firewall_hostname:442 (using your BorderWare Firewall Server hostname).

3. Type your User Name in the box that appears, then click Apply.

4. Follow the steps for logging in using your security card (see the sidebar below).

5. Enter your Firewall Server password.

At this point, the main RAC screen appears with several icons, including Admin, Services, VPN (if installed), Backup and Restore, and others depending on your particular installation.

To configure proxies, select the Services icon, then select Proxies. From here, you can configure the inbound and outbound proxies. By default, the only access allowed from the external side of the firewall to the internal network is through the use of password-protected authentication using CryptoCard or SecurID protocols. (Note that while you can define additional inbound proxies that do not require authentication, doing so can create serious security problems, and as such proxies essentially bypass the proxy server protection.)

Using CryptoCard & SecurID

As mentioned earlier, this firewall system requires access by means of a CryptoCard or SecurID-type card. If you are using a CryptoCard, when you request a Telnet or FTP session on the firewall server, you are prompted with an eight-digit challenge number. You enter the PIN number on your CryptoCard, verify the challenge, and are given the proper response to enter as a password. (The next login attempt is given a new challenge and requires a new response.)

SecurID is a "time-based" one-time password system. When you attempt a Telnet or FTP session, you are asked for the current password displayed on your SecurID card. The firewall then asks your network's SecurID authentication server to verify your password.

Outbound proxies must also be defined. To define outbound proxies, you can select from a list of preconfigured proxies, including:

- America Online
- FTP
- Finger
- GOPHER
- Ident
- NNTP
- Log-rejected packets
- POP Mail
- Ping
- Telnet
- WWW

In addition, you can define additional outbound proxies— again, keep in mind that user-defined proxies can present security risks. The risk arises from any insecurities in the specific protocol used and any problems or insecurities in the internal server itself. For example, you might want to proxy Web connections from outside your system directly to a Web server inside your firewall. Outside users *might* not realize that they have passed through to your internal system; however, if there are any bugs or insecurities in, for example, your HTTP or server, hackers might gain access to your internal system. (This is why Secure Computing suggests using the Secure Server Net for these types of sessions.)

To enable any proxy, simply select the proxy from the list and choose the Apply option. From the screen that appears, select the Yes option to enable the proxy.

Authenticated Access/Secure Logins

The central feature of any firewall is its ability to prevent unauthorized logins through the firewall to the internal network. Firewall Server accomplishes this by allowing only Telnet and FTP through the firewall, and these only with CrytpoCard and/or SecurID cards for security.

To allow this outside access, you must create secure login users. Using the RAC, log in as described above, then select the Admin icon. From the next screen, select the Secure Logins. Next, complete the information on the screen that appears. This information will include:

- Username

- Destination IP address

- Authentication (either CryptoCard or SecurID)

Once you are set up as a secure login user, you can log into the internal network by enabling your security card and following the prompts and challenges to connect to the internal network. Finally, you will be prompted for your usual network login name and password.

Alarms

If an unauthorized access is attempted on the secure side of your intranet, you not only want to stop it, you also want to know about it. The BorderWare Firewall Server has an alarm system that monitors for network probes and can catch TCP or UDP (User Datagram Packet) probes from either side of the firewall.

The software is designed to monitor and warn you of common attacks, such as efforts to exploit security "holes" in networking services such as NFS or X-Windows. Also, hackers may attempt to gain access by repeatedly trying to connect to each port on your system. You can set alarms in the software to warn you about these various types of attacks.

To configure the alarms, log into RAC, select the Admin icon, then select Alarms. From here, you have several options (all menu-driven), and you can set up a variety of alarms using these settings, which you enter from the Add Alarm Rule screen:

- Rule Description: defines the general parameters and names the alarm rule.

- Interface: allows you to select either the internal or external side of the firewall.

- Alarm Threshold: defines the number of probes within another setting (Alarm Internal) that triggers the alarm.

- Service Ports: defines which ports you want the alarm to "watch."

Once the alarm is triggered, you can configure the system to send e-mail to a person or persons on the system to respond to the alarm.

Other Administration

This software allows you to perform a variety of other administrative tasks, such as remote administration, network diagnostics, and mail and news server configuration, if those services are installed on the Firewall Server machine.

Moving On

In this chapter, we have given you a brief overview of a comprehensive firewall security program from Secure Computing Corporation called BorderWare Firewall Server.

In the next chapter, we will take a look at another firewall security product.

8 Product Review: LT Auditor+

In this chapter, we review a software firewall security package by Blue Lance, Inc. called LT Auditor+. This firewall product is a software application that incorporates several security features. These features can help you identify and eliminate potential network security weaknesses.

LT Auditor+ is designed to protect the Novell Netware network part of your intranet from the rest of the corporate network, the Internet, and internal security breaches. It installs onto the various Netware servers and monitors the networks for intruders and internal abuses.

The idea behind this product is that the majority of security violations come from internal sources. The majority of this product is designed to prevent internal security breaches. It alerts you or anyone else you specify on the network to these security breaches in real time.

Product Description

For more information, contact Blue Lance, Inc.:

Blue Lance, Inc.
1700 West Loop South
Houston, TX 77027
(713) 680-1187
e-mail: sales@bluelance.com

LT Auditor+ provides a number of features that go beyond simple intruder detection. Its features include audit trails, software license metering, and monitoring of hardware inventory. We discuss these in more detail in this chapter.

You will need a copy of this product for each server that you wish to protect on your Netware network. The systems administrator for your network must configure and manage these installations as individual server firewalls.

LT Auditor+ lets you create user configurations that define the level of authorization for accessing programs and data. It monitors this access and can report both authorized and unauthorized activities. Specifically, it can monitor and filter logins to the server; access to bindery objects (under Netware 3.x), such as user account; access to files on the server; and the use of software applications. It can detect changes to the hardware inventory of workstations that log in to the server. You can also configure it to delete certain files on a regular basis as a security precaution.

When LT Auditor+ is running its checks, it uses filter statements to process the various security checks. Filter statements define how LT Auditor+ performs each individual security check. These filter statements are discussed in more detail later in this chapter.

License Metering

The software license metering feature of this product enables you to monitor licensing compliance through several reporting features and a queuing feature. For example, if a user requests an application that already has all its licenses used, the queuing feature stores the request, and when a license becomes available, it automatically sends the user a notification message.

Hardware Inventory

Included in this firewall toolkit is a hardware inventory module that keeps a running inventory of the network hardware, right down to the memory on the workstations. If a user removes RAM memory from a workstation, this module detects the missing memory and reports the finding to the server. This check is performed every time the user logs on to the server.

Bindery Filter

The bindery filter can report all bindery activity on a Netware 3.x server to an audit file. This feature protects the server from unauthorized use or reconfiguration. In addition, the audit files cannot normally be accessed even by the systems administrator, and they are stored in an encoded format, which makes it very difficult for an intruder to modify them.

All these modules report mishaps and security violations to a central report utility on each of the protected servers. You can also configure the software to combine these reports from multiple servers and create a single consolidated report.

The reporting features of LT Auditor+ enable you to produce numerous reports based on the audit information gathered by the filters and monitors. With a multitude of report options, you can customize these reports to show just the information that you need.

Platforms

This product, designed to run on Novell Netware 3.x and 4.x platforms only, loads as an NLM (Netware Loadable Module) on the server instead of a TSR on the workstations, which makes systems administration considerably easier and avoids using up valuable memory on the workstations. This also prevents the user from tampering with or disabling the program. LT Auditor+ can be installed in a fashion that requires the server to be "downed" in order to unload the NLM. This can help prevent someone from easily disabling the software in order to get to the server.

Blue Lance has recently announced a new version of LT Auditor that provides a Windows user interface. This new interface will enable the systems administrator to use a Windows-based workstation, either Windows 3.x or Windows 95, to administer the system and request reports.

System Requirements

The following is a list of the system requirements for this product.

- Netware 3.11, 3.12, or 4.x

- DOS 3.x or newer

- One copy of LT Auditor+ per server to be protected

- IBM-compatible 286 or better workstations

- 2MB free server memory

- 30MB or more free volume space for audit files

Installing LT Auditor+

Before you install this product, be sure that your system meets the requirements listed in the preceding section. You must also have proper user authorization to install the software and to write into the SYS:SYSTEM directory on the server. Authorization is granted by the systems administrator under the "Supervisor" login authority.

The first step in the installation of this product is to install the system interface. The following steps will guide you though this installation.

1. Insert Disk One into the floppy drive of the workstation and enter the following:

    `A:INSTALL`

2. After a start-up screen, you see a screen that lists the servers available for installation on your network.

3. Choose the server that you want to install LT Auditor+ onto and press Enter.

4. Select the volume onto which you want to install the software.

5. The installation routine will now prompt you for the complete path. Enter the path to the desired directory. The files will now start to copy onto the server in the selected volume and directory.

6. Insert additional disks as directed.

7. Upon completion of the installation of the files onto the server, you will be able to select another server or exit the installation routine. If you wish to install this software package onto another server, you can repeat steps 3 through 7.

The next step to the installation is the loading of the Netware NLMs. The NLMs must be loaded in order for LT Auditor+ to audit and monitor the system. The following will guide you though this process. This must be done for each of the servers onto which you have installed LT Auditor+.

At the command prompt on the file server, enter the following:

```
LTASTART
```

Doing so loads the following NLMs:

■ LTAPLUS.NLM

■ LTMETER.NLM

■ LTADELP.NLM

For optimum security, you can install the NLMs with the */U* parameter, which prevents the NLMs from being unloaded at the command prompt on the file server:

```
LOAD LTAPLUS /U
LOAD LTMETER /U
LOAD LTADELP /U
```

Downing the file server is now the only way that the LT Auditor+ NLMs can be removed.

The next step in the installation process is to install the Hardware Auditor feature. You need to install it only if you want to be able to monitor hardware inventory on workstations.

Note: The HWA.EXE (the Hardware Auditor program file) is an executable file, not a TSR program.

The following steps will help you install this feature via the system login script on a Netware 3.1x system. The system login script is executed each time a user logs his or her workstation onto the network. The login script will automatically execute the HWA.EXE file and scan the workstation hardware every time the user logs onto the server. The system login script is used by every workstation on the network, so you would have to modify just this one script to affect all the users of the server. This would obviously need to be done on every server on which you plan to protect the workstation hardware.

1. Log in to the network with Supervisory rights.

2. Run the SYSCON utility.

3. From the main menu, select the Supervisor option.

4. Select System Login Script from the submenu.

5. Add the following line to the script:

```
#fileserver\path\HWA.EXE
```

 **TIP**

In the preceding example, fileserver *is the name of the fileserver and* path *is the path to the executable file HWA.EXE.*

Starting LT Auditor+ & Selecting Server

This section discusses the various procedures in using LT Auditor+. By reviewing these options, you will gain some insight into the firewall-related features of this product.

Assuming that LT Auditor+ is in your path, you can start it by running the LTA program. (At the DOS prompt, type **LTA** and press Enter.) Press Enter to get past the initial page and bring up the main menu.

To start LT Auditor, you enter the following command at the file server command prompt.

`LTASTART`

LT Auditor will load all the other NLMs that are needed to run the security checks.

Selecting a Server

The Servers option on the main menu enables you to select the file server on the network from which you are going to run reports and process filters or other utilities. Here are the steps in selecting a server:

1. Select the Servers option on the main menu.

2. On the pop-up menu, highlight the desired server and press Enter.

Attaching to Other Servers

To select a file server to which you are not currently attached, follow these steps:

1. Select the Servers option on the main menu.

2. On the menu that pops up, press the INS key; a list of servers to which you are currently not attached shows up.

3. Highlight the desired server and press Enter.

4. Enter the user name and password.

5. Now the server is added to the first list. Highlight it on the list and press Enter.

Configuring LT Auditor+

A filter is a kind of auditing tool that can arrest unauthorized activity rather than merely log it. LT Auditor+ acts as a firewall in selectively filtering access requests using a configuration that is based on Netware network authorization. The filter is an extra layer of security above the normal Netware level.

A filter in LT Auditor+ is made up of statements, and statements consist of components. Each component is made up of elements. A component is a filter category, and an element is a setting for that category.

Table 8-1 shows an example of a filter statement.

User	A/O	Path	Include	Excl	Oper	Log	Alert
<ALL>	A	SYS:HOME	<NONE>	<*.*>	[OCERTWMD]	BOTH	<NONE>

Table 8-1: A sample filter statement.

Each column heading (for example, USER) is called a component, and each component value (for example, <ALL>) is an element.

All filters are created in the same way, by adding new statements and corresponding components and elements.

Files/Directory Filters

The file and directory filters direct how LT Auditor+ monitors file and directory activity. This filter has eight components in the filter statement. With these eight filter statement components, you can specify a wide range of file- and directory-monitoring filters.

Login Filter

This filter controls the way the program monitors all the login and logout activity. This filter has four components.

Bindery Filter

The bindery filter statements are constructed of six components. As the name suggests, this filter specifies how LT Auditor+ monitors bindery activity.

Metering Filter

The metering filter controls the way LT Auditor+ monitors software application usage. This is done to ensure compliance with the software licensing agreements. This filter is constructed of six components.

Auto-Delete/Purge Filter

For security or disk management reasons, LT Auditor+ can purge files from the hard disk of the server. This filter specifies how this will happen. There are five filter statement components in this filter.

Hardware Filter

The hardware filter dictates how LT Auditor+ will monitor the workstation hardware. This filter statement contains three components.

Adding a Filter Statement

Here are the steps to add any filter statement to LT Auditor+.

1. From the main menu, select System Configuration | Filters. Then, select the type of filter statement you wish to enter.

2. Press the INS key, and you will enter an edit mode that will enable you to enter a new statement to the filter.

3. After you set all components in the filter statement, press Esc and choose Yes to save the changes. The arrow keys will enable you to move between the various fields (components) in the filter statement on which you are working.

4. To save the setting, press the Esc key and select Yes to the Overwrite Existing Filter prompt.

Editing a Filter Statement

Here are the steps to edit any filter statement in LT Auditor+.

1. Select System Configuration from the main menu.

2. Select Filters from the System Configuration menu.

3. Select the filter that you wish to edit from the Filters menu.

4. Select the statement that you want to change, and press Enter. Then, you will enter an edit mode that will enable you to edit the filter statement.

5. After resetting all of the components in the filter statement, press Esc and choose Yes to save the changes to the statement.

Reports

LT Auditor+ is big on reports, which can be customized using the query feature. There are several reports for each feature of the program, and each report has several options. This section briefly outlines the different reports available in the package.

Audit Trails

Audit trail reports are query-based reports. Selecting options from any one of several screens will produce a plethora of reports. Each report category in the following list can be fine-tuned via these numerous option screens.

- *Journal.* Consolidated, chronological report including file login and bindery activities.

- *File Activity.* Who opens, writes, renames, and deletes files.

- *Login Activity.* Who performs logins and logouts, and where and when.

- *Bindery Activity.* Who creates, renames, and deletes bindery objects.

Metering

The *metering reports* revolve around the Metering filter functions that monitor application usage. Using metering reports, you can find out the following:

- *Application Usage.* Who opened what application and for how long.

- *Exception.* Unsuccessful attempts to open applications if the licenses were not available.

Hardware

Hardware reports are about the hardware inventory. Using these reports, you can monitor the following:

- *Current.* Current hardware inventory.

- *History.* Past changes in hardware inventory.

Server

Server reports is the smallest report category. However, due to the multitude of reporting options, there still can be a lot of reports produced on the server.

■ *Server*.   Shows when NLMs are loaded and unloaded and volumes are mounted and dismounted.

Moving On

In this chapter, we looked at the various features of LT Auditor+ and outlined procedures for installing and using the product. Please refer to the LT Auditor+ manual for complete instructions on using the software.

9 Product Review: Modem Security Enforcer

In many intranet systems, some portions of the system are connected to other parts via telephone lines and modems, often using public (as opposed to dedicated) telephone lines. In addition, many of your intranet users will access their own computer via a remote system and a modem, using notebook computers while traveling, for example. Any system that employs a telephone connection and a modem presents at least one additional point of potential security breach—the telephone connection.

In this chapter, we review a firewall product called Modem Security Enforcer. The Modem Security Enforcer is a hardware/software product designed to eliminate data security problems encountered when using a publicly switched telephone network for access to a private network. The product is installed between the RS-232 port of the modem and the computer and works by "separating" the connection between these two devices.

When you use this product, you must first secure access into the Modem Security Enforcer. After you have secured this access, the software allows a through connection between the modem and the protected computer network.

Product Description

For information about this product please contact:

IC Engineering, Inc.
PO Box 321
Owing Mills, MD 21117
(410) 363-8748
Web Page: http://www.bcpl.lib.md.us/~n3ic/iceng.html

Modem Security Enforcer is actually a hardware/software product that operates as a firewall by protecting your intranet system at what is often considered the most vulnerable point—the incoming modem, or modem system. It is here that anyone who either has, or can guess, a valid telephone number has at least the opportunity to get from the outside world to the inside of your system.

Modem Security Enforcer is designed to block unauthorized access by requiring the user to enter a series of passwords. It can also be configured to call the user back automatically as an extra security measure.

Modem Security Enforcer operates by monitoring the modem on the protected computer system. When the modem receives a telephone call, it notifies Modem Security Enforcer, which then sets up an interactive "conversation" with the potential user. At that point, a variety of security measures might be used, depending on the configuration options you have selected.

As described more fully later in this chapter, this system can be set up so that only certain telephone numbers are allowed remote access, because the internal computer can actually call the remote user back. No, it's not exactly like the movie *War Games*, but it is similar. The administrator can create a list of authorized users and their telephone numbers and can configure the system to recognize users from that list. When a user tries to log in from a remote location, the system first identifies the user by requesting a series of passwords and then hangs up the telephone connection. After a time delay (which is also configurable), the system dials the number that it knows to be the correct one for that user, based on its internal list. So, unless a hacker calls from Jim Smith's house, he won't be able to access the system using Jim Smith's user account.

 **TIP**

The callback option is mainly useful for routine remote access from locations such as satellite offices or employees' homes. Since it is not convenient to reconfigure the user access list every time a user wants to log in, the system is not well suited for authenticating mobile users, such as an employee who logs in frequently from unpredictable locations while traveling. In these cases, using the callback option may be more trouble than it is worth, but we still recommend using the password and other security features described in this chapter.

If access is granted, the user is notified and transparently connected to the host computer. If access is denied, a through connection is not allowed, and the system is locked out from further access attempts for a selectable time period. This happens whether the callback option is engaged or not.

Thus, the Modem Security Enforcer provides an added level of protection for the security problem inherent in PBXes and like equipment by creating a protection scheme superior to that provided by the host computer. It solves security problems for large and small computer centers by placing a separate physical device ahead of the computer, providing a firewall between outside access and the host computer itself. Even if the host computer is a firewall server, this piece of equipment can be a nice, additional protective barrier. Any internal knowledge of the host computer is of no use in gaining computer access, because no connection is made between the modem and the computer until the Modem Security Enforcer has validated that the user is authorized for access.

The Modem Security Enforcer can be set up so that it cannot be programmed by someone who is not on site. So, even if a potential hacker knows about the Modem Security Enforcer, that knowledge alone cannot be used to modify the Modem Security Enforcer in order to gain access to the host computer.

Benefits

This product offers a variety of firewall benefits to intranet users. One segment of the intranet, for example, may be accessed primarily through a modem or a modem center. If so, the added layers of protection afforded by Modem Security Enforcer provide additional assurance that logins are by legitimate intranet users. Furthermore, the callback feature described previously can be very useful in an intranet setting, because most routine connections to a particular modem system will likely originate from established locations, with which the callback feature works best.

In addition, Modem Security Enforcer provides additional logging capabilities and can help the systems administrator trap unsuccessful login attempts by disallowing high-volume, repetitive attacking programs access to the system at all. These are brute-force programs that pound away at the login prompt. These programs generate thousands of passwords and try them all at the login prompt.

The Operation of Modem Security Enforcer

The uses and benefits of Modem Security Enforcer as a firewall are perhaps best evaluated by looking in some depth at the possible installation and configuration options available with the system. By reviewing the following information, you may see features or options that would be useful for your organization's intranet.

 **TIP**

Even if you are not presently using an intranet, if your organization routinely allows remote access via modem and public telephone lines, you should review the features and options available with this product.

Operational Overview

Authorized users are issued an account, which consists of the following:

- A login name

- A password

- A callback number

- A cumulative count of successful accesses

- A count of unsuccessful access attempts since the last successful access

 **TIP**

In addition to individual account transaction information, Modem Security Enforcer keeps a global record of all successful accesses and the unsuccessful access attempts that led to a lockout.

When the maximum security provisions are in place, the steps to successful access include the following:

1. The user calls the host computer via his or her modem.

2. The system modem answers the call and alerts the Modem Security Enforcer. At this point, the user's modem acknowledges the connection.

3. Depending on the speed of the modem, the user may be required to press the <ENTER> key.

4. The Modem Security Enforcer issues an identification request to the user. (This message is customizable.)

5. The user enters his or her login name.

6. The Modem Security Enforcer asks for the user's password. (This message is also customizable.)

7. The user enters his or her password.

8. The Modem Security Enforcer informs the user that the user will be called back.

9. The Modem Security Enforcer directs the system modem to hang up the call.

10. The user either manually hangs up his or her modem, or the user's modem detects loss of carrier and automatically hangs up the phone line.

11. The Modem Security Enforcer retrieves the user's Callback Telephone Number and instructs the host computer's modem to dial it.

12. The user's modem automatically answers the callback.

13. The system modem notifies the Modem Security Enforcer that the call has been answered by the user modem.

14. The Modem Security Enforcer once again requests the user's password.

15. The user enters his or her password.

16. The Modem Security Enforcer sends a configurable connection message to the user.

17. The Modem Security Enforcer establishes a communications path between the modem and the host computer.

18. The user conducts an interactive session with the protected equipment.

19. The user hangs up and the system modem notifies the Modem Security Enforcer.

20. The Modem Security Enforcer sends a logoff message to the host computer.

21. The Modem Security Enforcer and the modem are ready to receive another call.

Customization Options

Many of the options in Modem Security Enforcer are customizable by the systems administrator:

- *Access Time.* If the Access Time elapses between the time the system modem answers the initial call and the final acceptance and through connection to the host computer are established, the access procedure aborts, in which case, the Modem Security Enforcer instructs the system modem to hang up the call.

- *Error Maximum and Lockout Time.* If the number of incorrect Login Name or Password entries reaches the Error Maximum, the Modem Security Enforcer goes into a Lockout State. The Modem Security Enforcer is frozen for Lockout Time minutes, specified by the systems administrator. During this time, the Idle light on the front of the Modem Security Enforcer flashes. (Pressing the button on the front of the unit will cancel this state.) At the conclusion of the Lockout Time, the modem is instructed to hang up the call, and the Modem Security Enforcer and the system modem are ready for another call.

- *Maximum Time.* After successful access and during activity between the user and the protected equipment, if the Maximum Time is reached or there is a period of time during which no characters are sent in either direction that is equal to the No Activity Time, the Modem Security Enforcer sends the Logout message to the host computer and instructs the modem to hang up the call.

- *Operational Modes.* Less secure operational modes can be selected for the Modem Security Enforcer. By pressing the button on the front of the Enforcer, you can individually disable the requirements to enter the initial password, to call the user back, or to request a password after the call back. The Modem Security Enforcer can also be taken out of Protected mode, which allows unrestricted access from the modem to the host computer.

In environments such as large computer centers, many telephone lines may exist that can be accessed as a group by outside users. For these situations, the rack-mount version Modem Security Enforcer can be used. All individual Modem Security Enforcer units (one per line) can be configured to intercommunicate. User accesses and failures, user password changes, and system programming, when performed on any line, are automatically passed to all other Modem Security Enforcer units in the group. The button control also selects the mode setting for all of the units in the group.

Platforms

This product can operate on almost any platform because it works outside the host computer system. Thus, the system could be installed in a Novell Netware environment as easily as a Windows NT or UNIX environment.

Installing Modem Security Enforcer

Before you install Modem Security Enforcer, you should establish that the existing modem and host computer are compatible with one another, connected, and fully operational. If they are not, you should resolve any problems between those two parts of your intranet before attempting to connect this product. The modem should be placed into auto-answer mode, so that dialing the modem number results in the modem answering the line and connecting through to the host computer.

To install the Modem Security Enforcer, follow these steps:

1. Plug the power transformer into the Modem Security Enforcer unit and the wall plug. (The Idle, Protect, and Init PW lights should be on, with no others illuminated.)

2. Disconnect the RS-232 cable connecting the modem to the host computer.

3. Connect the host computer to the DTE connector on the rear of the Modem Security Enforcer. (This is located above the power connector.)

4. Connect the modem to the DCE connector on the rear of the Modem Security Enforcer.

Note: Be certain that all connectors are correctly seated for positive contact.

Configuring the Modem Security Enforcer

This section discusses several of the configuration procedures for this product. By reviewing the various configuration options, you will gain a good understanding of the features of this product.

Changing the User Password

When you log in to the system they add a leading character to the login to initiate an interactive login. For example:

```
+John Doe
```

Rather than being taken directly to the Active State after supplying the password, you will see the following message :

```
Enter New Password:
```

If you press Enter at this time, no change will be made, and the Active Message will be displayed.

If you change the password to another character sequence, followed by <ENTER>, you will see the following message:

```
Repeat:
```

Re-enter the new password at this time. John Doe's password is now changed and the Active message displayed.

Using the System Administrator Menu

Repeat the procedure in the preceding section using the System Administrator's login name and password. For example, use "Super" rather than "John Doe" and "SU" rather than "JD."

 **TIP**

No errors are permitted in the entry of the "Super" login name; if you make a mistake, you must hang up and start over.

In place of the Active message, the System Administrator menu will be displayed:

- ■ 0 Exit: exits programming mode
- ■ 1 Stats: displays the current statistics
- ■ 2 List: lists the accounts
- ■ 3 Account: creates accounts
- ■ 4 Parameters: changes system parameters
- ■ 5 Copy: please refer to sidebar
- ■ 6 Format: formats messages
- ■ ?: displays help text

This time, the Access light will turn off, and the Program light will turn on.

Stats: Displaying Access Statistics

The first menu option will display the statistics on the Modem Security Enforcer. For example, the following message might be displayed:

```
Successes-Lockouts: 0004 0001
```

The first number is the cumulative, overall number of successful accesses the Modem Security Enforcer has received. The second number is the cumulative number of times a user has unsuccessfully attempted to access the Modem Security Enforcer and made Error Maximum mistakes (the factory default is set to 7).

Copying

Option 5 of the System Administrator menu gives you the ability to copy parameters and the user account database from a single Modem Security Enforcer unit to all others. When this option is selected, Locations 10 and above are broadcast. (This does not alter the individual Unit IDs, the Mode, or the Single Unit push-button bit.) After changing and verifying parameters and user accounts, this option should be activated. It requires nominally two minutes for completion. DTE/DCE communications of receiving units, in the Active State, are not disturbed during the copy process.

Neither Location OE nor OF are altered by a copy operation; it is intended that the push button be used to modify the Mode. Location OF contains the Single Unit push-button bit and is not transmitted to prevent affecting that control. For initial system setup, any communications parameter bits that are altered from the factory settings in Location OF should be handled individually, as should the Unit ID.

List: Creating & Canceling Accounts

Menu option 2 will produce a list of all Accounts in the Modem Security Enforcer. A message such as the following will be displayed:

```
Super: Tel # = , Accesses = 0003, Failures = 00
John Doe: Tel # = 5551212, Accesses = 0002, Failures = 00
```

Menu option 3 enables you to create accounts. After entering option 3, the following message appears:

```
Account:
```

Using upper and lowercase letters, enter a login name. A maximum of 15 characters may be used. The following message will be displayed:

`+ to Add:`

If you make a mistake in typing the new login name, press Enter. If you enter the name correctly, however, type +.

The following message will be displayed:

`Enter New Password:`

Enter the password desired; you can use any number of characters and any of the 128 ASCII characters, with the exception of <ENTER>.

When you enter the password, the following message appears:

`Repeat:`

Re-enter the same password. Then, the following message will be displayed:

`Callback #:`

Enter the telephone number to be dialed to reach the user. If fewer than 10 digits are to be dialed, suffix the telephone number with F until a total of 10 characters have been typed. If no callback number is to be used for this account, type FFFFFFFFFF. (If you do this, callbacks will not be made for this account, even if the Modem Security Enforcer is in the Callback mode.) After you type the last digit of the telephone number field, a current listing of the new account will be displayed, showing *Accesses = 0000* and *Failures = 00*.

Next, the Account prompt will be displayed. Type John Doe and press <ENTER>. The information regarding this account will be shown, followed by this message:

`# to Cancel:`

Type #. This cancels the John Doe account. Press <ENTER> to the redisplayed Account message, and the menu will reappear.

Parameters

The parameters option enables you to change some of the defaults of the Modem Security Enforcer. The changes are made by specifying the hexadecimal location and entering the new value. In this section, we go over some of the more important parameters.

All parameters are assigned specific locations. The contents of the parameter locations can be read and modified through the use of menu option 4.

After you select option 4 on the menu, the following message will appear:

```
Location:
```

Enter 00. The following line will appear:

```
00 4D M
```

The 00 on the left indicates that Location 00 is being examined; 4D is the hexadecimal contents of Location 00; and M is the ASCII character represented by the hexadecimal value 4D.

Press the spacebar to examine the next location. The following line will appear:

```
01 53 S
```

This indicates that Location 01 contains hexadecimal value 53, which is ASCII character S. Continue pressing the spacebar until Location 06 is displayed, with contents 55. Type 40. This changes the contents of Location 06 to 40, and Location 07 is next displayed. Type -, and Location 06 will be redisplayed, showing that the contents are now 40.

Enter 55 to restore the data.

Press <ENTER>, and the Location message will reappear. After you press <ENTER> again, the menu will be redisplayed.

This process demonstrates the use of the Parameters Menu option. Upon selection, the two-character hexadecimal location of the desired parameter is entered. The hexadecimal contents and ASCII value of that location are displayed, the latter of which is useful for certain parameters.

To change the contents, type the replacement hexadecimal value; to return to the Location message, press <ENTER>; to back up to the previous location, type -; and to advance to the next Location, press the spacebar (or any other character). To exit from the Parameters submenu, press <ENTER> at the Location message.

 **TIP**

While you are in the Parameters option, be careful to avoid inadvertently changing locations where modifications are not intended.

Here is a list of the parameters that can be changed:

- *No Activity Time.* This value sets the maximum number of minutes to be permitted with no activity between the DTE and DCE.

- *Maximum Time.* This value sets the maximum number of hours to be permitted for a single access.

- *Access Time.* This value sets the maximum number of minutes that a user is permitted to remain in the Access state.

 **TIP**

This parameter should be kept as small as possible for security reasons. The less time a hacker has to experiment with passwords and login attempts, the less likely it is that the hacker will gain access.

- *Error Maximum.* This value sets the maximum number of errors that are permitted while in the Access state.

- *Lockout Time.* As mentioned previously, if access times or error parameters are exceeded, the Modem Security Enforcer will enter a Lockout state.

- *Carrier Detect Delay*. This value sets the number of seconds that the Modem Security Enforcer will delay after receiving indication of carrier detection from the modem.

 **TIP**

If the modem sends messages upon connection, this delay value must be set to exceed the time period for all such messages.

- *Default Baud Rate*. This value sets the baud rate used for access via the DTE port.

- *High Speed Baud Rate*. This value sets the baud rate used for access via the modem when the High Speed line from the modem is active.

/////// **TRAP**

Take care to ensure that this parameter is entered properly; incorrect values will cause the modem to not be able to communicate with other modems.

- *Initialization Message*. This message is sent to the DCE (modem) on power-up.

- *Login Prompt Message*. This message is initiated from the Idle state upon notification of access.

- *Password Prompt Message*. This message is sent when an initial password is to be received.

- *Calling Back Message*. This message is sent to the user just before hanging up the line in preparation for calling the user back.

- *Active Message*. This message is sent to the user after access has been authorized, just before entering the Active state.

■ *Logoff Message.* This message is sent to the DTE port upon disconnection from the modem, either forced or natural.

■ *Hang Up Modem Message.* This sequence is sent to the DCE port (modem) to force a hang-up.

■ *Extension Dialing Message.* This message is sent to the modem when it is determined that a callback is being made to the user, and the user's telephone number is from 1 to 6 digits in length.

■ *Local Dialing Message.* This message is sent to the modem when it is determined that a callback is being made to the user, and the user's telephone number is 7 digits in length.

■ *Same Area Code Toll Dialing Message.* This message is sent to the modem when it is determined that a callback is being made to the user, and the user's telephone number is 8 digits in length.

■ *Long Distance Dialing Message.* This message is sent to the modem when it is determined that a callback is being made to the user, and the user's telephone number is 9 or 10 digits in length.

■ *Unit ID.* This text is sent when the Unit ID code, F5, is encountered in any of the preceding message texts.

■ *Change Password Character.* This is the ASCII value of the character that is used to permit users to change their passwords, by preceding the login name with this character.

■ *Lockouts.* These are the locations where the overall number of lockouts accumulated is stored.

■ *Login Name Length.* This value is the maximum number of characters permitted in a login name and is expressed as a hexadecimal value.

■ *Password Offset.* This setting is the number of bytes from the beginning of the account to where the user's password is stored and is also a hexadecimal value.

   If passwords are not to be stored, this location should be set to FF.

- *Telephone Number Offset*. This setting is the number of bytes from the beginning of the account to where the user's telephone number is stored.

- *Accesses Offset*. This location contains the Accesses Offset, which is the number of bytes from the beginning of the account to where the user's cumulative number of accesses is stored.

- *Failures Offset*. The Failures Offset is the number of bytes from the beginning of the account to where the user's number of failures since the last successful access is stored.

- *Next Account Offset*. This setting is the number of bytes from the beginning of the account to where the next user's account begins.

Using Modem Security Enforcer

After you configure the Modem Security Enforcer, using it is quite simple. The front panel contains 10 indicator lights in three groups. These lights have the following meanings:

Status Indicators

The status indicators are green. Only one of the four status lights illuminate at any one time. The four states are:

- *Idle*. The Modem Security Enforcer is currently inactive. It is ready to receive a Carrier Detect indication from the modem to initiate access. A character from the DTE will initiate access from that port.

- *Access*. A potential user is currently attempting to gain access to the protected equipment but has not yet succeeded or failed. The user may be in the process of entering the login name or password, or the modem could be in the process of calling the user back.

- *Active*. A user has successfully gained access to the host computer and is in communication with it. A time-out, loss of carrier from the modem, or loss of DTR from the DTE will cause an exit to the Idle state.

■ *Program*. The systems administrator has accessed the Modem Security Enforcer. System programming is now accessible via the menu. Selection of the Exit option, loss of carrier from the modem (if accessed from the DCE side), or loss of DTR (if accessed from the DTE side) will cause exit to either the Idle or Access states.

Indicator Lights

The mode indicators are amber. They indicate the various states of the Modem Security Enforcer:

■ *Protect*. The Modem Security Enforcer is currently protecting the DTE from access.

■ *Initial Password*. After the system receives the login name from the user, the user will be prompted to enter a password.

■ *Callback*. After receiving the login name and initial password from the user (if Initial Password selected), the Modem Security Enforcer instructs the modem to call the user back at the telephone number stored under that account.

■ *Callback Password*. After calling the user back, the user will be requested to enter a password.

■ *Lock Indicators*. These four red lights represent the different lock states of the unit.

Moving On

In this chapter, we examined a product called Modem Security Enforcer, which acts as a firewall between an access modem and a host modem. It is a single piece of equipment that installs between the modem and host computer and protects the computer from being accessed directly until the entire authorization process is complete. In the next chapter, we will review another firewall-related product.

10 Product Review: Internet Scanner

In this chapter, we review the product Internet Scanner from Internet Security Systems. This software is unique in that it is not designed to specifically prohibit or allow specific types of data from entering or leaving the secure portions of your intranet system. Rather, it works as a roving security tester.

During its "patrols" of your network system, Internet Scanner checks for holes in your internal (or secure) network and alerts you to these potential security breaches.

Thus, the product is not a traditional firewall as discussed in the previous part of this book. It works great as a firewall tester, however, and in fact acts as a type of "roving" firewall. It works as a firewall because it protects a trusted network from an untrusted one. Moreover, it can help you identify a variety of internal attacks in addition to the external attack warnings.

Product Description

Following is the contact information for Internet Security Systems, the developer of Internet Scanner.

Internet Security Systems
5871 Glenridge Drive, Suite 115
Atlanta, GA 30328
Phone: (404) 252-7270
E-mail: CNUGENT@ISS.NET
Web Site: www.iss.net

Internet Scanner works by simulating many different network attacks. It reports the security breaches it finds during the simulated attacks. Under the premise that network security is only as strong as its weakest link, Internet Scanner will help you tighten the security on your network by playing devil's advocate and pointing out the weak spots in your intranet.

Since this product was released in 1991, it has gained widespread acceptance as the premier testing tool for network security. Although this product's main function is to act as a security testing tool, it has been found to act well as a roving firewall.

The Internet Scanner scans your system, automatically testing for more than 135 security vulnerabilities, such as weak passwords or holes in UNIX system architecture. It examines hosts, services, ports, daemons, and domains. It scans much more comprehensively than any (human) systems administrator can. You can run a scan at any time, and you can also configure the software to scan automatically at regular intervals.

The reporting features of this product are very useful and comprehensive. The reports are produced in HTML format, viewable with either a Web browser or a text editor. In addition to reporting any security breaches it locates, Internet Scanner includes information in each report on how to correct the network security breach. Included in this corrective information are hyperlinks to Web sites that contain patches and more information on the security breach.

Platforms

Internet Scanner is a UNIX-based product. It is designed to run on the following operating systems:

- SunOS
- Solaris
- HP/UX
- IBM AIX
- Linux

Internet Security Systems has released a similar product, called Intranet Scanner, which also runs on Windows NT.

Installing Internet Scanner

There are two types of installation of this product: the download method and the disk method. In this section, we review both methods of installation.

Downloading Internet Scanner

You can install Internet Scanner from a downloaded file from the Internet Security Systems FTP site. This file will be a UNIX tar (tape archive) file. To install this file, follow these steps:

1. Log in as *super user*.
2. Copy the downloaded file to the directory in which you want to install the Internet Scanner software.
3. Extract the files from the archive by entering this command at the UNIX command prompt:

   ```
   tar xvf iss-sun.tar
   ```

4. At this point, an *iss* directory has been created. Change to that directory by entering:

   ```
   cd iss
   ```

5. Run the installation script file by entering the following command:

   ```
   ./install.iss
   ```

The installation will be complete after the script has finished.

Disk-based Installation

You can install Internet Scanner from 3.5-inch disks. These are UNIX tar floppy disks. To install them, follow these instructions:

1. Log in as *super user*.
2. Change your working directory to the directory in which you want to install the Internet Scanner software.

3. Insert Disk 1 into the floppy drive on the UNIX workstation from which you are performing the installation.

4. To extract the files from Disk 1, enter the following UNIX command:

```
tar xvf /dev/fd0
```

5. Repeat step 4 for each of the remaining disks.

6. At this point, an *iss* directory has been created. Change to that directory by entering:

```
cd iss
```

7. Run the installation script file by entering the following command:

```
./install.iss
```

The installation will be complete after the script has finished.

Configuring Internet Scanner

Before you begin scanning with this product, you might want to fine-tune the operation of the software. You can specify a number of options applicable to your network environment and shorten the duration of the scan by disabling scanning operations that will not be necessary to your installation. For purposes of showing you the different uses of this product, we list the major settings and briefly describe each.

Configuring this product correctly is important so as to not waste time on scans you do not need and to ensure that the network is being properly protected. Because this product can scan for such a variety of different vulnerabilities and in such an automatic way, "overloading" the scans would be easy for a systems administrator. The downside of scanning for too many things too often can be slow system response time while the software is scanning. A good way to balance comprehensive scanning with sensitivity to system resource overloading is to limit the scope of scans during peak hours of system usage and to run more comprehensive scans at night or other off-peak periods.

Some General Operational Settings

The following sections describe a variety of scanning options from which you can choose to best meet your organization's needs.

Scan Always

This option instructs the Internet Scanner main program to try to connect to the host. There is no need to use this option if the *ping test* shows that the host is alive, because it would simply waste time. (A ping test determines whether a particular host is present and active. It is named after the "ping" of a submarine sonar to determine whether other ships are present.)

Half-open Scan

This option tells the software to do an exhaustive TCP port scan by using various TCP packets to determine the status of a port. This can require an additional two minutes per host during the scan, whether it is a manual or automatic scan.

Verbose Raw Output

This option toggles a more detailed explanatory notes section on the reports created by the product.

Parallel Processes

This option sets the number of parallel scans that can occur at one time. The more scans you allow to be performed at one time, the faster the overall scanning process. Increased scanning places an increased processor load on the system, however. This value (number of scans) will vary greatly depending on the speed of your system and/or its workload.

Ping Timeout

This sets the wait time for a response to the ping test. The only reason to change this option would be if your network has a long response time.

TCP Scan Connections/Process
This option sets the maximum number of service connections.

Phase Limit
This sets the number of times the software will conduct the half-open scan.

Ports to Scan
This enables you to select additional TCP ports to scan. By default, the software will select all the standard TCP ports.

Maximum Wait
This is the time that the Internet Scanner will wait for the program to execute before it will cancel the scan on that program.

Web Browser
This enables you to specify the Web browser that you will use to view the HTML pages in the reports.

RPC Options
Remote Procedure Call options (used in UNIX systems) are configured as follows:

Scan RPC/UDP as Backup
This option sets the software to scan for RPC and UDP (User Datagram Protocol) services if the program could not first find the portmapper.

Scan RPC/UDP Always
If selected, this option will cause Internet Scanner to do a manual scan of RPC services. This will lengthen the overall scan time.

NIS Domain Name
You can supply the correct domain name for the hosts with this option.

Network File System (NFS)-Related Options

To test for NFS-related breaches, use the *NFS Directory Depth* configuration option. This sets the limit to how far down Internet Scanner recursively searches into writeable directories. If you want to turn this option off, set it to 0. You would want to limit this option to reduce the amount of search time.

Brute Force Options

Internet Scanner uses several options called Brute Force. Brute Force refers to password cracking attempts and other "sheer force" type attempts. Here is a description of some of those options.

Maximum Connections

This option enables you to set the number of TCP port connections during this phase of testing. Lowering this setting will allow for greater bandwidth for parallel processing.

Connection Delay

This sets the time-out delay for TCP port connections.

Use Bruteforce Lists

This option can be set to Miscellaneous, UNIX, or VAX/VMS, depending on your installation. You can reduce scan time by making sure that you are not testing systems that do not pertain to your network.

Firewall Options

As noted at the outset of this chapter, this product is designed to probe, test, and try to fool your firewalls. Here are some of the relevant settings that you would need to set to test your firewalls.

Source Port

This enables you to specify the source port from which the connection will be made.

Gateway Host

This option enables you to bypass firewall security by packet rerouting. This will help to uncover additional vulnerabilities.

Socks Host

Because misconfigured Socks daemons allow undesired connections through gateway hosts, this option will attempt to open connections through the Socks service.

NetBios Options

Here are some options that help you scan your system for problems related to your NetBios.

NetBios Permutations

When it is attempting to connect to the shares (the shared resources on the network), the software will try different combinations of found usernames in various permutations.

Extensive NetBios Checking

This option causes the software to use words from the NetBios Dictionary as share passwords. This will naturally increase the effectiveness of the scan. As mentioned previously, however, this option will increase the scan time.

Using Internet Scanner

After you have optimized the settings of this package for your installation, you are ready to scan the network. The Internet Scanner software requires you to log in as *root* to run a scan whether it is a manual or automatic scan.

Running a Manual Scan

The method that is described in this section is for manual scans of the network system. The next section covers the method for setting up automatic scans.

To start the software package, enter the following UNIX command:

```
./XISS
```

Now, select the Start Scan option to start a scan of your intranet system. This is a manual scan, and after its completion, the results are sent to a report file that you can review to ascertain whether the software located any potential breaches.

Setting Up an Automatic Scan

To use this product as a "roving firewall" that alerts you to possible new security violations or breaches in security, you must set it up to run automatically.

The utility that you use to perform this function is the Addcron utility. Addcron is a tool for helping you place Internet Scanner into a cron job automatically. A cron job is a UNIX command batch file. Then, the cron job will run Internet Scanner at set intervals. To start Addcron, log on as *root* and enter the following UNIX command:

```
./addcron
```

The utility will guide you through a series of questions that will enter the Internet Scanner into a cron job.

Now that it is set to run automatically, you will be alerted to security problems at the scheduled intervals that you have specified.

Analyzing Scan Results

After Internet Scanner finishes scanning the intranet, whether manually or automatically, it records the vulnerabilities it found in a report and rates them on a "risk level" scale. To view the report, simply load it using a text editor or Web browser.

If you are viewing the report with a Web browser, clicking on a particular vulnerability activates a link to a Web site that either has a patch for the problem or has more information on the security breach that was found.

Moving On

In this chapter, we reviewed the features and functions of the software product, Internet Scanner. In the next chapter, we continue our review of firewall products.

Product Review: CyberSAFE Challenger

Based on a different security model than most other firewall software systems, CyberSAFE Challenger is a firewall product that stands out. CyberSAFE Challenger is built on the Kerberos security model, which we discuss later in this chapter.

This system is different from most other network-level firewalls in that CyberSAFE Challenger's use of Kerberos is built on user authentication rather than packet filtering. This product implements the use of an authentication server (which houses the software) that authenticates the user's login. After the user is authenticated, access is granted, and the user will not encounter any other security prompts. This is referred to as a "single sign-on."

CyberSAFE Challenger also comes with an add-on product called Security Toolkit, which we explore later in this chapter. The Security Toolkit enables programmers to secure in-house programs using the CyberSAFE Challenger via the Kerberos security model. This toolkit comes with a GSS-API (Generic Security Service Application Program Interface) to help C language programmers implement security authentication, integrity, and confidentiality in their applications.

The CyberSafe Challenger authentication server (firewall) is designed to run on the following network operating systems:

- Solaris
- HP-UX
- AIX
- NEXTSTEP
- Sun OS
- Dynix
- BSDi
- NCR

Understanding Kerberos

To understand CyberSafe Challenger, you must first understand Kerberos. Kerberos is a standard for network security in a distributed network environment and is the security model upon which CyberSafe Challenger is built. In fact, the Kerberos model and the product are intertwined. In this section, we explore the major concepts of this security model.

To the network user, the Kerberos system is transparent after the initial authentication. After authentication, authorized users have access to any application that incorporates Kerberos.

Running in the background, Kerberos protocol provides secure authentication between clients and the server to which they seek access. To incorporate Kerberos authentication, applications are modified to use special functions that provide the authentication. These applications are referred to as *Kerberized* applications. The more applications that your network has that are Kerberized, the more transparent the Kerberos system is to the user.

Kerberos Design Goals

Kerberos, at the network level, is concerned with the authentication of the users. Authentication is the process of verifying the user's identity. This is performed by using a piece of information that only the user and the authentication server know. Knowing this secret piece of information verifies the identity to the Kerberos system. Usually, the secret is a key generated from a password.

The goals of Kerberos authentication are as follows:

- *Secure authentication.* Two network entities must be able to securely authenticate each other. These entities can be users, applications, or network servers. Kerberos provides a means that supports one-way and two-way communication between network entities. It also provides a protocol to prevent the capture of clear-text passwords by network intruders.

- *Reliable network services.* Because authentication is used throughout the network services, the authentication service must be highly reliable. Kerberos provides for back-up authentication service in the event that the first one is unavailable.

- *Transparent to users.* Users should be unaware of the authentication process. After the user initially logs in, the Kerberos security scheme should be transparent. This transparency is best when applications on the network have been Kerberized.

- *Scaleable as network grows.* Even though the Kerberos protocol has been optimized for larger networks, the Kerberos model works for all networks regardless of size. (After it is implemented in a small network, Kerberos automatically scales as the network grows.)

Kerberos Security Levels

Three levels of security are available in Kerberos. Each of the levels builds upon the previous level.

Authentication

The first level is enforced by communication between client and server to authenticate the client. This level ensures that the user of the application is authenticated.

Safe Messages

The safe messages level provides message integrity. The safe messages level uses a checksum of the message to ensure that the message was not tampered with during transmission. This message is sent in clear-text format, so it is still visible on the network to prying eyes.

Private Messages

This is the highest level of security available in the Kerberos security model. This level provides message integrity and message privacy. A private message is encrypted before it is sent between client and server. This hides the context of the message during transmission. This level also uses a checksum to ensure that the message was not tampered with during transmission.

All Kerberized applications incorporate the first level of security. The rest of the security levels are incorporated as the security needs of the Kerberized application demand.

Using CyberSafe Challenger

Now that you understand the basics of the Kerberos model, we explore the general use of CyberSafe Challenger. CyberSafe Challenger is basically an implementation of Kerberos with tools to help you implement your other applications with the Kerberos security model.

CyberSafe Challenger uses an encrypted database to house all the authentication information for the users. This is an authentication server on the network, a computer onto which CyberSafe Challenger is installed.

This server receives all the authentication requests from the users and applications. It is the central depository for all the authentication that CyberSafe Challenger performs on the network. Fortunately, CyberSafe Challenger provides for a backup authentication server in case the first one is unavailable, for example, due to a hardware failure on the main authentication server.

Logging In

The only part of the CyberSafe Challenger that the network user is going to see every day is the login prompt. CyberSafe Challenger replaces the workstation login in a manner that is transparent to the user. These are CyberSafe Challenger functions that run the authentication routines. At the time of login, the CyberSafe Challenger issues the user all the authentication that he or she will need to access all the applications. This even includes authentication to use applications on remote systems that have been Kerberized.

The users will hold the authentication until they log out of the system or the authentication expires. Authentication can expire based on time limits.

Administrating CyberSafe Challenger

To administer CyberSafe challenger, you must have administrative privileges, which are configured in the admin_acl_file on the master authentication server. CyberSafe Challenger includes two programs that help you manage this firewall product:

- *kadmin.*   This program runs in a secured session. It can be run over any network client on the system. Additionally, you do not need root access to the location of the authentication database. This utility enables you to perform various administrative tasks, such as adding, deleting, changing, and modifying a password authentication.

- *CyberSafe Administrator.*   This program lets you perform the same administrative tasks as the kadmin program, but using a graphical user interface. Like kadmin, it runs in a secured session. At the time of this printing, CyberSafe Administrator runs over any UNIX network client. Counterparts for Windows and Macintosh clients are under development.

In addition to using these programs, a prudent systems administrator will want to review the audit log file created by the CyberSafe Challenger's utility files. All the messages are put into the /usr/admin/messages directory. These messages are retrieved via the syslog daemon. They are available in five categories that CyberSafe Challenger calls *levels*. These levels are as follows:

■ *LOG_ERR.*   Prints error messages

■ *LOG_WARNING.*   Prints warnings

■ *LOG_NOTICE.*   Prints application server errors

■ *LOG_INFO.*   Prints information pertaining to current activity

■ *LOG_DEBUG.*   Prints current state of database

The syslog daemon, when given the previously listed level option, will produce a report either to the screen or printer on that category.

Using the CyberSafe Application Security Toolkit

CyberSafe Corporation makes an add-on component for CyberSafe Challenger called CyberSafe Application Security Toolkit. This toolkit helps application programmers to incorporate Kerberos security into their applications. Doing so assists your organization to closely knit all its applications to the CyberSafe Challenger.

Understanding GSS-API

This toolkit helps the programmer implement GSS-API in applications. GSS-API is a set of C language functions that are used to secure distributed applications. The GSS-API provides a programming interface enabling servers, clients, and applications on the intranet to use the security services provided by CyberSafe Challenger. These services include:

■ *Authentication.*   The user's identity is verified, and an application can be guaranteed that it is talking to its authentic counterpart.

■ *Integrity.*   This service provides the programmer the ability to detect a tampered message when it is received by an application.

■ *Confidentiality.*   This is the ability to secure a message so that it is not visible during transmission.

Because the GSS-API programming interface is designed to be generic, the API does not have to be updated as the network that it rides upon changes or evolves. This toolkit will help your programmer ensure that your applications not only conform to the CyberSafe Challenger security model, but also maintain mechanism and transport independence.

The GSS-API provides a uniform interface to a variety of security mechanisms. Additionally, GSS-API standard is transport independent, thus permitting its use in a wide range of network environments. Figure 11-1 shows a diagram of the architectural view of the GSS-API and the network transport.

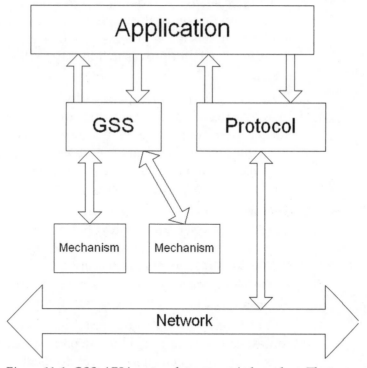

Figure 11-1: GSS-API is network transport independent. The transport must therefore be provided by the application.

From an application programmer's perspective, the design goals of this interface provide a one-time programming investment that will pay off as the mechanisms and transports change on the network.

Securing an Application With the Security Toolkit

In this section, we briefly explain how to secure an application with the provided toolkit. Because the details in implementing GSS-API vary by application, we outline the general steps in securing any application.

1. *Obtain credentials.* Credentials prove the identity of the application or user of the application. In securing an application, this is the process by which an application identifies itself and proves its identity to the security system.

2. *Establish a security context.* Security context is the means by which the secured application communicates among its various parts. For example, in a client–server application, if 20 clients are communicating with a server application, each client will have a unique security context, and the server will manage all 20 security contexts.

3. *Send and receive secured data.* After credentials are acquired and the security context has been established, the data can be secured and sent. GSS-API uses a unique session key to encrypt and decrypt messages. A session key is a temporary encryption key used by different parts of the secured application to communicate information.

4. *Terminate the security context.* In the GSS-API, the security context can be terminated by any part of the application. This means that, in a client–server application, either the client-side or the server-side of the application can end the unique security context between them.

The previous general steps will guide you through the process of Kerberizing your applications. After an application has been Kerberized, it will carry that security protection with it through further development and across different networks. It is a worthwhile investment in programmer time to have that done.

Moving On

In this chapter, we have examined a firewall product called CyberSafe Challenger, based on the Kerberos security model. In the next chapter, we look at several other products that you may want to use in your intranet for firewall protection.

12 Other Firewall Products

In this chapter, we list a number of firewall products and services, including those mentioned in the book, and provide a few comments about each one. The comments about each product are brief but are supplemented by pointers to each manufacturer's Web site, where more information is available. The listing also includes pointers to several firewall-oriented "directory" sites. Those sites contain links to many more firewall manufacturers and resources.

In addition to comments on each product, we've provided platform/OS information, a URL for the vendor's Web site, and an indication of National Computer Security Association (NCSA) certification, if it's applicable. The NCSA has developed a special certification program for network hardware and software, under which each product is submitted to increasingly severe attacks. The test evaluates the product's ability to withstand these attacks while allowing "significant business functions" to be accomplished. NCSA certification is just one of several ways to assess the quality of a given product. Consult the NCSA site (listed below) for more information about the certification process and the latest listings.

Directory Sites

Although we've made every attempt to provide a complete, up-to-date listing of firewall products, the pace of technology's advance makes it likely that this chapter (or at least parts of it) will be outmoded within the next six months. With that in mind, we've tracked down several Web sites that take advantage of the immediacy of Web publishing to keep readers abreast of current firewall products, trends, and technologies. In addition to providing a wealth of information about firewall technology, these sites also provide links to other informational pages and to vendors' home pages.

Firewall Fiesta

http://www.sevenlocks.com/TOCFirewallComparisonCharts.htm
Seven Locks Software's links page provides jumps to information about more than 60 firewall vendors and their products.

National Computer Security Association (NCSA)

http://www.ncsa.com/ncsafws.html
The NCSA Web site provides a wealth of information concerning almost every aspect of firewall security. The most valuable part of the site, though, is the listing of NCSA-certified firewall vendors and packages. In addition, NCSA gives a complete explanation of the rigorous requirements for earning that certification.

Serverwatch

http://serverwatch.iworld.com/tools/firewall.html
The Serverwatch Web site is, by its own description, "designed to be the ultimate resource on the Web for timely and accurate information on Web server technology and supporting tools." The site provides brief, to the point descriptions of current products, as well as regular updates on the latest wares for Macintosh, UNIX, and Windows platforms. A free newsletter is also available.

Firewall Product Listing

Now, on to the core of this chapter: product listings. The products here range from simple firewall software packages to routing hardware to full firewall-in-a-box solutions designed for complete electronic and physical network isolation. Not surprisingly, the prices vary just as widely, from just a few hundred dollars to many thousands. To keep the material as current as possible, we've provided a few general specifications for each product. Point your Web browser at the URL for each company to learn more about product specifics and pricing.

AbhiWeb AFS 2000

Vendor: AbhiWeb
http://www.abhiweb.net/afs.html
Platform(s): UNIX (RISC)
NCSA Certified
The AFS 2000 is, according to AbhiWeb, a "plug-and-play" secure Internet access server. The combination router and firewall box is designed to be connected to existing networks, and, with a few simple configuration selections, provides full, secure net access through a proxy firewall. The box is designed to be placed, without modification, into the user's existing network.

AltaVista FireWall

Vendor: Digital Equipment Corporation
http://www.altavista.software.digital.com/products/firewall/nfintro.htm
Platform(s): Intel (Windows NT, BSD/OS, UNIX);
Alpha (Digital UNIX, Windows NT)
NCSA Certified
AltaVista firewall uses a GUI interface for easy configuration of application gateways for standard Internet services such as SMTP, FTP, and NNTP. A generic TCP-application gateway is also available for other services. AltaVista's security features include user authentication, real-time reporting, complete logging and reporting, and anti-spoofing protection.

ANS Interlock

Vendor: ANS CO+RE Systems, Inc.
http://www.ans.net/InterLock/
Platform(s): UNIX
Interlock's primary strength is its ability to combine full network
security functions with hardware-based local-access controls,
including UNIX passwords, Pinpad cards, and the Enigma Logic
DES Gold Card. Also provides granular access control, sophisticated auditing, and 24-hour support.

Black Hole

Vendor: Milky Way Networks, Inc.
http://www.milkyway.com/mainmenu/index.html
Platform(s): Multiple
NCSA Certified
Black Hole provides an extensive set of security services, including full authentication, one-time password use, mail screening,
real-time alert messages, and comprehensive logging. Virtual
Private Networks can be easily configured, and Black Hole can be
set up to run in a dual configuration for additional security.

BorderGuard 2000

Vendor: Network Systems, a StorageTek Group
http://www.network.com/
The BorderGuard 2000 is a bridge router designed for firewall
routing and data protection. Routing is controlled by Network
Systems' Packet Control Facility, supporting TCP/IP, DECnet
Phase IV, Novell IPX/SPX, Appletalk II, and XNS. Data encryption
and compression are also supported.

BorderWare Firewall Server

Vendor: Secure Computing Corporation
http://www.border.com/
Platform(s): Intel
NCSA Certified

BorderWare's Firewall Server is billed as an easy-to-use firewall package combining packet filters, circuit-level gateways, and application server functions into one package. The software is unique in that it utilizes a "fail-safe" design; a number of miniature firewalls inside the software keeps any compromised area of the system from affecting the uncompromised sections. Other features include extensive logging and a high degree of transparency on the user's end. For a detailed description of BorderWare Firewall Server, see Chapter 7.

Brimstone

Vendor: SOS Corporation
http://www.soscorp.com/products/Brimstone.html
Platform(s): Intel (BSDI); SunOS; Indy/Challenge (IRIX)
Brimstone supports the most popular access controls and user authenticators, and features a Graphical User Interface (GUI) for administrative control.

Centri Firewall/Centri TNT

Vendor: Global Internet
http://www.gi.net/
Platform(s): Intel
Using the Windows NT OS, Centri Firewall provides complete security through use of TIS Gauntlet technology. Centri is administered through a simple GUI, and provides application proxies, packet filtering, address translation, and port mapping. Centri TNT (Trusted Network Transport) acts as a "personal firewall" for users on Windows NT networks. Both products maintain total end-user transparency.

Challenger

Vendor: CyberSafe Corporation
http://www.cybersafe.com/Products/chalengr.htm
Platform(s): AIX 3.2.5 and 4.1; AT&T/NCR (SVR4) UNIX 2.0; BSDi 1.1; HP-UX 9.0x and 10.01; Macintosh System 6 and System 7; MS-DOS 5.x or later; NEXTSTEP/NEXTSTEP Intel 3.2; Sequent DYNIX/ptx 2.1; Solaris 2.3 and 2.4; SunOS 4.1.x, 5.3 and 5.4;

Windows for Workgroups 3.1; Windows 3.1; Windows NT 3.5
Challenger allows users to enter a single password for access to all
authorized network services. Access is transparent and secured.
Challenger is compatible with a tremendous variety of platforms.
For a detailed description of Challenger, see Chapter 11.

CONNECT:Firewall

Vendor: Sterling Software
http://www.csg.stercomm.com/connect/Firewall/Firewall.html
Platform(s): SunOS
CONNECT:Firewall is a proxy server firewall emphasizing
simplicity and security. Strong user authentication and logging
facilities combine with a Motif GUI for ease of use and robust
network defense.

Controller

Vendor: Actane
http://www.actane.com/
Platform(s): Intel
Controller claims to be the first firewall controllable entirely via
SNMP, and utilizes Actane's Object Oriented Transparent
Proxying for security. Actane also touts Controller's easy setup
and management.

CryptoWall

Vendor: Radguard
http://www.radguard.com/wall.htm
Platform(s): n/a
NCSA Certified
CryptoWall is a data-encrypting hardware firewall. Designed to be
incorporated into an existing network, CryptoWall is tooled for
subnet-to-subnet TCP/IP communications.

CyberGuard FireWall

Vendor: CyberGuard Systems Corporation
http://www.cyberguardcorp.com/
Platform(s): Motorola 88100 RISC (CX/SX proprietary UNIX OS)
NCSA Certified
CyberGuard FireWall is a fully-integrated firewall hardware/
software solution. CyberGuard provides extensive protection by
combining a RISC-based UNIX box, a propriety UNIX OS, and a
secure network device (CyberGuard's LAN/SX). Address hiding,
packet filtering, and a strong user authentication team with highly
customizable configuration via a GUI administration tool to
provide a total-security solution.

Cypress Labyrinth Firewall

Vendor: Cypress Consulting, Inc.
http://www.cycon.com/
Platform(s): BSD UNIX
Cypress labyrinth utilizes complex address translation rules and a
combination of proxy rules, circuit-level gateways, and spoof rules
to build a "labyrinth-like" firewall structure.

Digital Firewall for UNIX

Vendor: Digital Equipment Corporation
http://www.digital.com/info/internet/resources/security/
2.html
Platform(s): DEC Alpha; OpenVMS
NCSA Certified
Digital Firewall comes preconfigured but maintains a high level of
flexibility to accommodate almost any use requirement. In addition, the firewall is exceptionally scalable, allowing it to grow as
the user's needs expand. The software employs an easy-to-use
GUI interface, making maintenance and configuration simple. The
technology used in Digital Firewall has protected Digital's own
80,000-node network for five years.

Eagle

Vendor: Raptor Systems, Inc.
http://www.raptor.com/prodinfo/prodinfo.html
Platform(s): UNIX; Windows NT
NCSA Certified
Raptor's Eagle provides extensive application-level security features, including multiple methods of user authentication. Users may access the system via a multiple-use password, a Bellcore single-use password, or a SecureID SmartCard. Further security is provided by Raptor's EagleConnect Encryption and auto code-checking features. System operators are kept constantly informed by Eagle's real-time Suspicious Activity Monitor.

ExFilter

Vendor: ExNet Systems Ltd.
http://www.exnet.com/
Platform(s): SunOS
ExFilter is a packet-filtering firewall program for the Sun3 and Sun4 architecture.

FireDoor

Vendor: Equivalence
equival@ozemail.com.au (e-mail)
Platform(s): Windows NT; Windows 95
FireDoor is a small package meant to be used in a school or small office. The program allows any number of users to concurrently access a single Internet connection, subject to stringent user authentication and security controls.

FireWall-1

Vendor: CheckPoint Software Technologies, Ltd.
http://www.checkpoint.com/
Platform(s): Intel (Windows NT); SunOS; Solaris; HP-UX; Bay Networks Routers
NCSA Certified

FireWall-1 achieves security, transparency, and extensibility through CheckPoint's "stateful inspection technology." All protocols are protected, and multiple gateways are supported. The system offers security monitoring via real-time audits, alerting, and log-viewing.

FireWall IRX Router

Vendor: Livingston Enterprises
http://www.livingston.com/
Platform(s): Windows; SPARC; RS/6000
The FireWall IRX Router is a network router designed to physically separate your intranet from any external connection. The FireWall IRX offers exceptionally detailed packet filtering controls, as well as packet logging (a feature not available on all routers). Configuration and control are handled through a unique graphic user interface.

FireWall/Plus

Vendor: Network-1 Software & Technology, Inc.
http://www.network-1.com/
Platform(s): Intel
NCSA Certified
FireWall/Plus combines Network-1's FireWall/Plus software package with a Pentium-class Intel box for a total firewall solution. The firewall software offers frame, packet, and application-level filtering, operating on the basis of "nothing is permitted except that which is allowed." The software can be upgraded dynamically to avoid downtime, and setup is claimed to be less than 30 minutes in most cases.

Galea Network Security

Vendor: Galea Network Security
http://www.galea.com/
Billing itself as "The Fast Firewall Company," Galea asks that all requests for information be directed to info@galea.com.

Gauntlet Internet Firewall

Vendor: Trusted Information Systems, Inc.
http://www.tis.com/docs/products/gauntlet/index.html
Platform(s): Intel BSD/OS; SunOS; HP-UX; Solaris (available Q3
96); NT (availableQ4 96, early 97)
NCSA Certified
Gauntlet Internet Firewall is a hardware and software-based
application gateway firewall. The package provides extensive
application proxies, including Telnet, rlogin, HTTP, gopher, SMTP,
pop3, x11, FTP, rsh, SQL, RealAudio, and printer. Gauntlet also
allows Java blocking at the firewall, and provides real-time notification of unauthorized activity.

Guardian Firewall System

Vendor: NetGuard, Inc.
http://www.netguard.com
Platform(s): Windows NT; OS/2
Guardian establishes security through the use of sophisticated,
user-defined filtering rules and strong user-access controls, including restrictions on time of day and service-specific restrictions.

GFX Internet Firewall System

Vendor: Global Technology Associates, Inc.
http://www.gta.com/firewall.html
Platform(s): BSDI/OS (Proprietary hardware)
NCSA Certified
GFX is a hardware/software firewall solution. The GFX box
operates on a "hardened" BSDI/OS, and provides security
through address translation, inbound-service proxies, logging,
and packet filtering. A unique feature of the GFX devices is
"double-wall" construction. Essentially, the system is built with
two walls, an inner and an outer, joined by a "private DMZ network." If a breach of the outer wall is detected, the DMZ shuts
down to protect the inner wall from further attempts at incursion.

Horatio

Vendor: SAGUS Security, Inc.

http://www.sagus-security.com/

The Horatio firewall provides high-security user access controls and all the services normally associated with firewalls. In addition, it carries a B2 security rating and utilizes Nortel Entrust encryption and digital signature technology.

IBM Internet Connection Secured Network Gateway

Vendor: IBM

http://www.ics.raleigh.ibm.com/firewall/info.htm

Platform(s): RS/6000 (AIX)

NCSA Certified

Secured Network Gateway supports advanced packet filtering, alerting, reporting, address hiding, and application gateway proxies for the RS/6000. In addition, several user authentication methods, including standard password, SecureNet cards, and SecurID cards are supported. Secured Network Gateway automatically performs hardening procedures on installation, disabling untrusted UNIX and TCP/IP services, and protocols.

I.C.E.Block

Vendor: J. River, inc.

http://www.jriver.com/

Platform(s): UNIX

I.C.E.Block is a packet-filtering firewall designed to protect any IP-based network. The program boasts simple installation and configuration, along with easy-to-use administration tool and easily understandable logging and auditing.

Interceptor

Vendor: Technologic, Inc.

http://www.tlogic.com/intercpt.htm

Platform(s): Intel

NCSA Certified

Interceptor is an application proxy firewall that ships with preconfigured proxies for most major Internet applications. The package is normally sold as a complete hardware/software solution, but the software may also be purchased separately. Interceptor also offers remote management facilities compatible with Macintosh, Windows NT, Windows 95, and UNIX workstations.

Internet Scanner SAFEsuite

Vendor: Internet Security Systems

http://www.iss.net

Platform(s): Windows NT 3.51 and 4.0; IBM AIX 3.2.5 and higher; HP-UX 9.05 and higher; Sun OS 4.1.3 and higher; Sun Solaris 2.3 and higher; Linux 1.2.x (with kernel patch); Linux 1.3.x prior to 1.3.75 (with kernel patch); Linux 1.3.76 and higher (no patch required)

SAFEsuite, as its name implies, is a collection of programs designed to provide comprehensive network security assurance. The package includes Intranet Scanner, for locating security holes in your internal network; Web Security Scanner, which evaluates your Webserver application and its CGI scripts for possible security problems; Firewall Scanner, for checking your firewall application's configuration (including packet filtering and proxy services); and System Security Scanner, which continuously monitors your system's security in real time. ISS also maintains a database of current known vulnerabilities on its Web site. For a detailed description of Internet Scanner, see Chapter 10.

INTOUCH NSA—Network Security Agent

Vendor: Touch Technologies, Inc.
http://www.ttinet.com/
Platform(s): DEC AlphaStation
INTOUCH NSA is a unique product. Consisting of INTOUCH software operating on a dedicated 64-bit AlphaStation connected to your LAN, the unit scans all LAN packets, and then reconstructs user activity and checks for rule violations. The scans may be customized by the adminstrator. Administrators may also review what activity took place during a violation, and can view a real-time reconstruction of the session in question.

IWare Connect

Vendor: Quarterdeck Corporation
http://www.quarterdeck.com/
Platform(s): NetWare Server & Windows Clients
IWare Connect offers complete network security by concealing each workstation's identity and defeating break-ins with a Windows-based IP filter.

KarlBridge/KarlRouter

Vendor: KarlNet, Inc.
http://www.karlnet.com/
The KarlBridge/KarlRouter utilizes packet filtering at full Ethernet speed. The FlashROM-based device can function as a firewall between networks. The device also provides authentication, encryption, and security features.

LT Auditor+

Vendor: Blue Lance
http://www.bluelance.com/
Platforms: Intel (Windows)
LT Auditor+ allows systems administrators to track any illegal entry into their system and alert the systems administrators. The software also provides powerful audit reporting capabilities. For a detailed description of LT Auditor+, see Chapter 8.

Mediator One

Vendor: ComNet Solutions Pty. Ltd.

http://www.comnet.com.au/

Platform(s): Intel

Mediator One's firewall secures your network utilizing security-hardened application proxies and other sophisticated tools. The firewall is exceptionally modular, with each module handling one protocol. New modules are "plug and play," and the whole package is managed via an intuitive GUI.

Modem Security Enforcer

Vendor IC Engineering, Inc.

http://www.bcpl.lib.md.us/~n3ic/iceng.html

The Modem Security Enforcer is a hardware/software product designed to eliminate data security problems encountered when using a publicly switched telephone network for access to a private network. The product is installed between the RS-232 port of the modem and the computer, "splitting" the connection between these two devices. For a detailed description of this product, see Chapter 9.

NETBuilder Firewall

Vendor: 3Com Corporation

http://www.3com.com/

NETBuilder Firewall is a packet-filtering router. Filtering functions are assigned per port rather than per box, providing a high level of user control. As shipped, NETBuilder is capable of filtering most standard Internet services. Users may also create new filters using a built-in generic filtering language.

NetFortress

Vendor: Digital Secured Networks Technology, Inc.

http://www.dsnt.com/

Platform(s): Automatically self-configures to all major platforms. Billed as "The NetFortress—Not A Firewall," this product is a hardware device that operates at the network layer, encrypting both the application-layer and transport-layer headers, providing exceptional security with almost no maintenance.

NetGate

Vendor: SmallWorks, Inc.
http://www.smallworks.com/
Platform(s): SPARC (Solaris or SunOS)
NetGate is a small, no-frills, command-line package. NetGate uses rules-based packet filtering to monitor activity on TCP/IP networks. SmallWorks claims NetGate's primary virtues are speed and low price.

NetLOCK

Vendor: Hughes Electronics
http://www.netlock.com/
Platform(s): MacOS; Intel; UNIX
NetLOCK is a unique software security package designed to allow worry-free data transmission across LANs, WANs, and the Internet. The package automatically seals data to be transmitted in a "cryptographic envelope," which can be decrypted only by an authenticated receiving site. User transparency is accomplished through Hughes' dynamic key generation, which also eliminates the need to use a key server.

NetSeer

Vendor: enterWorks.com, A Telos Company
http://www.enterworks.com/prods/ns/index.htm
Platform(s): SPARC (Solaris)
NCSA Certified
NetSeer is a flexible, scalable packet-filtering firewall package. Virtual private networks over the Internet are supported by NetSeer's firewall-to-firewall encryption. Bidirectional filtering allows administrators to filter incoming and outgoing traffic, and IP remapping hides intranet structures from potential interlopers. NetSeer also provides extensive detection capabilities and sophisticated reporting of in and outbound traffic.

NetRoad FireWALL

Vendor: Ukiah Software, Inc.
http://www.ukiahsoft.com/
Platform(s): Novell NetWare
FireWALL protects networks by restricting access to a narrow, single-gate access channel. The software scrutinizes all activity through this gateway carefully. FireWALL also provides IP/IPX address concealing.

NetWall

Vendor: Bull S.A.
http://www-frec.bull.fr/
Platform(s): Intel; UNIX (Bull's secure version)
NetWall's security is provided by dynamic packet filtering and application proxies. A user-friendly GUI simplifies management and configuration, and offers CP8 Smarcard user authentication.

The Norman Firewall

Vendor: Internet Security, Inc.
http://www.inter-secure.com/
Platform(s): Pentium; HP PA-RISC
The Norman Firewall utilizes packet checking rather than packet filtering. Accomplished via a proxy, this process actually scans the entire contents of incoming packets, checking for viruses and looking for forbidden material. Additional security is provided by a user-defined "hot word" database—a list of keywords that cause the firewall to set the offending packets aside for examination by the administrator.

ON Guard

Vendor: On Technology Corporation
http://www.on.com/
Platform(s): Windows NT; Netware
NCSA Certified
ON Guard is a "UNIX-free" Intel PC-based firewall designed to secure IP and IPX networks. It utilizes a proprietary operating

system called Secure32OS, and eases setup tasks by providing an Express Configuration Wizard. ON Guard uses address translation, along with packet and application-level screening, but remains transparent to the user and requires no proxies.

PERMIT Security Gateway

Vendor: TimeStep Corporation
http://www.timestep.com/
PERMIT Security Gateway is an Ethernet hardware gateway that functions as a proxy agent. PERMIT utilizes advanced address-based packet encryption, forwarding, and blocking.

PORTUS

Vendor: Livermore Software Laboratories, Inc.
http://www.lsli.com/
Platform(s): RS/6000 or compatible (including PowerPC), AIX 4.1 and 4.2; Hewlett-Packard 9000 Series, HP-UX 10; Solaris 2.5
NCSA Certified
According to LSLI, PORTUS "is an application firewall designed to repel the most sophisticated attack from skilled and determined crackers." PORTUS takes the approach that all functions not explicitly allowed are denied. All proxy activity is logged, and any OS proxies or daemons that PORTUS considers untrustworthy are disabled and replaced with secure versions developed by LSLI.

Private Internet Exchange (PIX) Firewall

Vendor: Cisco Systems
http://www.cisco.com/warp/public/751/pix/index.html
Platform(s): Real-time secure kernel
NCSA Certified
PIX is a rack-mount firewall device that uses address translation to shield your intranet's internal structure from potential intruders. Cisco claims no user impact from the device, which is configured via a Windows 95-based utility. PIX supports up to 16,000 simultaneous connections, and performs address translations as fast as 45Mbps.

PrivateNet Secure Firewall Server

Vendor: NEC Technologies
http://www.privatenet.nec.com/
Platform(s): BSD UNIX
NCSA Certified
NEC's PrivateNet is sold as a total firewall solution. The package
includes a Pentium-class box running BSDI UNIX and the
PrivateNet System Software. Security is achieved via varying
schemes—applications connecting from inside your internal
network are managed by NEC's SocksPlus circuit-level proxy
technology, whereas external connections are handled by "security-hardened" application-level proxy servers.

Secure Access Firewall

Vendor: Ascend Communications
http://www.ascend.com/
Platform(s): Ascend MAX; Ascend Pipeline
NCSA Certified
Secure Access is a software package designed to provide firewall
services for Ascend's own Pipeline and MAX lines of remote
networking hardware. Ascend's approach provides firewall and
routing services in one solution. The firewall maintains a high
level of security by opening ports only for the current session and
then closing them at the close of the session. Unused ports are
locked shut.

Secure RPC Gateway

Vendor: Le Reseau netwerksystemen BV
http://www.reseau.nl/
The Secure RPC Gateway is designed to allow Remote Procedure
Calls to be safely initiated across intranets or the Internet. The
product uses a secure portmapper, SSL, and data relay programs
that communicate only with the client for which they are working.
Le Reseau also provides a Java-blocking HTTP proxy.

Sidewinder

Vendor: Secure Computing Corporation
http://www.sidewinder.com/
Platform(s): UNIX
NCSA Certified
Sidewinder provides user-transparent firewall protection using rules-based filtering, split DNS, full inbound audits, and a unique Strike Back facility. Strike Back allows the firewall to take action against unauthorized incursions. This action can range from ejecting the offending user to tracking the user and attempting to gain more information about the source of the incursion, while alerting the systems administrator to the attempted incursion.

Site Patrol

Vendor: BBN Planet
http://www.bbnplanet.com/
Site Patrol is sold as a complete package of hardware, software, and services. Included are complete firewall software, hardware solutions, and installation. Also included are 24-hour monitoring and response services, firewall management services, and regular security updates and alerts.

Solstice Firewall-1

Vendor: Sun MicroSystems, Inc.
http://www.sun.com/solstice/Networking-products/
FW-1v2.html
Platform(s): Intel (Windows NT and Solaris); SPARC (Solaris)
Firewall-1™ provides robust security while maintaining flexibility and scalability. Based on Sun's Stateful Multi-Layer Inspection technology, FW-1 provides application-level filtering, along with advanced authentication for more than 120 integrated services, including secure Web browsers and servers, FTP, Mbone, and more.

SmartWall

Vendor: V-ONE Corporation
http://www.v-one.com/
Platform(s): Pentium (BSDI UNIX)
Sold as an integrated hardware/software solution, SmartWall "is
a dual-homed, application-level gateway firewall" providing
"token-based authentication and encryption with fine-grained
data access control." SmartWall also provides mutual authentication, secure Telnet, secure remote administration, and firewall-to-
firewall encryption.

SunScreen

Vendor: Sun Microsystems, Inc.
http://www.sun.com:80/950523/screen.html
Platform(s): Sparc
NCSA Certified
SunScreen is a complete firewall security package including hardware, software, and associated services. The software, SunScreen
SPF-100, utilizes rules-based packet screening and packet vector-
ing, along with built-in encryption and authentication to create a
secure data pipe. The hardware is a microSPARC-II-based firewall
blackbox, accompanied by a 486-based remote administration
station. The black box holds the packet-screening, encryption,
and other essential software, whereas the administration station
includes the SunScreen program, the administration interface,
configuration database, and log browser.

TurnStyle Firewall System

Vendor: Atlantic Systems Group
http://www.asg.unb.ca/
Platform(s): Pentium (BSD UNIX); SPARC; Apollo; Alpha
NCSA Certified
TurnStyle Firewall System is a turnkey firewall setup scalable to
small or large organizations: all hardware and software is provided for the user. The system utilizes Atlantic Systems' ASG
Secure Link Protocol, which allows a secure tunnel to other
firewalls using SLP. SLP currently employs DES encryption, with
the option to add other algorithms.

WatchGuard Security System

Vendor: Seattle Software Labs, Inc.

http://www.sealabs.com/

Platform(s): Windows NT or Windows 95; Linux

The WatchGuard firewall features an "Intelligent Defense Device," a melding of transparent proxies, dynamic packet filtering, and address translation. WatchGuard can be installed in Internet firewall configuration, in GroupGuard mode to protect departmental systems, or in HostGuard format to protect single machines housing mission-critical information.

WebSENSE

Vendor: NetPartners Internet Solutions, Inc.

http://www.netpart.com/

Platform(s): WindowsNT

WebSENSE is essentially a net-address blocker. Meant to provide the network administrator with control over user access to outside sites, WebSENSE maintains an extensive database of URLs and newsgroup addresses, which are placed into categories that may be turned on or off by the administrator. NetPartners plans to integrate WebSENSE into CheckPoint's FireWall-1, and also functions as a reseller for several other firewall packages.

Part 3:

Appendices

Appendix A

E-Mail Privacy & Security

There are times when things just need to be private. In this chapter, we'll discuss some ways of keeping your e-mail and other online files that way. Of course, it's not difficult to keep something *totally* secret. The trick is keeping something secret in such a way that you have control over which parts are made available and to whom. It's this controlled access that brings about all the difficulties. Sometimes you want to transmit data so that only those it is intended for can read it. Sometimes you want to keep data private and not let outsiders get to it, but it needs to be available to insiders. Sometimes you want some of the information to be public and the rest of it to be private. There are all sorts of situations and all sorts of methods for addressing them.

Here is a list of basic e-mail privacy tips. Each aspect of this list (password creation, e-mail encryption, anonymous remailers, and so on) is discussed in greater detail throughout this chapter. If such topics as cryptographic algorithms and the specifics of computer security leave you cold, you can skip over those sections. The important information every e-mail user should know is contained in this list and the do's and don'ts of password making that follow.

1. Most computer intrusions happen through insecure passwords. Take special care when generating your passwords and change them frequently.

2. Make sure your mail gets to the person for whom it is intended. This is a detail you can't be too careful about.

3. If you're paranoid about having your password intercepted because you've sent it over an unsecure network, change it immediately.

4. If you need to send a message, and you don't want your name attached to it, use an anonymous remailer.

5. If you want to encrypt your mail, you can use a program like PGP, RIPEM, or crypt, depending on what platform you're on and how much protection you think you need.

6. Remember: your e-mail is not really private, so take precautions accordingly.

7. If you don't want people reading your deleted messages and other files on your machine, you can use a program like Norton Utilities (for both Mac and Windows) to zap all of the hidden, deleted files. A program such as this can be used to remove all traces of the deleted files from your drive by completely erasing and *zeroing out* all space on your disk that is marked as free.

8. If you suspect that your e-mail account has been tampered with, contact your ISP or systems administrator immediately.

BflSpk: Password Tricks

The password is the first layer of protection. This is far and away the biggest security hole in any computer system. Most computer intrusions happen by hacking users' insecure passwords. You should put a great deal of thought into your password to make sure that it cannot be easily cracked. Although it is rare, all the heavy technical news you hear about security breaches and brilliant crackers is true.

The number one thing you need to do to keep your e-mail private and secure is to change your passwords frequently. Some systems age the passwords and tell users when the time comes to make a change. This only sort of works; people become emotionally attached to their passwords (we know we do) and take delight in trying to fool the system administrator. They simply change their password and then change it right back again. To deal with this sort of childish chicanery, old passwords have to be archived so they can be compared to current passwords. This is tedious for the systems administrator, but necessary if security is a real concern.

How *Not* to Construct a Password

There are certain passwords that people use over and over. Crackers know this. If you consider the following suggestions, you can maximize the security of your passwords:

- Don't set up an account and use the account name as the password, even as a temporary measure. This happens frequently when new users are added to a system.

- Don't use a word you find in a dictionary. There is a common trick used by crackers—they simply set up an automatic loop to apply the words of a dictionary to the account until one of them opens it up. This goes for foreign words and common abbreviations, too.

- Don't use short passwords of three or four characters. There are not enough of these to prevent a scan from being made (in a very short time) of all the possible combinations. Never use a password of less than six characters.

- Don't use the name of a person. There are two ways this can be broken. One is simply by using a dictionary of names. The other is by using the names of the people you know.

- Don't use your birthday (or some other special date). This is such a common password scheme that it is one of the first ones checked by someone breaking in. Don't use your social security number or phone number, either. It's best not to use any number that can be looked up.

- Don't use common words or dates (or anything) spelled backwards. The cracker simply tries each one in both directions.

- Don't use all letters or all numbers.

- No matter how good it may seem, don't use a password that you find in this book or in any other book. The people that break in to computers also read books. Where do you think they get all the ideas about bad passwords?

- Ideally, don't even write your password down. If you have to, store it in a safe place, away from your computer. Don't write it in the back of your MS Word manual or leave it on the bulletin board behind your desk or in other obvious places.

- If you're signing on to a new system, think up your new password before you log on. Sometimes, people feel like the meter's running and they need to think up something quick when prompted for their password. So, they look at their surroundings and choose the first thing they see. Not smart. Someone wanting to break in will often visit the site of the target system and look for these clues.

- Finally, something not directly related to construction, but which should be pretty obvious—never tell anyone your password. As the little man at the door of the Emerald Palace said, "Not nobody, not nohow!" You would be positively amazed at how many crackers can barely string two lines of code together, but are adept social engineers. They're very good at coaxing someone's password out of them with some sob story or tale of woe. Don't go for it. Your password should be absolutely secret.

 **TIP**

If you suspect that someone has gained unauthorized access to your e-mail account contact your ISP or systems administrator immediately.

How to Construct a Password

What you want for a password is a random selection of letters and numbers and punctuation. Along with this, you will need some way to remember it without writing it down. Most of the "great safe crackers" in history have simply been astute enough to look in certain hiding places for the written combination. Here are some ways to create a secure password that you can remember:

- Come up with some fictional word that you can pronounce and spell in some personal way. For example, say "for drum lee" in your mind and type "4drumly." Or, say "oh but yes they are too" in your mind as you type "Obytr2." Or, say "base on balls" while you type "B@snBalls."

- Take a couple of words and insert some punctuation such as "hen&fruit" or "Yall*drill."

- Make up a multisyllable word and leave out the vowels (or the consonants, or anything else you like). For example, the word "BaffleSpeak" could become "BflSpk."

- There are random password generators available on the Internet. They generate passwords that are pronounceable so you can remember them as sounds after a few repetitions.

- Pick some sort of phrase or saying and use the first letter from each of the words—for example, "The traveling salesman and the farmer's daughter." While you say this in your head, type "ttsatfd." It would be even better to add a couple of capital letters, as in "TtsaTfd," or add some numbers as in "1ts1fd" (for "one traveling salesman, one farmer's daughter").

- Construct a password from some sequence that you can reconstruct if you forget the word. For example, if you have a personal address book you carry with you, take the last letter from the first name of the first 8 people in the book. We just did this and got "kjjsjscc." This gives a bit of a convoluted password that could be hard to remember, but it can always be recreated. Just don't lose your address book!

Anonymous Remailers

Normally, when e-mail is sent from one person to another, every effort is made to include the name and address of the sender. You may find yourself in a position in which you'd like to send mail but you don't want the receiver know where it came from—there are ways to do that.

The simplest (and least effective) method to achieve anonymity is to simply change the name of the sender in your e-mail software. But this is only a facade since the sender can be traced directly by the other information in the header of the message. All received e-mail has the address of the sender. The only way to not have your return address appear on the mail is to have someone else send it so that their return address will appear there instead. That's exactly what an anonymous remailer does. You send the mail to the remailer, it strips off all of the return address information and inserts its own return address by sending the mail on to the intended recipient.

▨▨▨▨ TRAP

This may seem obvious, but when sending mail that does include your address, be careful about who exactly you're sending it to. People have actually lost their jobs because they've accidentally sent a message about the boss to the boss. We've seen a number of embarrassing incidents where someone on a group list intends to veer off from the list and complain about one list member to another, but they've used the "Reply to All" command by mistake. Oops.

Some people say all reasons for using a remailer are suspicious (illegal activities, terrorism, child pornography). But there are legitimate reasons. For instance, there are mailing list discussion groups on sensitive and personal subjects. Anonymous remailers allow the bashful to participate. Sometimes a corporate or government spokesperson wants to say something "off the record." For example, an anonymous remailer would have simplified the communications between the *Washington Post* and Deep Throat during the Watergate incident. In technical and intellectual discussions that may be over your head, remailers allow you to "think out loud" without publicly embarrassing yourself if your brilliant idea turns out to be a dim bulb.

There are security reasons for wanting anonymity, too. If sensitive information is to be sent from one place to another, it may be advisable to obscure the sender as well as the message so that snoopers won't know the message may be worth reading. If a message is taken out of the context of the identity of the sender this way, the contents mean very little. A combination of a remailer and encryption can be used to make messages even more secure.

There are a number of anonymous remailers (also called anonymous servers) around the world. There are a few remailers that have been in operation for a while, and there are new ones appearing and old ones dying all the time. There's a tendency for remailers to be short lived because there's no profit in them. An anonymous remailer allows mail to be sent to an individual, or to a newsgroup, and have the sender remain anonymous. With a couple of special exceptions (which we'll discuss in a minute), the sender information is discarded completely by the remailer, making it difficult to collect fees from a list of anonymous clients.

There are two classes of anonymous servers: the cypherpunk class and the mixmaster class. In addition, there was a penet class that became defunct in late 1996. The classification of remailers is quite informal. The whole thing has such a short history and sites come and go so quickly, it's difficult to formalize anything. There is a new class of remailers just appearing that are constructed to work as Web pages. An example can be seen in Figure A-1. Although these pages are simply front ends for existing anonymous remailer classes, they're very easy to use via a simple input form.

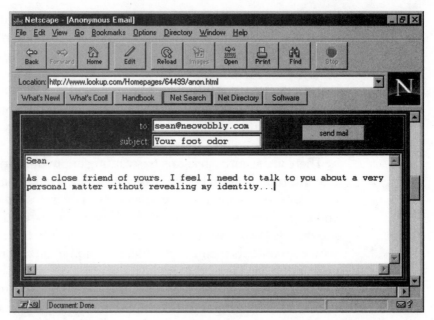

Figure A-1: The no fuss/no muss anonymous remailer at Noah's Place.

The Cypherpunk Class

The largest of the cypherpunk class of remailers appears to be the alpha.c2.org server. Whenever a message is sent through alpha.c2.org, it must begin with an encrypted reply block. The service then replaces the sender's address with its own and forwards the message to the recipient, original reply block included. Upon responding, the recipient includes the original reply block, which alpha.c2.org then decrypts to the original sender's actual address and forwards the mail to that address. This way, there are no files kept on the server, which means that not even the systems administrator can find the addresses.

There's one problem. The price paid for the higher level of security is reflected in the difficulty of use. You have to be able to do some fancy (and very specific) juggling to set up the encryption format part of the message. Fortunately, most of the difficulties come about when setting things up. Once you are up and running on the service, it's fairly easy to use. Getting yourself set up to use a cypherpunk remailer will certainly be educational and can approach becoming a hobby. With all of the crackers, hackers, and guys in trenchcoats playing cloak and dagger games on the Internet, boning up on encryption is not such a bad idea (see "Encryption" later in this appendix).

We won't attempt to describe the whole process here, but we will give you an idea of what has to be done and how the thing works. To set up an account, first you'll need to send for the instructions by sending a message to help@alpha.c2.org. Once you get the instructions, which includes the server's PGP public encryption key (see "PGP" later in this appendix), you will send the server a username, password, and an encrypted reply block. The name is, of course, any name you choose. The password is the one that will be used by the server to encrypt the alias before it's sent back to you. A reply block must be constructed by you. It is an encryption of your address with PGP, using the server's public key. Its exact format is in the instructions you receive from the server.

The Cypherpunks Home Page (http://www.csua.berkeley.edu/ cypherpunks/ Home.html) contains links to rants, papers, and articles about privacy and cryptography, a link to their FTP server, and pointers to other sites of interest, to name a few of its features (See Figure A-2).

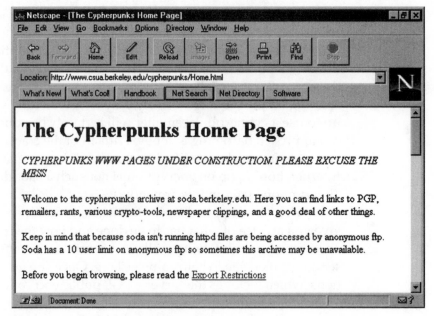

Figure A-2: The Cypherpunks Home Page.

The Mixmaster Class

This is the cutting edge of high-tech anonymity. The mixmaster class of remailers uses the latest in security technology—software based on the cypherpunk software (so it has the security of that class)—but it's not nearly as difficult to use. There is a trade-off, however. Since the security comes from using a special message format, there is special software used to create the messages. The message-formatting software comes as compilable source code for UNIX (it does not run on PCs or Macs). You should be able to run this software from a shell account on almost any UNIX system. It has been verified on a number of platforms including SunOS, Solaris, Linux, and FreeBSD. The original release of mixmaster was in the summer of '95, so it is the newest of the two classes.

The software can be acquired from FTP at obscura.com in the directory /pub/readmail, or ftp.ipunix.com. There are some restrictions on the mixmaster software. The software uses cryptography that cannot be copied outside of the United States. There are some instructions about this at the FTP sites. The client software and the server software are one and the same. The system configuration determines which is which. A server is a bit more difficult to set up. The mixmaster software does not use PGP encryption; it uses the RSAREF package from RSA.

Here is a list of the mixmaster remailers. You can get an updated list via FTP at obscura.com/pub/no-export or on the World Wide Web at http://www.obscura.com/~loki/remailer/active.remailers.html. To get the mixmaster public encryption key for any of these remailers, just send mail to it with the subject remailer-key.

```
mixmaster@obscura.com
mixmaster@vishnu.alias.net
mixmaster@aldebaran.armory.com
robo@c2.org
syrinx@c2.org
remailer@replay.com
remailer@utopia.hacktic.nl
remailer@crynwr.com
remailer@spook.alias.net
remailer@flame.alias.net
remailer@armadillo.com
mixmaster@anon.alias.net
secret@secret.alias.net
mixmaster@remail.ecafe.org
anon@ad.org
remailer@shinobi.alias.net
amnesia@chardos.connix.co
q@c2.org
mixmaster@mix.precipice.com
```

Encryption

There has been data encryption since there's been communication. It almost seems to be instinctive. Grade school children invent ciphers to map the letters of the alphabet to numbers so they can write secret messages. Throughout history, nations have devised cyphers to hide information from one another. It all comes down to, "I know what it says, and you know what it says, but *they* don't know what it says." Encryption is simply the conversion of data from a commonly readable form into a form that is only readable by certain people.

In its most basic form, encryption is a combination of input data (the text to be encrypted) and an algorithm that is used for the encryption. Since the text will eventually need to be made useful again, there is also a decryption method that reverses the actions of the encryption. To make the encryption more secure, there can be a key included with the input text. The key is a value of some sort thrown into the mix. It works just like a key in the real world. If you don't have the key, you cannot "unlock" the message. This means that the one doing the decryption will need to know the decryption key.

There are three basic types of encryption; each has its own purposes. There is one way to encrypt that is not intended to be decrypted. It is ideal for things like passwords that just need to be encrypted and compared to that which was previously encrypted. There is single key (or conventional) encryption, which uses the same key to decrypt the data as it did to encrypt it. Finally, there is public key (or dual key) encryption, which uses one key to encrypt the data and a different key to decrypt it. Single key encryption is also called symmetric, and dual key encryption is called asymmetric.

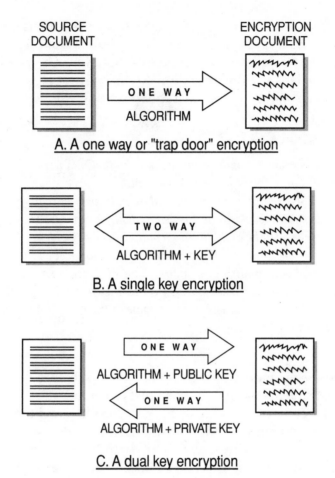

A. A one way or "trap door" encryption

B. A single key encryption

C. A dual key encryption

Figure A-3: The three basic types of encryption.

Encrypting and decrypting can be a lot of work. Before you go to all that trouble, you need to make sure that it's necessary. If it is, you need to make sure that doing it doesn't become an onerous chore.

One valid reason for using encryption is to prevent information from being accidentally discovered. An unauthorized person can, through unforeseen circumstance, wind up with a copy of sensitive information. This doesn't require that the data be deeply encoded in some 500 character key-deep, hairy-legged encryption scheme. Something very simple would work. In this circumstance, nobody is trying it crack the code. Instead, a computer user wants to protect data from the possible prying eyes of a systems administrator, let's say, or someone else who has root-level access to the system. A rather simple encryption scheme will do the trick.

▰▰▰▰▰ TRAP

Remember: your e-mail is not really private. On a network, systems administrators and anyone with root access can read your mail. Moreover, your messages will often be part of regular, routine system backups performed by your sysadmin. These backup files can be and have been subpoenaed as evidence in lawsuits involving employee misconduct. If you feel as though the content of your mail is innocuous, there's nothing to worry about. If you care whether your mail is potentially accessible to others, you might want to consider using some of the privacy methods discussed below.

There are more heavy duty encryption schemes designed to thwart the intentional snooper. Just remember the code of the ol' west, "There ain't no horse that can't be rode, and there ain't a cypher you can't decode." If one person can devise an encryption scheme, another can crack it. Use computer security methods as your first line of defense. Of course, if you are going to transmit data across publicly accessible data links, you'll need to encrypt anything that is sensitive.

Can Encryption Be Illegal?

There is all sorts of legal wrangling going on over encryption. And, like most legal situations, the wrangling seems to continue to muddy the water and add to the confusion. The United States, which treats encryption technology as a weapon, has banned the exportation of encryption software. Since encryption is about communications, and since communications is now worldwide, the governments of several countries have gotten involved. Boris Yeltsin issued a formal decree in Russia banning non-government-approved encryption. In the United States, the Clinton administration has been trying to get legislation passed that would put encryption hardware, namely the Clipper Chip, into all communications devices and force everyone to use it so the government could decrypt anything it wanted to. Nongovernmental encryption is flat out illegal in France, Iran, Iraq, and several other countries.

 **TIP**

There are sites on the Internet from which encryption software can be downloaded, and there are Usenet newsgroups for the discussion of encryption. Before accessing any data or software, you should check the laws in your country.

The exportation limitations in the U.S. have been a point of irritation for manufacturers and vendors. The United States export control policy categorizes certain encryption software and hardware as being "munitions-related" and subject to export laws under the Arms Export Control Act. This stuff requires licensing from the Office of Defense Trade Controls at the State Department and the Commerce Department. Export licensing requires a review from the National Security Agency. It has been found in the past that the approval time is greater than the life cycle of the software. Since encryption is built in to many software products, this ban has prohibited export of a lot of software from the United States.

In dual key encryption (one key to encrypt and one to decrypt), the United States government wants to have access to the decryption keys. There is legislation being considered that would require the decryption keys to be held in escrow by one or more government agencies, or possibly a private escrow company, so the government could get them if it wanted them. This would give the government the ability to decipher any transmitted messages it deemed suspicious.

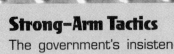

Strong-Arm Tactics

The government's insistence on labeling certain crypto algorithms as unexportable munitions has gotten under some people's skin. In Richard White's case, it has *literally* gotten under his skin. The Los Angeles civil libertarian has had the RSA encryption algorithm tattooed onto his arm (see "RSA," later in this chapter). This officially makes him contraband, living ammo! No word yet if White plans on doing any international traveling soon or whether the Feds have plans to confiscate his arm if he does.

Encryption Programs

Cryptography is a large field. There are thousands of ciphers and hundreds of books written on the subject. It is a science that goes back thousands of years. What we are going to discuss in this chapter are the most current and popular encryption methods and programs. Our list is by no means exhaustive.

crypt

This is a standard encryption utility on UNIX systems. It is in common use and will do a fine job of the low-level, "convenience" type encryption. However, don't use it to try to hide your latest Doomsday weapon plans.

Crypt is one of the oldest encryption methods still being used today. It is a software implementation of the Enigma machine devised by the Germans in World War II. Methods of cracking it are quite well known. It is implemented as a simple command line utility that can quickly encrypt and decrypt disk files. All it needs is a file name and a password. The password is used as the key. It is a symmetric cipher (the same key is used for encryption and decryption). Crypt is known to UNIX text-editing software, and encrypted files can be both read and written by supplying the password to the editor. The crypt utility has one curious feature: it is designed to intentionally use much more CPU time than it really needs when it is doing decryption. When the systems administrator detects unusually heavy use, he or she will be alerted to the fact that someone is attempting to break into something.

DES (Data Encryption Standard)

The other common UNIX utility, DES, was released to the public in 1977, the same year it was established as a United States government standard. DES is a strong, private-key algorithm developed at IBM. It has been repeatedly recertified as a government standard and will remain certified until 1998. There's a good possibility that it won't be recertified after that. Too much is happening in the area of data security.

On UNIX, DES is implemented as a command line tool (called des) that works almost the same as crypt, but the encryption algorithm is a bit more robust. It is des that is used to encrypt the system passwords kept in the /etc/passwd file. It has a variable algorithm that, as yet, doesn't seem to have been broken. (Crackers have other ways of going after the password file). This is a single key, or symmetric system, just like crypt. Both sender and receiver of an encrypted message must know the same key. This single key also makes it handy for use in encrypting and decrypting files by a single person, since the same key is used going in and out.

RSA

RSA is named after its inventors, Rivest, Shamir, and Adelman. Along with DES, it is considered to be one of the most effective encryption algorithms on the market. RSA has become a very popular cryptosystem. It is an asymmetric system, meaning that it has public and private keys.

RSA is not normally a stand-alone encryption method. It is commonly used in conjunction with DES or some other secret key method. To use this dual method, the sender of a message would encrypt the body of the message with DES using an invented key. Then, the intended receiver's public key is used to encrypt the invented key. The two parts together form the message. The receiver uses his or her private key to decrypt the invented DES key, then the DES key is used to decrypt the body of the message.

Skip This. It's Math.

It is a mathematical fact that it is much easier to multiply two prime numbers together than it is to factor them back out. Much easier. Modern encryption methods, like RSA, take advantage of this fact. Choose a couple of prime numbers, p and q, and multiply them together to find the modulus n; that is n = pq. The larger the prime numbers, the better. Now choose another number, e, such that e is less than n and it is relatively prime to (p-1)(q-1). (Two numbers are relatively prime if they have no factors in common.) Find d, which is the inverse of e mod (p-1)(q-1). This means that ed = mod (p-1)(q-1).

Simple, eh? We now have e, which is the public exponent, and d, which is the private exponent. The public key is the pair (n,e). The private key is d. The two large prime numbers that were so hard to come by are now discarded since they could be used to break the cipher.

The prime numbers p and q should be about the same size. The larger they are, the more secure the encryption. Prime numbers can be hard to find, but it isn't because there is a shortage. If primes of 512 bits are used, you can select any two from a group of 10 to the 150th power, which is more atoms than there are in the known universe.

RSAREF

RSAREF is a collection of cryptographic routines in C source code available at no charge from RSA Labs. The code includes, among others, RSA, MD2, MD5, DES. This is a set of both low-level and high-level functions. Included are functions that will generate keys, encrypt, decrypt, operate on multiple precision integers (required for large keys), perform modular exponentiation, and execute verification of digital signatures.

RSAREF is free, but there is limited access. The code is only available to citizens and permanent residents of the United States. It is also limited to personal and noncommercial use. You can find out about all the capabilities and limitations at the FTP site rsa.com or by sending e-mail to rsaref@rsa.com.

The Zip Family

The PKZIP utility is one of a family of programs used to compress files. The files can also be encrypted and decrypted while they are being compressed and decompressed. It is simply a matter of entering an encryption key (a password) during the compression process; the same key will be required for decompression. The PKZIP utility is a product of PKware. There is a shareware version for DOS, and a commercial version for DOS and Windows. There are several compatible programs in the ZIP/UNZIP family, such as Infozip.

PKZIP is a very popular utility that resides in one form or another on virtually every DOS and Windows computer. Internet FTP sites use this as a matter of course to compress files to be downloaded. Its primary purpose, however, is compression, not encryption. The encryption method has been broken and anything encrypted using any of the ZIP family of utilities can be decrypted in a matter of hours. It pretty much falls into that category of something that will "keep the honest people honest."

PKZIP is widely available on FTP sites, software libraries, and via online services like AOL and CompuServe.

Huffman Code

Like the ZIP family, Huffman Code is primarily a method of compression, but it can also be considered (and is sometimes used as) an encryption algorithm. It uses a type of encoding known as a "statistical code," since it operates on probabilities.

Huffman Code was designed to encode text, but can easily be extended to handle binary data as well. It works like this: A pass is made through the text to determine the number of occurrences of each character of text. Next, a code is assigned to each character found. To achieve compression, the shorter codes are assigned to the characters that occur the most often, and longer codes to the ones that are more rare. By looking up each character in the code table, the data is then rewritten as a string of these codes. The code table must be combined with the compressed data so the algorithm can be applied in reverse to decompress it. It is a simple matter for the encoder and decoder to use a standard table so that the table does not have to be included in the transmission of data.

As you can imagine, this is not the most secure code in the world. In the final analysis, it is only one step above A=1 and B=2. It can be handy for low-level security though, since it also does some compression.

 **TIP**

Probably the most interesting Huffman code utility is the one found on the Web page http://www.cs.brown.edu/people/amd/java/ ill/huffman.html. It is written in Java and operates interactively, demonstrating the steps taken by the algorithm to encode the text you enter.

SKIPJACK & the Clipper Chip

SKIPJACK is the classified encryption/decryption algorithm used in the Clinton administration's proposed Clipper Chip key escrow system. It uses an 80-bit key (as compared to the 56-bit key used in DES). It appears that, for now, Clipper is a dead (or at least dormant) issue.

Clipper is an algorithm in the SKIPJACK family. Clipper is only for voice and other low speed data, while other members of the SKIPJACK family, such as Tessera and Capstone, were designed for data encryption.

These methods were chosen by the NSA and NIST (National Institute for Standards and Technology) because it was assumed that commonly available computer-processing power doubles every eighteen months, making it 36 years before exhaustive search techniques could break a SKIPJACK encoded message in a reasonable time. Also, it was assumed that there was no significant risk of SKIPJACK being broken.

The United States government wanted to put this in place so they would be able to decrypt any message sent by anyone anywhere (telephone, video, digital data, whatever). The actual algorithm itself is classified and has never been released. Some selected individuals who were allowed a limited viewing declared the encryption as secure, but there was this nervous feeling in some quarters that the encryption algorithm has some sort of "back door" and could be decrypted without the key being taken out of escrow. One thing after another went wrong with Clipper. Each Clipper Chip encrypted message includes a LEAF (Law Enforcement Access Field) by which the key could be identified in escrow. Dr. Matt Blaze of Bell Labs discovered a way to create and insert a bogus LEAF that made the escrowed key value useless.

There was also the possibility that some sneaky citizen would simply encrypt with something else, say PGP, before passing their data through Clipper encryption, thus keeping the data encrypted even if the Feds used the key to unlock Clipper. After all of this, and not a small amount of protest from the Internet community, Clipper took on too much water and sank slowly out of sight.

PGP (Pretty Good Privacy)

PGP, created by Phil Zimmerman, is a very secure system for encrypting e-mail. It has successfully resisted even the most sophisticated forms of analysis. It is a public key encryption method, which means that there are two keys required. One key is used to encrypt the message, the other to decrypt it. This way, the encryption key can be published, or made public. Anyone wishing to send you a message simply uses your published key to encrypt the message, so that you're the only one who can decrypt it. Historically, one of the problems with ciphers has been that the 'bad guys' could get their hands on the key. With a public key system, the decryption key is never at risk because it never leaves home. Also, if the private key does become compromised, it is a simple matter publishing a brand new key to everyone who sends you messages.

```
-----BEGIN PGP PUBLIC KEY BLOCK-----
Version: 2.3

mQCPAizgA+EAAAEEAMzQAf9ffoq9tVD5oBxtVlPYAito4RBM+hJvX4irXzYgJWsA
Fhc4b/RfLcbGQVHwmoQ74cp/KhijXqGeLE2Tk62xo4u1mjfBevoOHUltOOWxrIbU
y6ros1cThAzVLo3lkh6OHR3DbfUJWld9WtmamGWFGHYvt1WSagSzG6zrQn1RABEB
AAG0G1hlbm9uIDxYZW5vbkBhbm9uLnBlbmVoLmZpPg===TNIL
-----END PGP PUBLIC KEY BLOCK-----
```

Figure A-4: The Mac version of PGP.

PGP is actually a combination of two cryptographic algorithms: RSA (Rivest, Shamir, Adelman) and IDEA (International Data Encryption Algorithm). The text of the message to be transmitted is encrypted with the symmetric IDEA algorithm. The key used to encrypt the text (which is also the one that will decrypt it) is itself encrypted using RSA. The output resulting from these two encryptions are combined to make up the transmitted message.

There is another way to use PGP that has some pretty neat implications for the future, in business and in personal use. It is possible to have PGP add a "signature" to a document. It doesn't encrypt the document; it only adds a bunch of characters at the end of the document that can act as a signature. Actually, it is stronger than a signature on a piece of paper, since the document cannot be changed without a new signature being attached. PGP can be used to verify that the signature and the document match. If even one character of the document is changed, the verification of the signature will fail. This way, signed documents can be transmitted around the world and kept on computers instead of paper. It's better than a paper signature because a signature can't be forged without breaking the PGP encryption.

PGP is available free in the United States for noncommercial purposes. The free version is in so many places on the Net that there are two FAQs on the Internet; one for PGP itself, and the other just for the locations.

A commercial version for use inside the United States can be purchased from:

ViaCrypt
9033 North 24th Avenue, Suite 7
Phoenix, AZ 85021
http://www.viacrypt.com

It is also possible to get a commercial version for use outside the United States by contacting:

Erhard Widmer
Ascom Systec AG
Dep't. CMVV
Gewerbepark
CH-5506 Maegenwil
Switzerland
IDEA@ascom.ch

PEM & RIPEM

RIPEM (Riordan's Internet Privacy Enhanced Mail) is an implementation of PEM (Privacy Enhanced Mail). PEM is a standard for transmitting encrypted e-mail. It uses RSA, so it's considered "munitions" quality encryption and cannot be exported outside the United States and Canada.

RIPEM is available via FTP to citizens and permanent residents in the United States at ripem.msu.edu. Look in the pub/crypt directory, where you'll see a file named GETTING_ACCESS that will explain what to do next. The RIPEM implementation of PEM runs on several platforms, including MS DOS, Macintosh, OS/2, and Windows NT, and has been shown to work on over 15 UNIX systems. RIPEM can be configured to work directly inside many popular mailers. If there is not an interface for your particular mailer, you can create one.

```
-----BEGIN PRIVACY-ENHANCED MESSAGE-----
Proc-Type: 2001,ENCRYPTED
Content-Domain: RFC822
DEK-Info: DES-CBC,2CFB5B1671A4BB20
Originator-Name: gareth
Originator-Key-Asymmetric:
 MFkwCgYEVQgBAQICAgADSwAwSAJBALGFCbQQ9ZtPmCgMeh7Zj24Y62/UL4TzPJ1j
 hVWdNekwk07uzr08bLULjynbn7QXnhQpda0XWe9wz2S9onP3T+ECAwEAAQ==
Key-Info: RSA,
 oCHndajjXeqfHi94FKb6kBfzakgnzaKqop6EVe0HP3F5B8A70YcrOGAWwNzKHE33
 IvPhzbvdfHtZDMd93iJ3ZA==
MIC-Info: RSA-MD5,RSA,
 AUIQn79tEN2auAYFzA1ppZ4JEMje6ND+u6Sv4jMqZ/xthJXs176W1G3rfbB89K7F
 3brXChO3R1dk1NK+wEnxcDK1NyhCN4U+
Recipient-Name: gareth
Key-Info: RSA,
 oCHndajjXeqfHi94FKb6kBfzakgnzaKqop6EVe0HP3F5B8A70YcrOGAWwNzKHE33
 IvPhzbvdfHtZDMd93iJ3ZA==

8fWHNanDACbZ11PQ3Y9kQ/5R5ROWC1x6dCP0mZBk9Cqu6Ktb3qWT4bebcoBvZNQF
xHhyOAWis3t9aLY4DIRY2ipUdvYQ18zWM1ybpXd/o3eFu6YedUi9kghFS68Y7qYD
PngMJc/5bUn09Y1uqHQw+5kGcOdiwaSZ6nXOByz2irAPDjiXf3UqvjIxZoXFpqvX
EAUTRfzpG4WtWzSM1T1Oy2vQ5eFr1fJGIF6/8eQ8WrDfBNIGm1W1X++vgMpOicEq
7VFJek7ecGrL9jIkvwvf48MP95/dxQ6iJ9aajV4sdXe3ZF9wqk1SxjQCMidscroV
SdmEV5cKczV8qeXFRJ6YcCQok87JmZDNxut/JZE7IOVXRe6vzI7Qfx68gH65/9S1
/DAPG4EJpkH4Wqc+1rHdhESH5XuEFehyYI3jV1+XxTKPAaX9+d3Ce9SmX+9e8R1c
Lc8U2qRkSmMBe7eFz5iMKM6ciC6R8BBGFiyYCWrfx1YPABxrEL44IbXUuBJkybnY
FqFbuXHwHCIsCbK6/0tjLfGnOs/P5MJZ3ig9d1xKDVV5P1NzjibLViHokF+vFaJz
i4eisGBhqnMyKA5JCxYhiSOEG/L1H4sdk1gv5HaZ+gGDQ2kXpFF9SfOKodEmcRer
OAc9oJe1T9te0ExFhHfQMzYYt8rYoi8HGuo4MMBG/OJg+tALJr6AS46hh/Spgp3D
x/Wur41Uqpp6MheNexL4LweYftj1nqScDXeQUhQ14xW4LKwssao2HsNoSBR/RuaJ
Z41FZq/LfugUA78Su4E/tc9xrc2YUhDrCANRTwM+BWu+5E8Ldfgib Tp/Av1BxWYv
pxCwSXiGWHz9Px4BdcrHGqy4sxyiTC6zmV2rQ+z1fThAuDOCvRqKTUNpW+1L/cHk
Z9zzgtFn30V9nNEcJR/oRpbuj5SOnIFH4ObTgP9yIpeR9NyvKn1XYNrxAzvHrV1M
```

```
kWQg5nn5iaPHMqR6CyRcZFnSxzRdBSfE/aQLWRKg61/rqqodhNRLBmWzxIrZ9wsV
ORgjYg4iDsxkJjsB81i+z2Ec+dsEB+Xh1ndOuRjZorb/PvbtMTZyksvF66cbLZir
hBfkusCg5T/k3B+tpq1XDxu+cbsvV/t2YjNUYeDS59SY3OeY3OHmiKt1RvTsRZI2
halnrqNcVrvU4Lc3Grju/IQQ/qeHyNihJ1E4ppOTEUaSI7HENyfUzROfRjW8T34v
1xILXTT2H6SrmPKSAQRxBK1GADkUWPW7gRcDz9sBFWZHA33fCe+ISsQ/jGc3O2Vw
opQuaqnuZBT22bXiZc8mD252cLOdBvei/fr8EzM1HMHYMVXnSRBgSgjfvVAwLNUQ
mA7QEE2aL8K4v6jOhIpzqg4ntcMFtVj4kIAy9uC95SO3iEHLO4sum95aSShuNYaS
nN6zbOrk3/HifJ4HW8SQdnLr78Dd+EkYeUWfOO+/xPdvxyaSP5YAZPitvId5d4ic
-----END PRIVACY-ENHANCED MESSAGE-----
Created with RIPEM Mac.
```

Figure A-5: RSA's RIPEM program.

MD (Message Digest)

This is a family of three functions designed specifically for cryptographic use. There are three versions: MD2, MD4, and MD5. There has been some theoretical work done on methods for MD, but there's no known attack other that "brute force." The rule of thumb for encryption is that speed of operation and level of security have an inverse relation. In other words, the quicker the encryption, the less secure the result. MD2 is the slowest to encrypt and decrypt; MD4 is the fastest. MD5 is functionally similar to MD4 except that it has added safety features and a more conservative design, which makes it slower.

MD is used for signature and document validation. It uses something called a "hash function," which takes a variable length message and returns a fixed length string. The string is called the "hash value." This is a one-way activity in that there is no decryption method. It's used as a validation method, since the input will generate exactly the same output. If the output is different, the input was different.

All three types of MD are publicly available for unrestricted use. You can find complete and detailed descriptions along with sample C programs in RFC 1319, 1320, and 1321.

SHS (Secure Hash Standard)

This is a hash function and is a United States government standard that was proposed by the NIST. It is intended to be part of the DSS (Digital Signature Standard). DSS is similar to MD5, but since it produces a larger hash value, its security potential is greater.

Kerberos

Kerberos is a secret key network authentication system developed at MIT. It uses DES for encryption and authentication. It's set up to provide real-time authentication of requests for network resources. It can be used to generate keys for a single session so that two parties can communicate privately.

Kerberos runs on a designated server on a LAN or intranet. The server handles all the key services from a single centralized location, using a database of all the keys and usernames. This means that there must be trust in the security of the server since, if it were compromised, its secret would be revealed. However, setting up Kerberos so that it can be easily used makes it functional for folks who need only a low-level security encryption method.

There is a version of Kerberos that is not secure. A flaw has been discovered in the random number generator of version 4 of the server. It allows an intruder to open the database of names and keywords in a matter of seconds. The release of version 5 has fixed the problem; now this sort of break-in would require a brute force attack against DES encryption. Since Kerberos 4 has been freely available on the Internet for several years, there are a number of locations still using it. If you are on version 4, it is important that you switch to version 5.

In Figure A-6, you will see the Cygnus Network Security page, one of several locations offering information on Kerberos and how to acquire the patch to move from version 4 to version 5:

```
http://www.cygnus.com
http://www.transarc.com
```

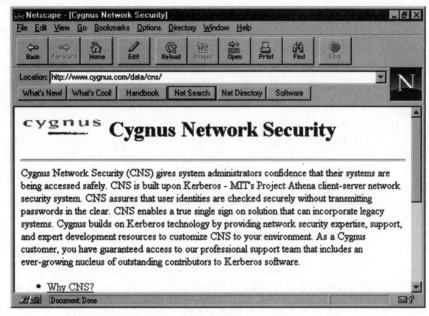

Figure A-6: Cygnus's Network Security page.

RC2 & RC4

RC2 and RC4 are two ciphers that are functional alternatives to DES. They have a variable length key. Use of the shorter keys renders an encryption that is less secure than DES, but a longer key can make the results more secure than DES. These algorithms are proprietary to RSA Data Security Inc. Several of the RSA Data Security packages are being used in commercial products such as Novell's Netware and PowerTalk from Macintosh. It is also going to be used by Visa and Mastercard for their SET (Secure Electronic Security) system.

There is an agreement between the Software Publishers Association (SPA) and the United States government that gives RC2 and RC4 a special status. The export approval process is simpler and quicker than normal. To be approved for export, the software must limit the size of the key to 40 bits. There can be 56 bits for foreign subsidiaries and overseas offices of United States companies. There can be another 40-bit "salt" value extension to the key thrown in to help thwart a brute force decryption. The salt value is then sent, unencrypted, with the message. This has become popular with software companies wishing to export, since it has some fair level of security and the approval cycle is short.

The Purloined Letter

There are still methods of sending secret messages that are quick and easy. All it requires is a little ingenuity. If the transmitted data doesn't look like it has a secret message embedded in it, it could slip through the fingers of a code cracker with only a glance.

Remember the invisible ink of your childhood? You would use lemon juice to write an invisible message between the lines of some innocuous text and the message would appear only after the paper was heated. The only reason the message was secure was that nobody know it was there. This same sort of thing happened in World War II with the microdot—the message was hidden as periods and commas used as punctuation. In the short story, "The Purloined Letter," by Edgar Allen Poe, a very valuable letter is spirited away by some miscreant. As it turns out, though, the thief had secreted it in plain view amongst a batch of other correspondence on the desk. The whole trick is to make the message not look like a message. The message is not the medium; it is the algorithm.

Take for example a large graphic or an audio clip. Setting the least significant bits to the value required to contain a message would have almost no effect on the displayability or listenability of the data. Since you can get one bit per byte, it wouldn't take a very large multimedia file to hold a sizable message. Of course, the message could be zipped, packed, and tarred and then written backwards. It could even be encrypted first. But the security of the message would primarily come from the fact that no one knows it's there.

This type of cryptography is called steganography (the art of hiding signals inside of signals). There are a number of steganographic programs (such as Stego, Hide and Seek, and StegoDOS). They can all be accessed via the Steganography page at http://www.stack.urc.tue.nl/~galactus/remailers/index-stego.html. See Figure A-7.

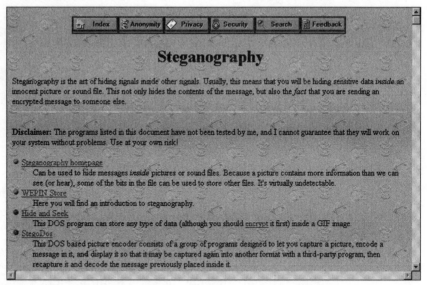

Figure A-7: The Steganography Web page.

Gone But Not Forgotten

If they're dastardly enough, other people in your office, or others with access to your PC, can perform "undeletes" in the directories on your PC and read the text of mail messages or other files you thought were long gone. On a UNIX machine, this is not as big a threat because the file system is very dynamic. It is conceivable that a file could be recovered after having been deleted, but the odds are against it. The disk space that was the deleted file could be used immediately by some process running in the background that needs a bit of workspace or gets a data block swapped out to disk. On a DOS/Windows or Mac machine, it is very easy to retrieve deleted files. Deleting a file simply marks it as deleted in the directory. If you don't want people reading your deleted mail messages and other files on your machine, you can use a program like Norton Utilities (for both Mac and Windows) to remove all traces of the deleted files from your drive.

Privacy & Security Cracks

All networked systems have holes in them through which unscrupulous, uninvited intruders can slip. The FBI estimates that $7.5 billion is lost annually to electronic attack. The *Wall Street Journal* reported that a Russian cracker successfully breached a large number of Citicorp corporate accounts, stealing $400,000 and illegally transferring another $11.6 million. Here's a very sobering statistic: the Department of Defense says that in 96 percent of the cases where the crackers got in, they went undetected. Hey wait, if they went undetected, how did they know it was 96 percent? Suffice it to say, this poses a significant threat to our increasingly interconnected digital society.

Hackin' & Crackin'

There was once a time when a person who was knowledgeable about programming and worked down at the bit and byte level of computers was called a "hacker." Those who broke into systems, stole data, or destroyed property were called "crackers." The hackers were the good guys and crackers were the bad guys. Somehow, the words hacker and cracker were eventually joined. They probably sound enough alike that the press got them confused. Anyway, the bad guys are now often called hackers and crackers interchangeably. What's left for the good guys? Do we just call them nerds?

If you want to delve into the world of hacking and cracking (and the debate over which is which), there's a notorious magazine called Phrack. It can be found online (where else?) at a number of FTP sites and at http://www.fc.net/phrack/. 2600: The Hacker's Journal is another long-standing print zine dedicated to hacking/cracking and phone hacking (or "phreaking"). It has an active (high noise) newsgroup called alt.2600.

If you know what the holes are in your system, there are things you can do to plug them up. Since most holes appear along with desirable functionality, most of the plugs are some sort of compromise between a level of safety and a level of utility. The only way to be absolutely certain that an unwanted intruder never gets into your system is to cut its wire to the outside world. Those that communicate over a dial-up link are the safest because they are usually offline.

 **TIP**

There is one very important thing you can do for security. In fact, this could turn out to be the most important thing you do to keep your system safe. Keep in touch with your service provider on security issues. These days, everybody has a Web page where they post information, so it has gotten to be very easy to make sure you have the most current information. Service providers and Net software vendors track system break-ins and (usually) keep their customers informed of problems. If you find holes in a system you are using, report them to the ISP or vendor. Remember, at the same time you're reading about a method of corking the bottle, there's a cracker reading a description of how to uncork it.

Holes in a Loosely Connected System

If you are operating a loosely connected system (for example, a PPP or SLIP connection with an ISP), there's virtually no way crackers can get directly to you. You simply don't have the facilities available for them to get in and monkey with stuff. You're not completely immune to danger, however.

One principal source of danger is the fact that your e-mail must pass over the Internet to get to its recipient. About all you can do is encrypt (as we talked about earlier in this chapter), since you have no control over where anything goes once you let it out of its PC cage. It's sort of like a tomcat. E-mail can wander around anywhere before it gets home, and you don't know what sort of adventures it may have had. Encrypting is sort of like having the cat neutered. It can go wherever it wants, but it's not going to get itself into trouble.

You must also consider the danger of downloading files containing a virus. We seem to be adding new viruses at the rate of three or four a day. The best method to avoid viruses is to only obtain files from sites that you suspect to be very clean, and to run a virus scan on the files once you receive them.

A single user dial-up system is under such complete control of the person at the helm, there's little that can go wrong if you take simple precautions. If you recognize the fact that your e-mail can be read and that you can contract a virus, and you take precautions, you should be fine. It's your service provider (or sysadmin on a LAN/WAN) that has all the real security worries.

Network Security Tools

The following section covers some of the software that systems administrators use to keep networks secure and to track down unwanted intruders. While you may not be directly involved in the security of the networks you use, we thought you might benefit from a brief discussion of some of the security issues that keep your systems administrator up at night. If some of the preceding material has already made your eyes glaze over and your palms sweat, you might want to skip over this section.

Packet Sniffing

Packet sniffers are handy dandy little TCP/IP debugging utilities that can monitor the traffic being sent over a network. They are intended to be used by systems administrators to tune and debug networks. But, like guns, they can be turned on the wrong target and used for evil purpose. You know the saying, "It's not sniffers that kill datagrams; it's people that kill datagrams."

A sniffer is a program that sits in a computer and reads all the packets that pass by on the network. Usually the TCP/IP stack ignores any packets or datagrams not addressed to it (or to some other address through it), but a sniffer reads all packets by changing the mode of operation of the TCP/IP stack. A computer that is configured to read all packets is said to be "promiscuous." On a local network, account and password information are passed around in the clear, so a sniffer can pick it up and read it directly.

Sniffers are very popular with crackers. You can see why. A sniffer installed on a system will gather every password and username that's used throughout the time it is installed. This could include the root password for several different systems.

The question is, how can one determine whether or not there's a sniffer running? If a sniffer is only collecting data and not reporting, it is necessary to go around to each machine and make a direct physical check. Whenever a sniffer is being executed, it puts the TCP/IP stack into promiscuous mode. This is so it will accept all the packets and acquire data from the entire network. It is possible to run a sniffer in non-promiscuous mode, but only the traffic in and out of the one host will be captured.

The sniffer sits there logging information to a file that the cracker will come back to and pick up later. If there is a lot of traffic on the network, the log file can swell and fill up the file system, thus shutting down the host and alerting the computer security person.

It is possible to use encryption to thwart sniffing. There are software packages that encrypt the data that passes over a LAN. This will prevent a sniffer from making heads or tails of it. Intruders can still get at the data, but it is of no use to them. During periods when the systems administrator is analyzing the system, the encryption can be disabled so the sysadmin's sniffer can gather useful information. Under normal circumstances, the data is encrypted.

 **TIP**

If you FTP, Telnet, or rlogin across an insecure network, your password has traveled in clear text over communication links that could be littered with sniffers. Change your password as soon as possible after one of these remote jaunts.

Running Finger

Outsiders can discover login names if the finger daemon is running. A finger command in the form "finger @host.domain" could return a login name that could subsequently become the target of a password attack. This opening can be closed in the /etc/inetd.conf file by specifying the host names that are allowed access to the finger daemon.

Trojan Horses

A cracker can get in and out of your system very quickly. If successful, they may leave some Trojan horse programs. These are programs that have the same name as some standard utility and work pretty much the same, but have some other features that benefit only the cracker. Examples of commonly replaced programs are sh, ksh, telnet, rlogin, and ifconfig. Things seem to be working OK, but they are really slowly turning toward the cracker.

▰▰▰▰ TRAP

Besides Trojan horses, there is an amazing amount of "volunteer" damage that can be done by innocent users adhering to requests that come in the form of administrative e-mail. Things like, "This is the systems administrator. Please temporarily remove your password so I can check your files for bad sectors" or "Please make your local disk sharable so I can run a thorough disk scan tonight." There are cases where the intruder coaxes the user to inflict damage with messages such as "Look for a file named c:\windows\system.ini. If you have this file on your system, delete it." Just because you get a message that says it comes from a systems administrator or other person of authority does not mean it's legitimate. If in doubt, e-mail or call your sysadmin/ISP and ask them to verify the request.

COPS (Computer Oracle Password & Security)

This is a UNIX utility that will scan your system and check for the kinds of security leaks that occasionally will open up during the regular activities of your systems administration. It will also catch a few holes that regular users can open up. It will scan for spots of possible trouble and report them; it doesn't fix them. It can be run manually, but it is best if it is set up so that it will run automatically at regular intervals and catch the holes that accidentally open up. It is very simple to use. It has minimal configuration settings and no command line arguments whatsoever; just run it and it generates a listing of everything it can find that looks the least bit funny.

It checks the access permissions on files, directories and devices. It checks the /etc/passwd and /etc/group files for passwords that are not set properly. It checks the /etc/hosts.equiv file for an opening that would allow someone on another host to override the security on this host. It checks the .rhosts files in each user's home directory since there are settings that can allow anyone onto the system. It checks the UUCP settings since it is possible, among other things, to copy executable programs from remote computers and execute them locally.

It will almost certainly report conditions that are really not a problem on your system. The sysadmin will simply scan its output and make sure that all the things it complains about are things that are not a problem. For example, COPS reporting that the /etc/motd (message of the day) is writable may not be a concern—it could be that it's meant to be used that way. However, things such as missing passwords will almost certainly be a problem.

COPS can be acquired via FTP from any number of sites. The file is normally named cops.tar.Z and contains the full make instructions. Once compiled, it is just a matter of modifying the COPS shell script and setting it up so that it includes the address of the person to whom the report should be mailed.

Could it be...SATAN?

The Systems Administrator's Tool for Analyzing Networks (SATAN) arrived on the Internet on April 5, 1995, at 14:00 GMT. He appeared in a swirl of publicity (both on the Internet and off) about how this evil program was going to be used by all sorts of sneaky and unprincipled people to perform unspeakable acts on computer hosts all over the world. Much to the doomsayer's chagrin, none of the bad stuff happened. What *did* happen was that systems administrators all over the world grabbed a copy of SATAN and used it to find the weak spots in their own defenses. Computer manufacturers (some of which had prior access to SATAN and thus were forearmed) issued bulletins containing patches to be inserted and procedures to be taken to make their systems more secure. The end result of all this: there have been fewer computer break-ins, not more, since SATAN tooled onto the information highway.

SATAN is software that finds holes in the security settings of a computer and then reports those holes. SATAN doesn't run on a PC or a Mac unless you're running some version of UNIX. SATAN is a World Wide Web-based tool that can be set up to gather information about hosts over the network. Along with the report it issues on the security holes, there is a brief tutorial on just what type of problems the hole can cause and what sort of workarounds could be used to close it up. SATAN speaks perl. If you come up with something that is peculiar to your installation and you would like to add it to SATAN, it can be done with a perl script.

There is a primary FTP site for SATAN:

```
ftp.win.tue.nl/pub/security
```

Security Resources

If security is an issue in your situation, you should subscribe to a Net security journal like RISKS Digest (http://catless.ncl.ac.uk/Risks/) and look into security topics at your ISP, Usenet Newsgroup, or BBS for the latest on known holes and security breaches. Usenet groups discussing security and encryption include:

```
comp.risks
comp.security.announce
comp.security.misc
comp.security.unix
alt.security.pgp
alt.security.keydist
```

"Prince Albert" in Cyberspace

A lot of computer break-ins, e-mail intrusions, and phony Net identities are little more than sophisticated, digital age versions of the phone pranks of our youth. Remember making prank calls when you were a kid, asking questions of store owners such as "Do you have Prince Albert in a can?" An affirmative response was rewarded with "Well, you better go let him out!" followed by lots of twittering and knee slapping. These escalated to "Good afternoon ma'am. This is the phone company. We're having a bit of trouble with the lines out your way and need to clear them. Could you please leave your phone off the hook and put it in a paper bag while we blow the dust out from this end? Thank you." Then, more vicious twists developed: "Good afternoon sir. This is the telephone company, and we're going to have to make some minor adjustments to your equipment. This is going to cost you $35 if we do it, or you could do it yourself if you'd like. Really? OK, you'll need a pair of scissors and a screw driver. I'll wait, yes. OK, turn your telephone over and remove the four screws in the corners and take the bottom plate off. Good. Now, the little red wire next to the brass name plate. Yes, that's the one. Cut it." Dial tone. More sinister laughter.

As wily teens have become more and more knowledgeable about computers and the inner workings of the phone system, these pranks have now become highly sophisticated. And, as our society (and the planet) becomes increasingly wired into one grid, these kids can potentially cause big problems, especially if they have malicious intent. The good news is that Net citizens are becoming more aware of these tricksters and, hopefully, are using more good sense online. Computer security types are constantly working on new ways to secure systems so that they'll be virtually impenetrable . . . at least for awhile.

Appendix B

Other Firewall Notes of Interest

This appendix adds some additional facts about firewalls to your "security suitcase" that you may not have otherwise gleaned from reading each of the chapters of this book. These facts are in no particular order, but each of them deserves merit in your decisions about security.

Policing Protocols

Network service access policy is a high-level, issue-specific policy that defines those services that will be allowed or explicitly denied from the restricted network, plus the way in which these services will be used and the conditions for exceptions to this policy. It is the network services access policy that determines which protocols and fields are filtered, that is, which systems should have Internet access and the type of access to permit. The following services are inherently vulnerable to abuse and are usually blocked at a firewall from entering or leaving the site.

- Trivial FTP (tftp), port 69, used for booting diskless workstations, terminal servers and routers; can also be used to read any file on the system if set up incorrectly.

- X Windows, OpenWindows, ports 6000+, port 2000, can leak information from X window displays including all keystrokes. (Intruders can even gain control of a server through the X-server.)

- RPC, port 111, Remote Procedure Call services including NIS and NFS, which can be used to steal system information such as passwords and to read and write to files.

- rlogin, rsh, and rexec, ports 513, 514, and 512, if improperly configured, can permit unauthorized access to accounts and commands.

Other services, whether inherently dangerous or not, are usually filtered and possibly restricted to only those systems that need them. These would include:

- TELNET, port 23; often restricted to only certain systems.

- FTP, ports 20 and 21, like TELNET; often restricted to only certain systems.

- SMTP, port 25; often restricted to a central e-mail server.

- RIP, port 520, routing information protocol; can be spoofed to redirect packet routing.

- DNS, port 53, domain names service zone transfers, contains names of hosts and information about hosts that could be helpful to attackers; could be spoofed.

- UUCP, port 540, UNIX-to-UNIX CoPy, if improperly configured can be used for unauthorized access.

- NNTP, port 119, Network News Transfer Protocol, for accessing reading network news.

- Gopher, HTTP, ports 70 and 80, information servers and client programs for Gopher and WWW clients; should be restricted to an application gateway that contains proxy services.

While some of these services such as TELNET or FTP are inherently risky, blocking access to these services completely may be too drastic a policy for many sites. However, at many sites, not all systems require access to all services. For example, restricting Telnet or FTP access from the Internet to only those systems that require the access can improve security at no cost to user convenience. Services such as NNTP may seem to pose little threat, but restricting these services to only those systems that need them helps to create a cleaner network environment and reduces the likelihood of exploitation from yet-to-be-discovered vulnerabilities and threats.

System managers should also be aware that there are services available through which users can obtain access to FTP and other Internet services through e-mail. For example, the UNIX Mail Robot allows Web documents to be retrieved through e-mail and there are sites that provide Internet via e-mail. If especially tight security demands that such access be restricted, there may be additional controls to impose on outgoing and incoming e-mail.

Firewall Testing

The following sections look at tests that may be performed to determine the effectiveness of a firewall. We have focused on the sort of self-tests that a firewall administrator might carry out to make sure that a firewall is properly installed and maintained. This is the testing that NCSA carries out as part of its firewall certification program.

About Self-testing

By now you should have a clear idea of the role that policy plays in the design and deployment of firewalls. For the most part, security policy is common sense. It is also common sense which decrees that you test your firewall once you have installed it. Most experts also recommend ongoing testing to make sure the firewall continues to work as intended.

Consistent, periodic testing is an important part of maintaining an effective firewall. Placing trust in an invalidated configuration, or in a configuration that was only validated at installation is dangerous. For example, any "quick change" to a firewall configuration to support a special project or one-time access may have unforeseen effects on the security posture of the entire configuration. While self-testing is no guarantor of invulnerability, it serves the purpose of making sure that the castle walls are not crumbling, the gates are closed, and that the moat is full of water.

The following sections address three groups of people. The primary audience is people who have installed, or are planning to install, a firewall product in their enterprise. We also address a broader group of less technical readers, hoping to further familiarize them with the problems that must be addressed by firewalls and the people who maintain them. In other words, even if you are not the person in your organization who will be called upon to test the firewalls defending the organization's networks, we hope to give you a better idea of what this entails. The third target is anyone responsible for contracting with an outside company for firewall testing. For example, if your organization does not have the technical resources for in-house self-testing, or if you want to arrange an objective outside test, the following information will help you understand some of the areas that such testing needs to address.

Note that discussions about testing may seem to be addressing "all networks," when in truth the material specifically applies to TCP/IP networks. There may be some distant and contrived applicability to IPX, Netbui, or SNA, but readers are advised to consult other works and practitioners for advice in those areas. The manual techniques listed herein are intended to serve as a familiarization with a given firewall configuration and as an adjunct to automated testing techniques.

Black Box Testing

In the olden days of personal computing, when the end-user battle du jour revolved around the relative merits of 6502 versus Z-80-based systems, there was a game called "black box." Somewhat similar to the modern MS-Windows Minesweeper game, the object was to shoot "probes" into the "black box" and determine the location and nature of what was inside, based on how it responded to the probes.

This concept can be applied directly to firewall testing. In fact, it is the basis of in-place validations. By shooting probes at our firewall, what can be determined? By observing the network traffic what can be learned? From locations both without and within the organization, it should be possible to deduce the salient features of the network security policy—in theory without previous knowledge. This testing can be divided into two parts: port scanning and on-the-wire observation.

Port Scanning

Port scanning is the least-common-denominator of both network-based attacks and validation testing. In lay-language, a port scanner systematically works its way across all of the 65,000 possible service-connection ports on a TCP/IP connected host or device. This is a valuable service to both the hacker-of-systems and the erstwhile-maintainer-of-systems, as it reveals what avenues of attack, or legitimate services, may be available on the target.

Stand-alone scanning software is widely available for UNIX-based platforms as well as for Windows workstations. Scanning capabilities also are incorporated into automated testing tools (more on these later). A scanning session might yield output such as:

```
icebox# scan 2.5.160.199.1
UltraScan 4.9
      Scanning firewall.ncsa.com
      Port 21      FTP
      Port 25      SMTP
      Port 53      DNS (udp)
      Port 80      HTTP
      Port 113     AUTH
      Port 32812 ???
UltraScan Done.
icebox#
```

Naturally, the resulting list will vary widely, depending upon the purpose of the target of the scan and the policy governing its configuration. The useful part of scanning is accounting for what the scan turns up and making sure that only things that are authorized under policy are present (for example, finding out what is running on port 32812 in the above case). Firewalls vary widely in how they implement services. Likewise the OS platforms upon which they are installed have sundry built-in or necessary services that cannot be disabled. However, it is possible to establish some generic guidelines for self-test scanning:

- *Baseline scans.* Run a baseline scan on any configuration before connecting it to the Internet. Having pristine state scans of firewalls and any other network-attached devices is a useful aid in tracking down things that change—due to causes legitimate or nefarious.

- *Scan from multiple locations.* It makes sense to scan from numerous locations. At a minimum these include scanning from a "typical user" location on the protected network, the DMZ (network immediately outside the firewall), and a "foreign" external site (perhaps a dial-up ISP account).

  Note that correlating output from these scans should provide a clear picture of the network security policy. Differences between DMZ and foreign scans may indicate unwarranted trust of the DMZ that should be investigated or the effect of filtering at the router. Scanning from inside the protected net also provides a picture of what an attacker who managed to dial-up, or gained physical access, would see. This often provides interesting food for thought.

- *Scan all ports.* Despite the time that it may take, ensure that scanning attempts all ports from 0 to 65535. Stopping a scan at port 10000 (as some automatically do) leaves a large section of unmonitored perimeter.

- *Scan all systems.* Scan everything. Although it spills over into the policy area, ensuring that the service offerings of all systems, even inside the protected network, are recorded and understood contributes greatly to site security.

- *Use automation wisely.* Review the output. Scripting of scan tests is a great time-saver; however, reviewing the output for anomalies requires some clever automation or a diligent administrator (organizations are urged to acquire one or the other, if not both).

- *Protect your tools.* A most pernicious work of Trojaneering is a tool that tells you that things are just fine (regardless of what is actually there). Likewise having baseline or periodic reports "adjusted" by unfriendlies has no good outcome. Techniques for protecting tools range from read-only file systems and removable media to air-gapped (unplugged from the network) systems and beyond.

- *Keep records offline.* You want to keep your test records out of harm's way. Once again, removable media, or even paper copies, safely locked away, may prove to be invaluable should things go awry.

On-the-wire Observation

In the not-too-distant past, network analyzers were bulky, expensive devices that required a pilot's license to operate properly. The top end of the product category is still expensive and complex, but there are now cheap-if-not-free products for monitoring network traffic. Most network monitors provide a semi-interpreted play-by-play of what is going past the monitoring system in real time. Note that, as in the case of port scanners, the network monitor (commonly called a "sniffer," which is a trademark of Network General Corporation) is a tool that can be used effectively by persons wearing either color of hat.

Network monitor software is available as part of some operating system distributions (such as snoop, which ships with Sun's Solaris). A popular free product, tcpdump, is available as source code for many other Unix platforms. There are also a number of PC-based products that work with packet drivers and allow the use of "retired" 286 or 386 PCs as dedicated network monitoring stations (a noble and cost-effective alternative to the dust-collector-and-doorstop retirement plan).

Please note that the cheap-if-not-free network monitoring products are generally applicable to nonswitched Ethernet networks. If the configuration under the test utilizes less common network media, the type of monitoring described may well require special equipment.

"Quiet Wire" Observation   It is important to be familiar with the "signature" of the network when quiescent. In addition to the ports that are active (ready to respond to incoming calls), services that broadcast information are a concern worth noting. Depending upon the configuration and point of connection relative to hosts/router/firewall, different types of traffic will be visible.

With the DMZ disconnected from the Internet router, and no clients initiating traffic, a network monitor should see relatively little (if any) traffic. While it is of little utility to save trace files in this mode, it is very helpful to have notes of the type of broadcasts or session requests seen and which devices originate requests.

Control Testing   As a control, it is useful to observe the trace of a connection originating on internal clients "leaving" the firewall bound for an external destination. The source address will vary depending upon the particular firewall implementation, as some products cause all sessions to "appear" to be originating from the firewall's own IP address. Products that implement Network Address Translation (NAT) by definition may not allow the client's true IP address to be seen on the DMZ.

Observing the behavior of inbound connections, both to provided services and to services not permitted by the firewall, improves familiarity with how normal production traffic on the network will appear. A worthwhile control exercise is to observe a network monitor while running a port scan. Scanners that run highspeed linear scans are particularly visible to network monitor tools. Other more stealthy scanners insert delays between probes and target ports in a semi-random order (depending upon the type of network monitor being used, some scanning techniques are not visible).

"Live Wire" Observation   On a busy network, a wide-open network monitor can scroll information past at an incredible rate. The utility of watching everything is limited, with a couple of exceptions. In the event that something goes wrong at the ISP or backbone level, being able to note the direction and type of traffic passing through (or to) the firewall is an aid to diagnosis. Port scans may be observed as well. In the event that the firewall's logging/alert system reports unusual activity, it is very handy to have a network monitor available to observe, decode, and possibly record it.

System Logging Verification

It is critical that the personnel supporting a firewall be familiar with the outputs of the logging/alerts system. Configurability of logging/alerts facilities is a great help in reducing the amount of material to be reviewed by the administrator, however, it is important to verify the kind of events that are logged by the system and the format in which they appear.

Since logging facilities vary considerably by product vendor, a meaningful universal list of "what ought to be logged" is difficult to establish. The point is to attempt violations of the security policy and to note how (or if) the attempt is logged. Here are some tactics to try:

- *Log on to the FTP and Telnet proxies.* Try logging on to the FTP and Telnet proxies (if the firewall has them and they are enabled) numerous times as a nonexistent username. Note whether the events are logged singly as "failed-access attempts" or if each attempt is logged separately. This behavior reveals how brute-force password-guessing attempts may show up in the logs. Likewise note whether the IP address of the offender is listed.

  Perform the same test from the DMZ, a foreign site, and the internal network. On non-NAT systems attempt the test from a foreign network to the IP address of the firewall located on the protected network.

- *Test unsupported protocols.* Attempt to use a protocol not supported by the security policy to connect to the firewall, possibly rlogin or TFTP. Many systems reject such attempts without logging; however, on systems that do log the attempts it is a useful indicator. Perform the same test from the DMZ, a foreign site, and the internal network.

- *Test token authentication.* In configurations that utilize token authenticators, it is helpful to note what occurs when an invalid challenge/response cycle occurs on a legitimate user account.

- *Test mail.* On configuration that have SMTP proxies, the following dialogue should produce a number of log entries:

```
telnet IP-OF-FIREWALL 25
200 <welcome message>
HELO foo.bar.com
220 <hello message, likely with your real IP or host
name listed>
WIZ
500 <unknown command, possibly an insulting message>
DEBUG
500 <unknown command, likely a further insulting
message>
QUIT
```

This dialogue is a blatant attempt to lie about one's mail address as well as to exploit two hoary-old back doors in the Sendmail SMTP software.

- *Test automated tools.* Automated testing tools will certainly exercise a firewall's logging capability in the extreme and may generate such copious output as to swamp the firewall. If you have access to such tools it is useful to note what shows up in the logs (or possibly what the firewall does) during an all-out nonstealthy automated probe.

Configuration Testing

The point of configuration testing is to validate that the detail components of the configuration were correctly entered as the firewall was installed. The examples listed are by no means exhaustive, but should serve as a basis for devising tests appropriate for the installed configuration.

Misplaced trust of systems due to misconfiguration is a common (and dangerous) situation. In testing for misplaced trust, do not underestimate the risk of trusting IP addresses located on the DMZ network. Trust of DMZ IP addresses may increase susceptibility to address spoofing attacks and widens the zone of exposure should any other hosts/devices on the DMZ be compromised.

Socks

In a firewall configuration that uses SOCKS, the facility incorporates trust of certain clients based on IP address of origin. SOCKS incorporates address-spoofing protection, however, misconfiguration can result in external SOCKS clients being able to pass the firewall.

Using SOCKSified clients (such as Telnet and FTP) from a foreign network, configure the SOCKS HOST parameter to point to the external IP address of the firewall. Then attempt to access an IP address inside the firewall using the client software. Referencing by IP is more reliable in this situation than using a fully qualified domain name. Attempt the same test specifying the IP address of the firewall's interface on the protected network as the SOCKS HOST. Repeat the test from the DMZ.

HTTP Proxies

In the same manner as the SOCKS test, configure a Web browser to use the firewall's Web proxy (if one exists). Attempt to access a Web server inside the protected network. Also attempt to access a Web server outside the protected network. Success with either indicates a misconfigured HTTP Proxy.

Attempt the same test specifying the firewall's IP address on the protected network; also repeat the test from the DMZ.

DNS

Since numerous schemes for supporting DNS with varying degrees of opacity are common, a full DNS test is highly site-specific (and also policy-specific).

Ensure that fully qualified domain names (FQDNs) are resolvable from the internal network. The ability to Telnet to an external site by IP address, but not by FQDN indicates a DNS configuration problem.

User Services

Though pedestrian, formally exercising all of the end-user software in accessing external services is a reasonable validation as to which services the firewall does actually pass to the outside (and that users will be able to use the software with the expected results). Ensuring that services provided (or denied) to external hosts function (or fail) in accordance with policy is likewise helpful as a validation.

Automated Testing Tools

This list is alphabetical by origin and is by no means exhaustive. Inclusion in the list does not constitute endorsement. Omission from the list does not imply anything either.

- Bellcore: Pingware (http://www.bellcore.com)

- Dan Farmer: System Administrator's Tool for Analyzing Networks "SATAN," (ftp//ftp.win.tue.nl/pub/security/index.html#software)

- DoD's SPI Package (available only to DoD/DoE sites...you know who and how)

- Internet Security Systems: Internet Scanner (http://www.iss.net)

These products provide, in varying degrees, a means of launching scanning, probing, and other attacks at firewalls and other IP devices. Note that NCSA utilizes software from Internet Security Systems in the testing of network products.

Third-party Validations

In addition to self-testing, a range of security assessment services are available from consulting and auditing firms. Third party validation services offer a valuable cross-check of implemented security policy, as well as providing additional assurance for customers, stockholders, or management. Options to consider when arranging for such services include:

- *Scheduled/periodic*. The idea of periodic testing is much like scheduled tune-ups for a car. They serve to make sure everything is running smoothly and discover undesirable changes you might not have detected.

- *Unscheduled (surprise!)*. This type of test is designed to keep security staff on their toes and is sometimes incorporated in broader company audits. The idea is to see what happens when attacks take place unannounced and without warning (just like in the real world).

- *Physical security*. The importance of physical security should never be underestimated, but it is often overlooked when we focus on the bits and bytes. "You can't penetrate my firewall!" proclaims the proud engineer. "But we can steal it on your lunch break" replies the savvy attacker. Perimeter and site-access controls as well as heavy seclusion of the hardware and pipes may be required, and whatever physical protection you use should be tested from time to time.

- *Espionage/social engineering*. Anyone familiar with Ira Winkler's papers on social engineering will know that the best-laid plans of network administrators and MIS professionals can often be undermined by poor personnel practices and the natural human tendency to underestimate the duplicity of others. Tests in this realm should be considered if you have any doubts about any of your people or suspect that any of your competitors are developing a taste for espionage.

■ *Customized testing.* You may have specialized needs that
require custom test scenarios. Try to select a third party that
can demonstrate not only the technical skills required to
devise the test, but also a good understanding of your
business and the likely threats.

Future Issues

The past 12 months have been an exciting time for people involved
with internetwork security. From flawed attempts to implement
secure transactions, to high-profile Web-page hacks like the one in
August at the Department of Justice, the media attention accorded
to the previously arcane world of information security has been
unprecedented. The following are some of the developments that
might make the next few years even more exciting, notably IPv6,
the "next generation" of the IP protocol that underpins the
Internet and could help to solve some of the security problems
now facing Internet users.

Next Generation: The Protocol

You can call it Ipng, for Internet Protocol Next Generation. Or you
can call it IPv6, because it skips a whole revision number from the
current IPv4 (actually, IPv5 does exist, as the experimental Internet
Stream Protocol, ST-II). But whatever you call it, this latest version
of the Internet's underlying protocol is beginning to make the
transition from the theoretical, academic stage to the real-world,
testing phase. If it has been a while since you visited the IPv6
implementations page on the Web, take a look today (http://
playground.sun.com/)/

You will see an impressive list of projects, from full and complete IPv6 security for 4.4 BSD-Lite derived systems created at the
U.S. Naval Research Laboratory, to IPv6-over-ATM and a host of
other features that are now running on Digital UNIX. There are 14
host implementations and half-a-dozen router implementations.
One company, Telebit Communications A/S of Denmark, is
already selling an IPv6 router, the TBC2000, currently in use on
the world's first IPv6 network. You can read more about this
project at www.tbit.dk, a Web site running on an IPv6-capable
server.

In fact, many of the IPv6 implementation sites provide extensive documentation of the latest developments. The initial impetus for IPv6 came from the realization that the current version will eventually reach its limits due to the huge growth of the Internet. With IPv4 the Internet is running out of addresses to assign to new networks, and routing tables on the backbones are getting so large that they can't be accessed quickly and are starting to cause throughput bottlenecks. Here is how the Telebit Web site lists the main features of IPv6:

- IP's address space is expanded from 4 to 16 bytes, which permits the creation of far more addresses.

- Full interpretability with IPv4 facilitating a borderless transition to IPv6.

- Flow labeling for marking packets belonging to high-priority traffic, such as multicast video conferencing.

- Accommodation of non-IP address formats.

- Mandated Security Routines for packet-level encryption and authentication.

- Multicase and Anycast support.

- Neighbor Discovery Protocol, allowing hosts to discover their own network addresses. This leads to increased router look-up speed and reduced router memory requirements through efficient allocation of IP addresses. Network administration requirements are also reduced.

- Support of mobile hosts through algorithms to automatically forward packets from a base address to any other address.

- Simplified header format from 12 to 8 data elements. This reduces the computation required to process headers, speeding up routing.

To elaborate on the first feature, IP addresses jump from 32 to 128 bits in IPv6, which provides an address space that is 4 billion x 4 billion x 4 billion times the size of the IPv4 address space. However, whereas IPv4 headers have at least 12 information fields, plus variable-length options fields, the IPv6 packet is much simpler. Rather than including options in the IP header, IPv6 uses separate extension headers, located between the IP header and the transport-layer header (TCP, UDP, and so on) in a packet.

The IPv6 header always contains just eight fixed-length fields. The IPv6 option functions are where the enhancements for authentication, integrity, and security/confidentiality are to be found, along with routing (path selection similar to IPv4's source route), hop-by-hop (special options that require hop-by-hop processing), and destination-optional information to be examined by the destination node.

Apart from providing a vast increase in possible addresses, IPv6 provides an improved header format, quality-of-service capabilities, simplified and expanded support for options, plus authentication and confidentiality capabilities. However, these enhancements have been designed with transition in mind, allowing IPv6 to coexist with IPv4, so that IPv4 hosts will still be able to communicate with IPv6 hosts.

What Next?

This section was originally headed "And Finally," but then we realized there was probably nothing final about either firewalls or information security. However, we recognize that firewall technology and the firewall marketplace evolve at a rapid pace. Therefore, there may have been things we missed or some aspects of firewalls that we emphasized to the neglect of others.

If you are looking for further sources of impartial information about firewalls, you might want to check out the NCSA Firewall Buyer's Guide (editor at ncsafbg@ncsa.com) or the *Firewall Report* from Outlink Market Research (www.outlink.com).

Finally, as we're going to press, news of fresh Internet denial of service attacks was breaking. Sadly, this serves to underline our final point: To protect your networks you must remain vigilant. Whether you assign your own staff to keep track of the latest attacks, threats, patches, and fixes, or whether you subscribe to a service such as NCSA's IS/Recon, it pays to stay in touch with developments. Indeed, if you want to preserve the confidentiality, integrity, and availability of your networked information assets, you cannot afford not to.

Appendix C

Other Informative Firewall Resources

Okay, security experts...crank up your browsers (Netscape Navigator or Microsoft Internet Explorer will do) and let's start searching the terrabytes of information about electronic commerce and Internet security on the Internet and World Wide Web (WWW). You can search the Net using a number of search engines available including Yahoo!, excite, Lycos, and so on.

On the following pages we've listed many popular Web sites, Usenet groups, mailing lists, and other resources you might find interesting in your quest to stay "security-aware." There are many more resources being added each day, but these sites should get you started.

Usenet Forums on Security

Usenet (also known as Netnews) was originally developed for UNIX systems in 1979. It has become a worldwide network of thousands of Usenet sites, known as news hosts or news servers, running many operating systems (such as Mac OS, UNIX, MS-DOS, and Windows NT) on various types of computers. Millions of people share messages electronically over these Usenet sites. The messages are sent from news server to news server using UNIX-to-UNIX Copy Protocol (UUCP). People post their Usenet messages or articles to categories known as newsgroups instead of to individuals (as would be the case with e-mail).

A newsgroup is a great place to exchange ideas, ask questions, or discuss opinions and experiences. The following is a list of newsgroups on Usenet devoted to discussions of privacy, encryption, and other aspects of security.

- alt.privacy

- alt.privacy.anon.server

- alt.privacy.clipper

- alt.security.pgp

- alt-security.ripem

- alt.security

- alt.security.index

- alt.security.keydist

- alt.security.pgp

- alt.security.ripem

- alt.security.tscm

- comp.org.eff.news

- comp.org.eff.talk

- comp.society.privacy

- comp.security.announce

- comp.security.firewalls

- comp.security.misc

- comp.security.pgp.announce

- comp.security.pgp.discuss

- comp.security.pgp.resources

- comp.security.pgp.tech

- comp.security.unix

- comp.virus

Mailing Lists for Security Enthusiasts

A mailing list is simply a list of the e-mail addresses of everyone who wants to send and receive mail about a certain topic. There are thousands of lists, with new ones being created every week. Adding your e-mail address to a mailing list is a way of joining these conversations. Once you have subscribed to a list, any mail you send to the list address gets sent back out to all the other e-mail addresses included on the list, and any mail from any of the other subscribers also gets sent to you.

Below we provide addresses for mailing lists that we think you might be interested in joining; however, there is a compendium of mailing lists you might want to investigate. This compendium is Stephanie da Dilva's list of Publicly Accessible Mailing Lists, originally created by Chuq Von Rospach. It includes the mailing list name, a short description, and information on how to subscribe for each one. The list itself is currently in 22 parts, arranged alphabetically and stored on a machine at MIT. Simply address an e-mail to mail-server@rtfm.mit.edu to find out more information.

Computer Security Sites

- Alert — *mailto:request-alert@iss.net*
- Best of Security — *best-of-security-request@suburbia.net*
- COAST Security Archive — *coast-request@cs.purdue.edu*
- Risks — *risks-request@csl.sri.com*

Encryption

- Cypherpunks — *majordomo@toad.com*

Firewalls

- Internet Firewalls — *majordomo@greatcircle.*
- Academic Firewalls — *majordomo@net.tamu.edu*

Hacking

- Computer Underground Digest — *cu-digest-request@weber.ucsd.edu*
- Phrack — *phrack@well.com*

Privacy

- Computer Privacy Digest — *comp-privacy-request@uwm.edu*
- Privacy Forum — *privacy-request@vortex.com*

WWW Security

- WWW Security — *www-security-request@nsmx.rutgers.edu*
- Secure Socket Layer — *ssl-talk-request@netscape.com*

Viruses

- Virus-L — *listserv@lehigh.edu*

Frequently Asked Questions (FAQs) on Security

FAQs are lists of frequently asked questions (and their answers) in a particular topic area. Most mailing lists and network newsgroups regularly provide updated FAQs. It is important to read the FAQ for a particular newsgroup before beginning to post messages. Here are some sources of FAQs covering various aspects of security:

- Computer Security — *comp.security.misc*

- Cryptography — *http://www.rsa.com/faq*

- Hacking — *alt.2600*

- Internet Firewalls — *http://www.v-one.com/pubs/fw-faq.htm*

- Internet Security and Related Topics — *http://www.iss.net/ sec_info/addsec.html*

- World Wide Web Security — *http://www.genome.wi.mit.edu/ WWW/faqs/www-security-faq.html*

Miscellaneous Security Organizations

The following organizations are sources of a wide variety of security-related information including advisories about newly discovered flaws in software with the potential of jeopardizing security, Frequently Asked Questions (FAQs), software tools and white papers, links to other relevant sites, and more.

- Computer Emergency Response Team (CERT), Carnegie Mellon University — *ftp://ftp.cert.org/pub/cert_advisories OR http://www.sei.cmu.edu/SEI*

- Computer Incident Advisory Capability, Department of Energy — *http://www.cs.purdue.edu/coast*

- Computer Operations, Audit, and Security Technology, Purdue University — *http://www.cs.purdue.edu/coast/coast.html*

- Computer Professionals for Social Responsibility — *www.cpsr.org*

- Computer Security Institute — *http://www.gosci.com*

- Computer Security Research Laboratory at the University of California at Davis — *http://seclab.cs.ucdavis.edu/security.html*

- Electronic Frontier Foundation — *http://www/eff.org*

- The Forum of Incident Response and Security Teams, National Institute of Standards and Technology — *http://csrc.ncsl.nist.gov/first*

- Information Systems Security Association — *http://www.uhsa.uh.edu/issa*

- Library of Congress Internet Resource Page, Internet Security — *http://lcweb.loc.gov/global/internet/security.html*

- National Computer Security Association — *http://www.ncsa.com*

- Safe Internet Programming, Princeton University — *http://www.cs.princeton.edu/sip*

- World Wide Web Consortium, W3C — *http://www.w3.org/pub/WWW/Security*

Appendix D

Intranets Redefine Corporate Information Systems

As with most cutting-edge topics, you can find a lot of useful information about the latest developments and products on the Web.

This appendix contains a "white paper" written by Netscape Communications Corporation. This white paper contains the latest information about Netscape's foray into the intranet market, along with a sampling of companies that are using the technology.

Keep in mind that this white paper was written by Netscape staff, and is designed to generate interest in their products. It is reproduced here with the permission of Netscape.

Intranets Redefine Corporate Information Systems

While the race to establish commercial Web sites has fueled the Internet's rapid growth, corporate applications based on Web technology are revolutionizing communication behind company firewalls. In fact, internal Web, or intranet, usage is predicted to overwhelm external Internet usage before the turn of the century.

Intranets, which run on open TCP/IP networks, enable companies to employ the same types of servers and browsers used for the World Wide Web for internal applications distributed over the corporate LAN. Because intranets are based on the same independent standard Internet protocols and technologies, they are accessible to every member within an organization, regardless of their choice of hardware platform.

Intranet servers enable real business functionality, such as publishing information, processing data and databased applications, and collaboration among employees, vendors, and customers. Across all industries, intranets are rapidly reshaping company-wide communication, collaboration, productivity, and innovation—and saving significant time and money in the process.

Contents

Introduction: The Exploding Intranet Market
  Why Intranets?

Applications Across the Enterprise
  Sales & Marketing
  Product Development
  Customer Service & Support
  Human Resources
  Finance
  Other Applications

Intranet Technology Today

Conclusion

Introduction: The Exploding Intranet Market

A critical mass of enabling technologies and market conditions is satisfying pent-up demand for a more dynamic way of linking people and information. Nearly a third of the Internet's 30 million users are accessing the World Wide Web. Web server software products, which deliver content to individuals (or clients), number more than 120,000 as of the end of 1995 (IDC), up from 130 in 1993.

The combined corporate Internet and intranet market will jump from $12 billion in 1995 to $208 billion by the year 2000, estimates Input, a research firm in Mountain View, California. In fact, two-thirds of all large companies either have a Web server installed or are considering installing one.

The key enablers of Web growth are:

1. The proliferation of PCs, LANs, and modems;

2. Open standards such as TCP/IP, HTTP, and HTML;

3. Cross-platform support;

4. Multimedia support and ease of use; and

5. Support for secure transactions.

With these enablers complementing existing systems' infrastructures, organizations are finding that an intranet provides a way for people to easily retrieve the information they need, when they need it.

Reflecting the shift in Web application development from the external network to within the enterprise, Netscape Communications Corporation reports that more than 50 percent of its Web server sales are earmarked for corporate intranet use.

Predictions for intranet growth have sprung from an examination of current corporate needs and market demands. Organizations of all sizes are facing major communication challenges, and in today's fast-moving, competitive environment, quick and easy access to departmental, corporate, and customer information is essential. By the turn of the century, intranet servers will outsell Internet servers 4.6 million to 440,000, according to IDC. More than connecting employees and business partners to vital corporate data, intranets let companies speed information and software to employees and business partners. They're also inexpensive to develop, maintain, and use.

Why Intranets?

Richard Villars, Internet analyst at IDC, says, "Any intranet offering must meet one or more specific needs better than an alternative to succeed," citing communication, collaboration, and distributed applications as the main areas where intranet technologies will influence future user implementations.

Companies are realizing that many of their current communication vehicles are too limited to cope with the market environment. Therefore, intuitive access to broad types of media make an internal Web an ideal solution for addressing these communication issues. Corporate intranets can provide information in a way that is immediate, cost-effective, easy to use, rich in format, and versatile.

But intranets do more than just solve the problems inherent in existing modes of communication. They provide the following benefits:

- *Freedom of choice.* Web technology is based on open standards and therefore doesn't lock companies into limited, costly choices. In fact, Web technology is available for nearly all leading operating systems and hardware platforms and can leverage legacy database systems.

- *Security.* Protecting information, even within a private corporate network, is critical. Netscape's Secure Sockets Layer (SSL) technology encrypts packets of information so that the information is transferred securely. Netscape has openly licensed SSL, making it the leading de facto security standard for Web-related products.

- *Ease of use.* Among the most fundamental innovations driving people to use Web technology is hyperlinking.

- *Hyperlinking* allows users to easily navigate and find information by simply clicking a word or graphic. With intranet clients such as Netscape Navigator, a single front end is used to access all internal and external resources—so users don't need to learn multiple software packages. According to a recent survey, 56 percent of managers said that ease of use was the single most critical factor for a corporate information system.

- *Cost-effectiveness.* Intranet applications are surprisingly inexpensive in initial purchase, training, and deployment. At less than $40 per user on an interdepartmental or company-wide basis, they cost far less than most other communication or workgroup systems. And the intranet's platform independence eliminates the need to distribute client software or create different versions of the same applications.

Applications Across the Enterprise

Convinced of these advantages, companies in industries ranging from aerospace to entertainment and banking to manufacturing have already implemented intranets and report significant savings in operations costs and improvements in staff productivity. Although the range of applications that can be developed to meet industry-specific or general needs is virtually limitless, intranet applications generally fit into one of three categories:

Communication occurs on a one-to-many basis between teams, departments, or entire corporations by posting information on Web pages, reducing bulky, easily outdated paper-based documents. This use of an intranet brings an immediate payback to organizations, eliminating the costs of producing, printing, and shipping corporate information.

Applications enable two-way interactions, such as logging help desk requests or enrolling for benefits. Whether an employee needs to develop a report, analyze data, or learn about the company's customers, using Web technology linked to legacy data can be an intuitive and efficient alternative to the frustrations of "telephone tag" or paper pushing.

Collaboration represents many-to-many interactions. This category includes newsgroups that facilitate direct exchanges of information between members, with posted information available to others, resulting in a corporate "knowledge base." People subscribe and can view a screen with subject lines, authors, and news article numbers.

Each of these items is the beginning of a "thread" that starts when someone sends out an article or e-mail; then, readers can trace these threads deeper as they wish.

These types of intranet applications improve communication and productivity across all areas of an enterprise. Companies are currently deploying intranets to solve communication needs in departments such as sales and marketing, product development, and others in the following ways:

Sales & Marketing

A fundamental challenge of sales and marketing departments is delivering up-to-date reference information to an often geographically distributed group of people. Having just the right information at the right moment can make a sale happen, and lacking that information can mean losing the deal to a competitor. An intranet can give immediate access to the following types of information:

- product specs, pricing charts, and new collateral sales leads

- competitive information—by means of immediate access to accurate information on company World Wide Web sites

- lists of key customer wins, including win/loss analysis

- program calendars documenting marketing activities and sales forecasts

- online training materials

- sales presentations

Transaction applications with a Web browser client, coupled with industry-standard databases, help marketing departments maintain and access a database of key customers and references. Salespeople can use transaction applications to place orders, check order status, and complete the paperwork surrounding a sale.

For example, by publishing multimedia files on the intranet, HBO is saving thousands of dollars previously incurred for printing, duplication of videocassettes, and distribution of marketing campaign materials among 200 to 300 sales representatives. The intranet eliminates the time and effort involved in distributing these materials and gives the sales force instant access from any location.

In just three months, Cadence Design Systems built a dynamic databased sales and marketing intranet. The system maps out each step of the sales cycle with links to sales support resources, uses Netscape forms to facilitate communication with headquarters, allows global account teams to securely share information, provides a repository of sales tools and reference materials in a variety of document formats, has links to relevant Internet sites, and accesses and distributes a daily news feed on the industry.

In collaborative applications, sales and marketing teams share expertise that improve their success rate in specific sales situations. Newsgroups might focus on issues surrounding winning deals against a particular competitor: weak points, rebuttals, and the latest tactics of the competitor as experienced by sales people in the field; feedback and discussion of various marketing programs, working solutions, and suggestions for improvement; and threaded discussions about specific accounts or issues to help sales representatives exchange information about the challenges of a particular segment or customer.

Product Development

Like sales and marketing departments, product development teams need up-to-date information to perform their jobs effectively. Product development applications often center on project management, with team members updating project schedules and sharing information about the progress of development or customer feedback. Of course, access to the sensitive information in these applications is restricted to team members through access controls. The types of information made accessible through intranet applications may include product specifications, designs, schedule milestones, and changes; team member listings and responsibilities; customer issues; and features of key competitive products.

National Semiconductor Corporation developed an intranet largely to help its customers get their products to market faster. Tim Stuart, information services consultant for National Semiconductor, says, "When we develop a new product, we go through cycles of learning. The faster you can get a product out and look at it, the better you can make the next generation of product. If you can learn faster, you can end up ahead of the competition."

Multimedia entertainment company Electronic Arts uses newsgroups to enable teams to discuss projects and collaborate by means of a Web. This way, Electronic Arts can quickly assemble virtual workgroups to tackle a project regardless of where employees are located. Employees can access the information they want, review the history of discussions, and come up to speed quickly if they're starting on a project already in progress. Web-based client-server applications enable Electronic Arts team members to request or submit specific information. Used in conjunction with a database, intranet applications allow team members to log and query product test results. These applications can also be used to submit a request to patent a recent development, and send the appropriate forms and information directly to the corporate legal department.

Collaborative applications facilitate the discussions and exchange of ideas that are such a critical part of product development—for example, in threads focusing on expertise on specific issues in product development; forums for brainstorming new ideas and critiquing proposed approaches; and customer feedback from sales, marketing, and customer service.

Customer Service & Support

The goal of customer service and support groups is to provide the best quality service in the most cost-effective, efficient way possible. Both publishing and transaction applications help customer service and support departments share customer feedback, creating a coordinated support system. Such intranet applications enable team members to share up-to-date status reports on problems so that all team members can respond to customer calls; get the most up-to-date information on the status of customers' orders; be alerted immediately to any important changes, such as special offers or issues; and train online to respond to customer queries and complaints.

For example, Mobil Corporation depends upon the Web to serve and communicate more effectively with its audiences. Mobil Internet Team's Shelley Moore explains, "People have always called or written to Mobil with comments or questions about products, services, or environmental issues. But we only got feedback from people who were motivated to write or call all over to find the right person within Mobil. With the Internet, we get a more immediate response."

Community applications enable service and support staff to delve more deeply into specific issues. Newsgroup threads provide a forum for detailed discussions of underlying factors with recurrent customer problems and an open exchange about which solutions have succeeded or failed thus far. In addition, newsgroups alert particular staff members to changes or other significant information.

Human Resources

Above all other departments within an organization, human resources (HR) must keep employees well informed of important company issues in addition to the details pertaining to their personal health and well-being. By using an intranet to publish corporate information and transaction applications to provide personal data, HR departments can free their staffs from answering routine questions and doing basic processing tasks. HR departments can publish information and enable secure transactions such as the following:

- benefits information and enrollment
- corporate policies
- company mission and goals
- job postings and internal job transfer forms
- searchable telephone directories
- the annual report
- employee development
- departmental and personal home pages
- classified bulletin boards of items for sale, housing, etc.
- medical referrals

For example, Biotechnology pioneer Genentech provides its employees with access to information on research seminars, company announcements, building facilities, the employee directory, commuting options, benefits, child care, how to place purchase orders, how to get business cards, safety equipment, and more. They look at the Web as an online employee handbook with information on how to do things at Genentech.

Client-server applications eliminate much of the routine paper processing that HR departments typically handle while providing employees with immediate access to their personal information. Access can be restricted to certain departments or users. Secure applications can enable online employee enrollment in benefit plans, such as 401K programs; employee surveys; employee lookup of vacation balances, options, etc.; and online submission of employee status change forms by employee survey managers.

Newsgroups hosted by HR departments are particularly valuable within large companies because they deliver a quick and cost-effective way of communicating with specific groups of people such as senior managers, people with 401K accounts, and employees with dependents. Such newsgroups simplify the task of informing employees about changes in corporate policy that would affect them, and provide a forum for discussion among those with shared interests.

Finance

Carefully monitoring financial indicators helps a company set clear objectives for its managers. It has always been a significant challenge to provide access to important financial information securely, in an easy-to-use, online manner. But with intranet applications, finance departments can more easily disseminate this information to key managers by securely posting corporate financial data or by providing simple forms-based query capabilities.

The purchasing side of financial operations can also benefit from intranet applications. Using the same products that enable "cybermalls" on the public Internet today, companies can simplify electronic software distribution, billing, and purchasing of supplies by providing an internal Web-based mall that offers all company-approved products.

Taking asset management a step further, at Allen-Bradley employees can "recycle" their old computer equipment by locating internal buyers through a Web-based, forms-based system tied to a relational database.

Other Applications

Numerous other corporate departments, such as legal or MIS groups, currently using paper-based forms or policies can reap the benefits of making transaction applications available through intranets. Not only does an intranet automate request processing and eliminate the possibilities of lost paperwork, but it completely erases the costs associated with paper printing and distribution.

Intranet Technology Today

Intranet applications have quickly become the foundation of many leading companies' IS solutions. A competitive, open marketplace is driving organizations like Netscape to enhance the range of capabilities, ease of implementation, administration, and data management in an intranet. As the Internet continues to mature into the mainstream platform for enterprise computing, internal Web sites are requiring better application development tools, "middleware" solutions for connecting to legacy systems, and system management tools.

A company's most valuable information resides in its legacy databases and on employee PCs. Vendors are developing tools to make it easy for end users to publish documents on the intranet and share their knowledge. For example, Netscape Navigator Gold eliminates the complexities of HTML authoring through an interface that makes creating and publishing "live" multimedia documents as easy as using a word processor, only within the same familiar browser environment used to navigate and access data.

Improved graphical development tools such as Netscape LiveWire Pro make it even easier to manage intranet sites and to build Web-based client-server applications that conduct complex transactions against databases, and mine the data in legacy systems and other corporate information sources. Administration tools are available to help intranet managers control links, expiration dates, and ownership, tasks that become increasingly critical as intranet sites evolve.

Already, some companies have more than 250,000 documents available on their intranets. As more people within an enterprise publish to the intranet and the number of legacy databases hooked to the intranet grows, information search and retrieval becomes more complex. Products such as Netscape's Catalog Server, which enables dynamic creation of "Yahoo!-like" indexes, and the Enterprise Server, with an integrated Verity text search engine, will become more essential for quickly pinpointing and serving information.

Increasingly powerful management tools are also enabling enterprises to support far-reaching, innovative systems without sacrificing control. Enhanced security and administration tools ensure that users are authorized to access the information they seek, while others provide integrated search technology to effectively locate information across distributed servers.

At the same time, recognizing the unique needs of enterprises to fine-tune the browser clients to their specifications, Navigator client administration features allow intranet site managers to customize options, such as restricting access to the external Web.

Developers can create advanced, customized applications today using the Netscape Server API, and can add functionality with server plug-in products.

Netscape is dedicated to developing innovative technologies that make it possible to build open applications that support live online content. These technologies, based on Sun Microsystems' Java scripting languages, as well as the integration of third-party plug-ins for functionality such as spreadsheets and presentations, or multimedia formats such as Adobe Acrobat and Macromedia Director, make Netscape the logical platform for applications that need to provide intelligent, compelling content to its users.

Conclusion

Driven by the powerful combination of openness and security, intuitive access to detailed information, extreme cost-effectiveness, and flexibility for customization in increasingly competitive times, the mounting popularity of these products is expected to sky-rocket. IDC predicts that by 1997, 80 percent of Web servers will be used for internal sites. And perhaps a more profound change brought about by corporate intranets will be cultural, not techno-logical, as we gain new tools that reassign the influence of infor-mation access within the enterprise as a whole.

Looking forward, Forrester Research predicts the move to a Full Service Intranet, adding that "by 2000, the intranet will grow far beyond a TCP/IP network that just supports the Web. It will have five core standards-based services—directory, email, file, print, and network management—that will overshadow proprietary NOS solutions."

The revolutionary, open Web-based products developed by Netscape Communications and other leading vendors are already redefining the way thousands of global corporations communi-cate, collaborate, and process transactions.

Today Netscape customers can choose from best-of-breed products, scaling seamlessly from the workgroup to the enterprise to the global Internet. Recognizing the needs of enterprises, Netscape's new generation of servers, clients, and tools are geared to making the Full Service Intranet a reality, providing companies with limitless possibilities for extending intranet technology.

Corporate Sales: 415/937-2555; Personal Sales: 415/937-3777; Federal Sales: 415/937-3678

If you have any questions, please visit Customer Service.

Copyright © 1996 Netscape Communications Corporation

Glossary

Abuse of Privilege   An action prohibited by an organization's security policy.

Application-level Firewall   A firewall that maintains complete TCP connection state and sequencing, and that monitors authorization at the application level. Application-level firewalls often re-address traffic so that outgoing traffic appears to have originated from the firewall rather than the internal host.

Authentication   The process of determining the identity of a user who is attempting to access a system.

Authentication Token   A portable device used for authenticating a user. Authentication tokens operate by challenge/response, time-based code sequences, or other techniques.

Authorization   The process of permitting a user to perform certain activities. This normally occurs immediately after the user is authenticated.

Bastion Host   A computer that is the central component in a network security architecture, often the main entrance to the network. It is usually the most critical, and therefore the best-secured, system in the network.

Challenge/Response   A method of authentication in which the server provides to the client a piece of information (the challenge) that was not known in advance, and the client includes the challenge—possibly in modified form—in its authentication information (the response). Because the server avoids repeating the same challenge, the authentication cannot be replicated at a later time using the same authentication information.

Chroot   "Change root." A function in UNIX that restricts a process from operating above a certain subdirectory by making the process think that the subdirectory is the root directory of the file system.

Cryptographic Checksum   A one-way hash function applied to a file to produce a unique "fingerprint" of the file for later reference.

Data-driven Attack   A form of attack that is encoded in innocuous-seeming data and is executed by a user or other software to implement an attack. In the case of firewalls, a data-driven attack is a concern because it may get through the firewall in data form and launch an attack against a system behind the firewall.

Defense in Depth   A security model in which every system on the network is secured as much as possible. Using this model does not necessarily decrease the need for a firewall.

Dual-homed Gateway   A system that has two network interfaces, each of which is connected to a different network. In firewall configurations, a dual-homed gateway usually acts to block or filter some or all of the traffic trying to pass between the networks.

Encrypting Router   See *Tunneling Router*.

File Server   The computer on a network assigned to the task of being a central storage site for all or most of the data used by workstations connected to it. Use of a dedicated file server allows a company to invest in one high-performance computer for this job and many medium-range computers for individual workstations.

File Transfer Protocol (FTP)   A protocol designed for the efficient transfer of files between computers over a TCP/IP network (an intranet or the Internet).

Firewall   A system or combination of systems that enforces a boundary between two or more networks.

Frame   A data-link layer packet that contains the header and trailer information required by the physical medium. Network layer packets are encapsulated to become frames.

Gateway   The term *router* is now used in place of the original definition of *gateway*. Currently, a gateway means a communications device/program that passes data between networks that have similar functions but dissimilar implementations.

Host   A computer that is connected to a network.

Host Address   The part of the IP address that uniquely identifies a node on the network.

Host-based Security   A security model designed to protect an individual computer from attack.

Insider Attack   An attack originating from within a protected network.

Internet Protocol (IP)   The Internet Protocol, defined in STD 5, RFC 791, is the network layer for the TCP/IP protocol suite. It is a no-connection, best-effort, packet-switching protocol.

Intrusion Detection   Detection of break-ins or break-in attempts either manually or via software-expert systems that operate on logs or other information available on the network.

IP Spoofing   An attack in which a system attempts to illicitly impersonate another system by using its IP network address.

IP Splicing/Hijacking   An attack in which an active, established session is intercepted and co-opted by the attacker. IP splicing attacks may occur after an authentication has been made, permitting the attacker to assume the role of an already authorized user. Primary protections against IP splicing rely on encryption at the session or network layer.

Local Area Network (LAN)   A data network intended to serve an area of only a few square kilometers or less. Because the network is known to cover only a small area, optimizations can be made in the network signal protocols that permit data rates up to 100MB per second. LANs are usually used in small- and medium-sized offices or parts of large networks contained within small physical areas.

Logging   The process of storing information about events that occurred on the firewall or network.

Log Retention   The length of time that audit logs are retained and maintained.

Log Processing   How audit logs are processed, searched for key events, or summarized.

Mail Gateway   A computer that connects two or more electronic mail systems and transfers messages among them. Sometimes the mapping and translation can be quite complex, and they generally require a store-and-forward scheme in which the entire message is received from one system before it is processed and transmitted to the next system.

Net Mask   A bit mask used to differentiate which bits in an IP address represent the network and subnet. This mask is often referred to as the subnet mask because the network portion of the address can be determined by the encoding inherent in an IP address.

Network Address   The network portion of an IP address, also referred to as a network number. For a class A network, the network address is the first byte of the IP address. For a class B network, the network address is the first two bytes of the IP address. For a class C network, the network address is the first three bytes of the IP address. In each case, the remainder is the host address.

Network-level Firewall   A firewall in which traffic is examined at the network protocol packet level.

Packet   The unit of data sent across a network. *Packet* is a generic term used to describe a unit of data at all levels of the protocol stack, but it is most correctly used to describe application data units.

Packet Switching   A communications paradigm in which packets are individually routed between hosts, without a previously established communication path.

Perimeter-based Security   The technique of securing a network by controlling access to all entry and exit points of the network.

Policy   Rules governing the use of computing resources, security practices, and operational procedures.

Port   A transport layer demultiplexing value. Each application has a unique port number associated with it. Commonly used port addresses for Internet applications are port 21 for FTP, port 80 for HTTP (World Wide Web), port 6667 for Internet Relay Chat (IRC), and so on.

Protocol   A set of rules, usually in a formal specification, that describes exactly how two or more computers will communicate with each other for a specific purpose. Protocols can be defined for anything from system-level to application-level communications.

Protocol Stack   A layered set of protocols that work together to provide a set of network functions.

Proxy   A software agent that acts on behalf of a user. Typical proxies accept a connection from a user, make a decision as to whether the user or client IP address is permitted to use the proxy, perhaps do additional authentication, and then complete a connection on behalf of the user to a remote destination.

Root   **1.** The top level of a disk drive or directory structure. In DOS, C:\ is considered to be the normal root on the vast majority of PCs. **2.** The superuser or system administrator account on a multiuser system such as UNIX.

Screened Host   A host on a network behind a screening router. The degree to which a screened host may be accessed depends on the screening rules in the router.

Screened Subnet   A subnet behind a screening router. The degree to which the subnet may be accessed depends on the screening rules in the router.

Screening Router   A router configured to permit or deny traffic based on a set of permission rules configured by the administrator.

Session Stealing   Same as IP splicing.

Socket   Generally speaking, a network connection of the type used by TCP/IP networks. Sockets allow multiple applications to access the network at the same time so that a user can FTP a file from one source while continuing to browse the intranet or download e-mail.

Social Engineering   An attack based on deceiving users or administrators at the target site. Social engineering attacks are typically carried out by telephoning users or operators pretending to be authorized users, in attempts to gain illicit access to systems.

Subnet   A portion of a network that may be a physically independent network segment and that shares a network address with other portions of the network. A subnet is denoted by a subnet number.

Subnet Address   The subnet portion of an IP address. In a subnetted network, the host portion of an IP address is split into a subnet portion and a host portion using an address (subnet) mask.

Trojan Horse   A software entity that appears to do something normal but which, in fact, contains a trap door or attack program.

Tunneling Router   A router or system capable of routing traffic by encrypting and encapsulating it for transmission across an untrusted network, for eventual de-encapsulation and decryption.

Virtual Network Perimeter   A network that appears to be a single protected network behind firewalls, but which actually encompasses encrypted virtual links over untrusted networks.

Virus   A self-replicating code segment. Viruses may or may not contain attack programs or trap doors.

Worm   A computer program that replicates itself and is self-propagating. Worms, as opposed to viruses, are specifically designed to spawn in network environments.

Index

A

AbhiWeb AFS 2000 (AbhiWeb) product
  listing   205
Access-control policy
  firewalls to implement   11
  issues to consider in   48, 117–18
ACK flag in TCP packet   87–88
Acme, Inc. sample firewall implementation   109–29
  completed system of   128
  defining the Internet connection as security
    issue for   112–13
  determining access as security issue
    for   113–17
  identifying weak spots in information flow
    as security issue for   117–18
  managing internal access to sensitive
    information as security issue for   124–
    26
  managing remote access as security issue
    for   118–22
  organization chart of   110
  sending remote information as security
    issue for   122–23
  technology background of   109–11
  virus detection and removal as security
    issue for   127
ActiveX (Microsoft)   33
Address routing   83

Allen-Bradley's use of intranet   299
alpha.c2.org cypherpunk remailer   234–35
AltaVista Firewall (Digital Equipment Corporation)
  product listing   205
  proxy server   102
Anonymous remailers (servers) for anonymous e-mail messages   232–37
ANS Interlock (ANS CO+RE Systems, Inc.)
  product listing   206
Application gateways
  capabilities of   90
  defined   89
  in screened host   104–5
  in screened subnet   106–7
Application-level technology   78, 89
Archie data exchange protocol   20
Arms Export Control Act   241
ARPANET
  established by DoD's Advanced Research
    Projects Agency   18
  users of   19
Audit trails of access to sensitive data   126
  LT Auditor+ to create   162
Authentification of users, Kerberos model's
  process of   194–95
Authentification server   93, 196
Authorization server to check logins   78
Automated testing tools, testing   276

B

Backup media, access to   67
Bastion host   103, 107
Batch processing defined   16
Berners-Lee, Tim   20–21
Black Hole (Milky Way Networks, Inc.)
    product listing   206
Blaze, Matt   247
Bookmarks in Web browsers   26
BorderGuard 2000 (Network Systems) product
    listing   206
BorderWare Firewall Server (Secure
    Computing Corporation)
    alarm system of   151–52
    authenticated access in   151
    circuit-level proxy technology in   91
    configuring   144–52
    data protection by, example of   120
    Firewall Server Console (FSC) and
        Remote Administration Console (RAC)
        of   144–45
    firewall technologies combined in   89
    installing   141–44
    as Internet "gateway"   138
    monitoring system activity using   145
    network address translation in   139
    packet-level screening in   139
    platforms for   140–41
    product description of   137–40
    product listing of   206–7
    product review of   137–52
    Remote Administration feature of   144
    reports created by   146–47
    Secure Server Net in   140
    security issues for   142
    selecting server components for   142
    specifications needed for   143–44
    transparent proxies in   138–39, 148–50
    using   144–52
    viewing logs using   145–48
    Virtual Private Network (VPN) to connect
        two servers in   140
Brimstone (SOS Corporation) product
    listing   207
Browsers, intranet   23
    Web browsers used as   26
Browsers, Web
    available free on the Internet   26

features of advanced   21, 26, 51
hardware requirements for   25
HTML tag support by   29
HTTP use of   27–28
selecting   51

C

Call blocker service   56
Callback features
    as security measures   166–68
    settings for   180
Caller ID service   56
Centri Firewall/Centri TNT (Global Internet)
    product listing   207
CERN, development of World Wide Web
    by   20
CGI (Common Gateway Interface)   32–33
Challenger (CyberSafe Corporation)
    audit log file of   197
    authentification of users by   195
    one-time passwords used by   93
    operation of   197–98
    product listing of   207–8
    product review of   193–201
    Security Toolkit add-on for   193, 198–201
Circuit-level gateway   90
Cisco router   83
Client
    hardware for   25
    software for   26
Client-server applications   298
Client-server system
    intranet as   23–24
    unique security contexts in   201
Clinton administration attempt to force use of
    Clipper Chip   241, 246–47
Clipper Chip   241, 246–47
Collaborative applications, intranet used
    for   295, 296
COM commercial domain   47
Component certification   94–98
Computer crime. *See also Crackers,* Hackers,
    and U.S. Department of Defense
    evolution of   3–4
    in financial institution, example of   55–56
Computer Emergency Response Team
    (CERT)   287

Computer Incident Advisory Capability   287
Computer Operations, Audit, and Security
  Technology   287
Computer Professionals for Social
  Responsibility   288
Computer security. *See also* Network security
  components of   9–11
  importance of   2
  issues in   48–49
  level A   61
  level B1 (Label Security Protection)   60
  level B2 (Structured Protection)   60
  level B3 (Security Domain)   61
  level C1 (Discretionary Security
    Protection)   58–59
  level C2   59–60
  level D1   57–58
  status of   3
Computer Security Institute   288
Computer Security Research Laboratory of the
  University of California at Davis   288
Computer security sites, mailing lists for   286
Configuration testing   276–78
  for misplaced trust   277
CONNECT:Firewall (Sterling Software)
  product listing   208
Connection load on intranet   24–25
Connections
  control testing of   274
  defined   24
Controller (Actane) product listing   208
COPS (Computer Oracle Password &
  Security)   262
Corporate espionage   2, 55, 279
Corporate information systems, intranets as
  redefining   289–301
Cost/risk matrix   68–71
Crackers   256–58
  hackers versus   257
  packet sniffers used by   260
  password   228–31
  Trojan horse programs left by   261
Cron job   191
crypt encryption utility   242–43
CryptoCard   149, 151
Cryptography. *See* Data encryption
CryptoWall (Radguard) product listing   208
Customer service and support, intranet used
  for   296–97

CyberGuard Firewall (CyberGuard Systems
  Corporation) product listing   209
"Cybermalls"   298
Cypherpunk class of anonymous server
  233–36
Cypherpunks Home Page   235–36
Cypress Labyrinth Firewall (Cypress Consult-
  ing, Inc.) product listing   209

D

Data compression   245–46
Data encryption   57, 238–55
  defined   238
  of e-mail   228, 234–35
  as internal control   61
  legal issues for   240–42
  mailing list for   286
  programs for   242–55
  public key (dual key or asymmetric)
    238–39, 241, 244, 247
  reasons for using   239–40
  single key (symmetric)   238–39
  "trap door" (one way)   238–39
  types of   238
Data exchange protocols and their uses   20
Data in a network security policy   65, 67
Data sharing, planning for   113–17
Datagrams
  data received from TCP in   39
  defined   40
Decryption keys   239, 241
Deleted files, security threat of recover-
  ing   228, 256
Demilitarized zone (DMZ)
  logging onto proxies from   375
  quiet wire observation with discon-
    nected   274
  in a screened subnet   106–7
  self-test scanning of   272
  testing IP addresses on   277
  testing unsupported protocols from   275
Denial of access as network security   64
Department heads' involvement in
  considering security   66
DES (Data Encryption Standard) encryption
  utility   243, 253
Development tools for an intranet   49
Digital Firewall for UNIX (Digital Equipment
  Corporation) product listing   209

da Dilva, Stephanie   285
Directory Web sites   204
DNS (Domain Name System)   47
  full tests of   277–78
  restricting access to   268
Documentation in a network security
  policy   66, 68
Domain Name System (DNS)   47
Drawbridge Packet Filter (Texas A&M
  University)   86–87
DSS (Digital Signature Standard)   252
Dual-homed gateway
  advantages of   102
  defined   100
  disadvantages of   102
  IP addresses for, two   101

E

Eagle (Raptor Systems, Inc.) product list-
  ing   210
EDU educational domain   47
Electronic Arts' use of intranet   296
Electronic Frontier Foundation   288
Emacs   26
E-mail privacy and security   122–23, 227–65
  anonymous remailers for   232–37
  data encryption for   238–55
  security holes for   258–59
Encryption. *See* Data encryption
Espionage
  corporate   2, 55
  testing for   279
Ethernet protocol
  on network access layer   80
  for physical networks   39
European Laboratory for Particle Physics
  (CERN), World Wide Web developed
  by   20
ExFilter (ExNet Systems Ltd.) product list-
  ing   210
External security controls   62

F

FAQs (frequently asked questions) for
  newsgroups about security   287
FBI (Federal Bureau of Investigation)
  Internet address of   54
  losses from security cracks estimated
    by   256
  National Computer Crime Squad of   4, 54,
    56–57
FDDI (Fiber Distributed Data Interface) on
  network access layer   80
Federal Express (FedEx), tracking software
  of   6
Finance, intranet used for   298–99
Finger daemon, login names discovered
  from   261
FireDoor (Equivalence) product listing   210
Firewall Buyer's Guide by NCSA   282
Firewall Fiesta of vendors   204
FireWall IRX Router (Livingston Enterprises)
  product listing   211
Firewall Report (Outlink Market Research)   282
FireWall/Plus (Network–1 Software &
  Technology, Inc.) product listing   211
FireWall–1 (CheckPoint Software Technologies,
  Ltd.)   88
  product listing of   210–11
Firewalls. *See* Intranet firewalls
Form as a Web page   33
FQDNs (fully qualified domain names)
  resolvable from internal network   278
FrontPage (Microsoft)   29, 51
FTP (File Transfer Protocol) data exchange
  protocol   20
  advantages of   36
  downloading files using   36–37
  mixmaster software available from   237
  restricting access to   268
FTP proxy, logging onto   275
Full Service Intranet   301
FWPD Certification Contract   96

G

Galea Network Security (Galea Network
  Security) product listing   211
Gauntlet Internet Firewall (Trusted Informa-
  tion Systems, Inc.) product listing   212
Genentech's use of intranet   298
GFX Internet Firewall System (Global Technol-
  ogy Associates, Inc.) product listing   212
Glossary   303–9
Gopher data exchange protocol   20
  restricting access to   268

GOV government domain   47
Groupware
    cost of   7, 23
    defined   4
    intranets versus   22–23
GSS-API, Security Toolkit to implement
    199–201
Guardian Firewall System (NetGuard, Inc.)
    product listing   212

H

Hacker's Journal   257
Hackers
    crackers versus   257
    firewalls against   13, 150
    importance of computer security against   2
    mailing lists for   286
    minimizing access time to deter   178
    programs used by   119
    protection by FBI against   54
    success of   55
    warnings of attacks by   151
Hardware
    composing a firewall   77
    in a network security policy   65, 67
Hash function   251, 252
HBO's use of intranet   293
Headers of packets   79
    information in   85
    three layers in   80
Helper applications   28
Hess, David   86
Home pages, internal   123
Horatio (SAGUS Security, Inc.) product
    listing   213
Host routing defined   85
"Hot" lists of Web site addresses   26
HotBot search engine   35
HTML (HyperText Markup Language)
    adding codes for   50–51
    release of specifications for   20
    tags used by   28–29
HTTP (HyperText Transfer Protocol)
    release of specifications for   20
    World Wide Web publishing based on
        27–28
HTTP proxies   277

Huffman Code compression and encryption
    algorithm   245–46
Human resources, intranet used for   297–98
Hypertext links (hyperlinks)
    advantages of   31, 292–93
    defined   30
    on images   32
    to request related information   21
    use of   30, 32

I

IBM Internet Connection Secured Network
    Gateway (IBM) product listing   213
I.C.E. Block (J. River, inc.) product listing   213
ICMP (Internet Control Message Protocol) on
    transport layer   80
IDEA (International Data Encryption
    Algorithm)   248
Implementation steps for an intranet   49–51
    attaching Web server to network as step 2
        in   50
    connecting data to the Web server as step 3
        in   50–51
    equipping the users as step 4 in   51
    setting up corporate network as step 1
        in   50
Inclusion concept for network security   63–64
Indexing software to search for
    information   21, 34–35
Information Systems Security
    Association   288
Interactive processing   16
Interceptor (Technologic, Inc.) product
    listing   214
Internal security controls   61, 62
Internet
    access through e-mail to services of   269
    computer criminal using   4
    firewalls as barriers between organization
        and, 11
    free software from   26
    growth of   5
    intranets connected to   50
    as network of networks   19
Internet Explorer (Microsoft)   26
    tags in   28
Internet Firewalls Toolkit (TIS),
    authentification server of   93

Internet Information Server (Microsoft)   25
Internet layer of header   80
Internet Network Information Center
    (InterNIC)   41–42
    domain names registered by   47
Internet Protocol (IP)
    datagrams received by   39
    used by HTTP   27
Internet Scanner (Internet Security
    Systems)   278
    Addcron utility of   191
    Brute Force options of   189
    configuring   186–90
    firewall options of   189–90
    installing   185–86
    NCSA use of   98
    Network File System-related options
       of   189
    ping test used by   187
    platforms for   184–85
    product description of   183–84
    product review of   183–92
    Remote Procedure Call options of   188
    reports created by   184, 191
    using   190–91
Internet Scanner SAFEsuite (Internet Security
    Systems) product listing   214
Internet Stream Protocol (ST-II)   280
InterNIC   41–42
    domain names registered by   47
INTOUCH NSA—Network Security Agent
    (Touch Technologies, Inc.) product list-
    ing   215
Intranet concepts   15–51
Intranet firewall concepts, technology
    and   75–108
Intranet firewall technology   78–93
Intranet firewalls
    basics of   1–13
    as computer security component   9, 57,
       76–77
    configurations of   98–108
    custom   12
    defined   1, 11, 76
    functions of   12
    guidelines for   108
    implementation of   109–29
    importance of   2
    as internal controls   61

mailing lists for   286
    in network security   53–74
    one-way passage of data through   113
    products for   7, 76, 133–223
    recommended by FBI   56
    resources for   283–88
    testing   269–80
Intranet Scanner (Internet Security Systems),
    monitoring for attacks using   127, 185
Intranets
    addressing on   43–44
    administration and management of   49
    advantages of   4–5, 21, 292–93
    appeal of   6–9
    categories of applications for   293–99
    connectivity features of   8
    cost of   7, 21, 23, 293, 299
    defined   4, 16
    ease of use of   7–8, 21
    groupware versus   22–23
    growth of   5–6
    implementing   49–51
    legacy support with   49, 299
    network infrastructure for   49
    planning   48–49
    services for   27–37
    software for   25–26
    today's technology for   299–300
"Intranets Redefine Corporate Information
    Systems" white paper (Netscape Communi-
    cations Corporation)   289–301
    intranet applications noted in, types
       of   293–99
    intranet market described in   291–92
    reasons to use intranets described in   292–
       93
    today's technology described in   299–300
IP addresses   40–44
    classes of   42
    destination   85
    dotted decimal form in   41
    in dual-homed host, two   101
    notation of   40
    source   85
    testing, on DMZ   277
    translation of   135
IP forwarding   102
IPv6 version of the IP protocol   280–82
    address space in   281

header of   281–82
main features of   281
router for   280
IRC (Internet Relay Chat) data exchange
protocol   20
ISAPI to run scripts   33
Isearch search engine   35
ISP (Internet service provider), IP addresses
assigned by   42
ISS Security Scanner   97
IWare Connect (Quarterdeck Corporation)
product listing   215

J

Java scripting languages, Netscape technologies based on   300

K

KarlBridge/KarlRouter (KarlNet, Inc.) product
listing   215
Kerberos security model (MIT)   93, 194–96,
201
authentification of user passwords using   194–95
data encryption using   252–53
design goals of   194–95
private messages feature of   196
safe messages feature of   196
security levels of   195–96
Keystroke-level monitoring of workstations   56

L

Labyrinth Firewall (Cypress), circuit-level
proxy technology in   91
LEAF (Law Enforcement Access Field)   247
Library of Congress Internet Resource Page,
Internet Security   288
"Live wire" network observation   274–75
Local area network (LAN)
encrypting data on   260
similarity of intranet to   4
workgroup connectivity using   18
Login attempts, station identification for
unsuccessful   126

Login banner warning against unauthorized
access   56
Lotus Notes server software as Web server   23
LT Auditor+ (Blue Lance)
auto-delete/purge filter of   161
bindery filter of   155, 160
configuring   159–63
files/directory filters of   160
hardware filter of   161
installing   156–58
login filter of   160
metering filter of   160
monitoring license compliance using   154
platforms for   155–56
product description of   154–55
product listing of   215
product review of   153–63
reports created by   155, 162–63
system requirements for   156
tracking hardware inventory using   155,
162
using   158–59
Lynx   26

M

Magellan search engine   35
Mailing lists on security issues for e-mail
addresses   285–86
Mainframe computers   16–17
MD (Message Digest) data encryption func-
tions   251
Mediator One (ComNet Solutions Pty. Ltd.)
product listing   216
Metering reports, LT Auditor+ to create   162
Microdots   254
Midas WWW   26
MIS staff involvement in considering secu-
rity   66
Mixmaster class of anonymous server   233,
236–37
Mobil Corporation's use of intranet   296–97
Modem
auto-answer mode of   172
baud rate of   179
callbacks by   182
disconnection from, message sent
during   180

failure to communicate of   179
forcing hang-up of   180
Modem Security Enforcer to "separate"
    connection between computer and   165,
    166
Modem Security Enforcer (IC Engineering, Inc.)
    account contents for   169
    advantages of   168
    changing user passwords using   173
    configuring   173–81
    copy operation of   175
    creating and canceling accounts us-
        ing   175–76
    customizing   171–72, 177–81
    displaying access statistics using   174
    example of use of   119–21
    indicator lights of   182
    installing   172–73
    limiting phone numbers having remote
        access using   166
    operation of   168–72
    platforms for   172
    product description of   166–68
    product listing of   216
    product review of   165–82
    status indicators of   181–82
    using   181–82
Moore, Shelley   296–97
Mosaic   26

N

Name server   47
National Computer Crime Squad (NCCS)
    (FBI)   4, 54, 56–57
National Computer Security Association
    (NCSA)
    certification of products by   203
    Firewall Buyer's Guide by   282
    functionality requirements of   94–96
    IS/Recon service of   282
    security requirements of   96–97
    test criteria of   94–98
    tools used by   97–98
    Web site of   204, 288
National Institute for Standards and Technol-
    ogy (NIST)   246, 252
    Forum of Incident Response and Security
        Teams of   288

National Science Foundation, NSFNET
    established by   19
National Security Agency   241, 246
National Semiconductor Corporation's use of
    intranet   295
Navigator Gold   29
NCSA Malicious Code Agreement   97
NET Internet domain   47
NETBuilder Firewall (3Com Corporation)
    product listing   216
NetFortress (Digital Secured Networks
    Technology, Inc.) product listing   216
NetGate (SmallWorks, Inc.) product list-
    ing   217
NetLOCK (Hughes Electronics) product
    listing   217
Netmasks   44
Netnews   284–85
NetRoad FireWALL (Ukiah Software, Inc.)
    product listing   218
Netscape Catalog Server (Netscape Communi-
    cations Corporation)   300
Netscape Communications Corporation,
    "white paper" on intranets by   289–301
Netscape LiveWire Pro (Netscape Communica-
    tions Corporation)   299–300
Netscape Navigator Gold (Netscape Commu-
    nications Corporation)   299
Netscape Navigator (Netscape Communica-
    tions Corporation)
    features of   26, 51
    popularity of   51
NetScape Secure Sockets Layer (SSL) technol-
    ogy   292
NetSeer (enterWorks.com) product list-
    ing   217
NetWall (Bull S.A.) product listing   218
NetWare (Novell)
    LT Auditor+ to protect   153, 155, 159–60
    NLMs of   157–58
Network access layer of header   80
Network Address Testing, products that
    implement   274
Network analyzer (monitor) products   273–75
Network communications protocol   27
    TCP/IP as   37
Network interface cards (NICs) in dual-homed
    gateway   100

Network security. *See also* Computer security
  approaches to   63–64
  designing a policy for. *See* Network security
    policy design
  handling exceptions to   64
  importance of   55–57
  integrating firewalls into   53–74
  recurring review of   72
Network security policy design
  analyzing risk/cost as step 2 in   68–71
  identifying security issues as step 1 in
    65–68
  implementing plan as step 3 in   71–72
  reviewing and updating plan as step 4
    in   72–74
Network security tools   259–65
Network services access policy   267–68
Network-level technology   78
NNTP, restricting access to   268
Norman Firewall, The (Internet Security, Inc.)
  product listing   218
Norton Utilities to zap deleted files   228, 256
NSFNET as "backbone" network   19

O

Octets
  in intranet addresses   43–46
  in IP addresses   40–41
ON Guard (On Technology Corporation)
  product listing   218–19
Open Windows   267
Operating system, access to root level of
  58–59
"Orange Book" of DoD   57
Order processing system, example of
  automated   118–19
ORG organization domain   47
OSI Reference Model, 38
Overprotection in network security,
  avoiding   66, 68

P

Packet
  authentification of   139
  blocked   84
  defined   39, 40, 79
  incoming   80, 83
  outgoing   80
  parts of   79
  source   83
Packet filters   79–89
  as firewall configuration   98–100
  information extracted from packet header
    by   82
  inspection module in   87
  rules used by   82–85
Packet sniffers, misuse of   259–60
Password crackers   228–31. *See also* Crackers
Passwords
  archiving old   229
  authentification servers software to
    produce   93
  disadvantages of   92
  expiration dates of   125, 229
  insecure   3, 10, 228, 260
  as internal controls   61
  Kerberos model's user authentification
    using secret from   195
  Modem Security Enforcer's use of   166
  preventing the capture of clear-text   195
  SecurID system for one-time   149
  sniffers to gather   260
  tips for creating   228, 229–31
  users' changes to   180
PEM (Privacy Enhanced Mail) data encryption
  system   249
Penet class of anonymous server   233
People in a network security policy   66, 67
PERMIT Security Gateway (TimeStep Corpo-
  ration) product listing   219
Personal computer, networked   17–18
Personal identification number (PIN)
  for CryptoCard or SecurID   149
  for smart card   93
Personnel security controls   62
PGP (Pretty Good Privacy) data encryption
  system   247–49
Phrack magazine about hacking and
  cracking   257, 286
Phreaking   257
Physical security controls   62, 279
Ping test   187
Pingware (Bellcore)   278
PKZIP/UNZIP utilities   245
Port scanning   97, 271–73
  semi-random   274

PORTUS (Livermore Software Laboratories, Inc.) product listing   219

Prime numbers used in data encryption   244

Privacy, mailing list for   286

Private Internet Exchange (PIX) Firewall (Cisco Systems) product listing   219

PrivateNet Secure Firewall Server (NEC Technologies) product listing   220

Procedural security controls   62

Product development, intranet used for 295–96

Product listing, firewall   205–23

Proxies

   inbound   139

   outbound   150

   transparent   138–39, 148–49

   user-defined   150

Proxy server   42, 89–91

   connections accepted or rejected by   91

   defined   89

   in dual-homed gateway   100, 102

   to permit and block access   78

   process used by   89–90

Publicly Accessible Mailing Lists   285

Q

Query processed by search tool   34–35

"Quiet wire" observation by network monitor   274

R

RC2 and RC4   254–55

Records of test results stored offline for better security   273

Redundancy in access to information   67, 68

Remote access as security issue   118–22

Reviews of firewall products   133–223

rexec   268

RIP, restricting access to   268

RIPEM (Riordan's Internet Privacy Enhanced Mail) data encryption implementation   249–51

RISKS Digest   264

rlogin   268

Routers. *See* Screening routers

RPC (Remote Procedure Call) services   268

RSA data encryption algorithm   243–44, 248

RSAREF data encryption routines   244–45

rsh   268

Rules (filter) table for screening router   82, 84, 86–87

   growing size and complexity of   100

S

Sacrificial lamb   103, 105

Safe Internet Programming, Princeton University   288

Sales and marketing, intranet used for 294–95

Salt value   254

SATAN (Systems Administrator's Tool for Analyzing Networks)   263, 278

Screened network   98–100

   advantages of   98–99

   disadvantages of   100

Screened subnet   106

   advantages of   107

   disadvantages of   107

Screened-host firewall   104

   advantages of   105

   disadvantages of   105

   <IndScreening routers

   advantages of   98–99

   common   83

   disadvantages of   100

   to filter network traffic   80

   packet filters versus   80

   rules for   80–82

   in screened host   104–5

   in screened networks   98–100

   in screened subnet   106–7

Scripts, CGI to run   32–33

Search engine software to search for files   21, 34–35

Secure Access Firewall (Ascend Communications) product listing   220

Secure RPC Gateway (Le Reseau netwerksysteen BV) product listing   220

Secure Server Net (Borderware), selective data access using   124

SecurID one-time password system   149, 151

Security breaches, list of Usenet groups discussing   264

Security controls, internal and external   61–63

Security issues

   example of. *See* Acme, Inc. sample firewall implementation

frequently asked questions (FAQs)
  about 287
  future 280–82
  Usenet forums on 284–85
Security organizations, listing of 287–88
Security review team, concerns for 73–74
Security Toolkit. *See* CyberSAFE Challenger
Server software 23
  defined 25
  sources of 25
Servers. *See also* individual types
  functions of 23
  hardware requirements for 24
  HTTP use of 27–28
  organization of 113–17
  overloaded 25
Serverwatch Web site of technology and
  tools 204
Services vulnerable to hacker and cracker
  attacks, list of 267–69
SET (Secure Electronic Security) system 253
SHS (Secure Hash Standard) 252
Sidewinder (Secure Computing Corporation)
  product listing 221
Site Patrol (BBN Planet) product listing 221
SKIPJACK encryption/decryption algo-
  rithm 246–47
Smart card defined 93
SmartWall (V-ONE Corporation) product
  listing 222
SMTP proxies, testing 276
SMTP, restricting access to 268
SOCKS, firewall configuration using 277
Software
  composing a firewall 77
  in a network security policy 65, 67
Solstice FireWall Module 87
Solstice Firewall–1 (Sun MicroSystems, Inc.)
  product listing 221
Source routing as hacking 83
State evaluation to check incoming and
  outgoing packets 87–89
Steganography 254–55
Structured Query Language (SQL) data-
  bases 6
Stuart, Tim 295
Subnet masks 44–46
Subnets
  created to isolate sensitive information,
    example of 124

defined 44
SunScreen (Sun Microsystems, Inc.) product
  listing 222
Supplies in a network security policy 66, 68
System auditing 59
System logging verification by firewall
  support personnel 275–76

T

Tags, HTML 28–29
TBC2000 (Telebit Communications A/S) IPv6
  router 280
TCP source and destination port numbers 85
TCP (Transport Control Protocol) on transport
  layer of header 80
TCP/IP technologies
  DoD development of 37
  open design of 5–6
TCP/IP (Transport Control Protocol/Internet
  Protocol)
  introduction of 18
  as network communications protocol for
    intranets 37, 50
Telnet data exchange protocol 20
Telnet proxy, logging onto 275
Telnet, restricting access to 268
Testing of firewalls 269–80
  automated tools for 278
  black box 270–75
  customized 280
  periodic 279
  self-testing as 269–70
  surprise 279
  third-party validations as 279–80
Token authentification, testing 276
Transaction applications, intranet used
  for 294
Transparent proxies in Firewall Server
  138–39, 148–50
Transport layer of packet 80
Trap and tracing service from telephone
  company 56
Tri-homed gateway 124
Trivial FTP 267
"Trojan horse" computer virus 67, 261, 273
Trusted Computer Standards Evaluation Criteria
  ("Orange Book") 57
TurnStyle Firewall System (Atlantic Systems
  Group) product listing 222

U

UDP (User Datagram Protocol) on transport
layer 80
  state evaluation to avoid ACK flag problem
    of 87–88
U.S. Department of Defense
  ARPANET network established by 18
  attacks on computer systems of 2, 55
  computer security levels set by 57
  cracker success noted by 256
  SPI Package by 278
U.S. export control policy 241
U.S. State Department 241
URL (Uniform Resource Locator)
  format of 48
  for product manufacturer. *See* individual
    product listings
  release of specifications for 20
Usenet data exchange protocol 20
Usenet forums on security, listing of 284–85
User authentication 91–93
  parts of 92
User authorization levels 59
User groups for allowing access 63
User management policy 10
User names
  sniffers to gather 260
  unique 125
User services, tests of accessing external 278
User training for an intranet 49, 51
UUCP, restricting access to 268

V

Veronica data exchange protocol 20
Victim machine 103, 105
Villars, Richard 292
Virus checking 127, 258
Viruses
  in downloaded files 258–59
  mailing list for 286
Von Rospach, Chuq 285

W

WAIS (Wide-Area Information Service) data
  exchange protocol 20
WatchGuard Security System (Seattle Software
  Labs, Inc.) product listing 223

Web page
  authoring software for 32, 51
  hiring outside company to create, example
    of 112–13
  HTML tags used for 28–29
Web server
  connecting data to 50–51
  migration to commercial 50
  off-site 112–13
  prevalence of 49
  projected use of 301
  sales of, earmarked for intranet use 291
Web sites of firewall product
  manufacturers 203, 204
WebSENSE (NetPartners Internet Solutions,
  Inc.) product listing 223
White, Richard 242
Wide area network (WAN)
  components of private 18
  similarity of intranet to 4
Winkler, Ira 279
World Wide Web Consortium, W3C 288
World Wide Web (WWW) 5
  access statistics for 291
  as based on HTTP 27–28
  complexity of 6–7
  creation by CERN and Tim Berners-Lee
    of 20–21
  as dominant service on the Internet and
    intranets 22, 27
  factors in growth of 291
  graphical user interface of 8
  security on, mailing list for 286

X

X Windows 267

Y

Yahoo! search engine 35
Yeltsin, Boris 240–41

Z

Zimmerman, Phil 247
ZIP/UNZIP programs 245

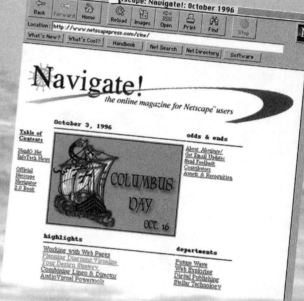

Design Online!

Interactive Web Publishing With Microsoft Tools

$49.99, 818 pages, illustrated, part #: 462-6

Take advantage of Microsoft's broad range of development tools to produce powerful web pages; program with VBScript; create virtual 3D worlds; and incorporate the functionality of Office applications with OLE. The CD-ROM features demos/lite versions of third party software, sample code.

Looking Good Online

$39.99, 450 pages, illustrated, part #: 469-3

Create well-designed, organized web sites—incorporating text, graphics, digital photos, backgrounds and forms. Features studies of successful sites and design tips from pros. The companion CD-ROM includes samples from online professionals; buttons, backgrounds, templates and graphics.

Internet Business 500

$39.95, 450 pages, illustrated, part #: 287-9

This authoritative list of the most useful, most valuable online resources for business is also the most current list, linked to a regularly updated *Online Companion* on the Internet. The companion CD-ROM features a hyperlinked version of the entire text of the book.

The Comprehensive Guide to VBScript

$39.99, 864 pages, illustrated, part #: 470-7

The only encyclopedic reference to VBScript and HTML commands and features. Complete with practical examples for plugging directly into programs. The companion CD-ROM features a hypertext version of the book, along with shareware, templates, utilities and more.

Books marked with this logo include *Online Udates*™, which include free additional online resources, chapter updates and regularly updated links to related resources from Ventana.

Web Publishing With Adobe PageMill 2

$34.99, 450 pages, illustrated, part #: 458-2

Here's the ultimate guide to designing professional web pages. Now, creating and designing pages on the Web is a simple, drag-and-drop function. Learn to pump up PageMill with tips, tricks and troubleshooting strategies in this step-by-step tutorial for designing professional pages. The CD-ROM features Netscape plug-ins, original textures, graphical and text-editing tools, sample backgrounds, icons, buttons, bars, GIF and JPEG images, Shockwave animations.

Web Publishing With Macromedia Backstage 2

$49.99, 500 pages, illustrated, part #: 598-3

Farewell to HTML! This overview of all four tiers of Backstage lets users jump in at their own level. With the focus on processes as well as techniques, readers learn everything they need to create center-stage pages. The CD-ROM includes plug-ins, applets, animations, audio files, Director xTras and demos.

Web Publishing With QuarkImmedia

$39.99, 450 pages, illustrated, part #: 525-8

Use multimedia to learn multimedia, building on the power of QuarkXPress. Step-by-step instructions introduce basic features and techniques, moving quickly to delivering dynamic documents for the Web and other electronic media. The CD-ROM features an interactive manual and sample movie gallery with displays showing settings and steps. Both are written in QuarkImmedia.

Web Publishing With Microsoft FrontPage 97

$34.99, 500 pages, illustrated, part #: 478-2

Web page publishing for everyone! Streamline web-site creation and automate maintenance, all without programming! Covers introductory-to-advanced techniques, with hands-on examples. For Internet and intranet developers. The CD-ROM includes all web-site examples from the book, FrontPage add-ons, shareware, clip art and more.

Make it Multimedia

Microsoft SoftImage|3D Professional Techniques 🌐

$69.99, 524 pages, illustrated, part #: 499-5

Here's your comprehensive guide to modeling, animation & rendering. Create intuitive, visually rich 3D images with this award-winning technology. Follow the structured tutorial to master modeling, animation and rendering, and to increase your 3D productivity. The CD-ROM features tutorials, sample scenes, textures, scripts, shaders, images and animations.

LightWave 3D 5 Character Animation f/x 🌐

$69.99, 700 pages, illustrated, part #: 532-0

Master the fine—and lucrative—art of 3D character animation. Traditional animators and computer graphic artists alike will discover everything they need to know: lighting, motion, caricature, composition, rendering ... right down to work-flow strategies. The CD-ROM features a collection of the most popular LightWave plug-ins, scripts, storyboards, finished animations, models and much more.

3D Studio MAX f/x 🌐

$49.99, 552 pages, illustrated, part #: 427-8

Create Hollywood-style special effects! Plunge into 3D animation with step-by-step instructions for lighting, camera movements, optical effects, texture maps, storyboarding, cinematography, editing and much more. The companion CD-ROM features free plug-ins, all the tutorials from the book, 300+ original texture maps and animations.

Looking Good in 3D 🌐

$39.99, 400 pages, illustrated, part #: 434-4

A guide to thinking, planning and designing in 3D. Become the da Vinci of the 3D world! Learn the artistic elements involved in 3D design—light, motion, perspective, animation and more—to create effective interactive projects. The CD-ROM includes samples from the book, templates, fonts and graphics.

TO ORDER ANY VENTANA TITLE, COMPLETE THIS ORDER FORM AND MAIL OR FAX IT TO US, WITH PAYMENT, FOR QUICK SHIPMENT.

TITLE	PART #	QTY	PRICE	TOTAL

SHIPPING

For all standard orders, please ADD $4.50/first book, $1.35/each additional.
For "two-day air," ADD $8.25/first book, $2.25/each additional.
For orders to Canada, ADD $6.50/book.
For orders sent C.O.D., ADD $4.50 to your shipping rate.
North Carolina residents must ADD 6% sales tax.
International orders require additional shipping charges.

SUBTOTAL = $ _____
SHIPPING = $ _____
TAX = $ _____
TOTAL = $ _____

Or, save 15%–order online.
http://www.vmedia.com

Mail to: Ventana • PO Box 13964 • Research Triangle Park, NC 27709-3964   ☎ 800/743-5369 • Fax 919/544-9472

Name _____
E-mail _____ Daytime phone _____
Company _____
Address (No PO Box) _____
City_____ State_____ Zip_____
Payment enclosed ___VISA ___MC ___ Acc't # _____ Exp. date_____
Signature _____ Exact name on card _____

Check your local bookstore or software retailer for these and other bestselling titles, or call toll free:

800/743-5369